The Michigan Historical Reprint Series

Reprints from the collection of the University of Michigan University Library

The Scholarly Publishing Office
the University of Michigan
University Library

THE

BAPTIST DENOMINATION:

ITS

History, Doctrines, and Ordinances;

ITS

POLITY, PERSECUTIONS, AND MARTYRS; FACTS AND STATISTICS OF ITS MISSIONARY INSTITUTIONS, SCHOOLS OF LEARNING, ETC.; THE INDEBTEDNESS OF THE WORLD TO BAPTISTS, AND THEIR DUTY TO THE WORLD.

BY D. C. HAYNES.

WITH AN INTRODUCTION BY JOHN DOWLING, D.D.

"And be ready always to give an answer to every man that asketh you a reason of the hope that is in you, with meekness and fear."—1 PET. iii. 15.

"Prove all things: hold fast that which is good."—1 THESS. v. 21.

NEW YORK:
SHELDON, BLAKEMAN & CO.
PORTLAND, ME.: MERRILL & WHITMAN.
1856.

PHILADELPHIA:
STEREOTYPED BY GEORGE CHARLES,
No. 9 Sansom Street.

PREFACE.

The object of this book is to furnish for the people generally, the information necessary to a correct judgment of the Church of Christ. It is an effort to bring to the masses, what belongs to them as much as to scholars, to whom it has, to a great extent, been confined.

With this view, the author has labored to press into one small volume, matter found in no one work, small or large; and, as far as it has been published, is scattered over several volumes, pamphlets, and papers. The different topics are, of course, treated with great brevity; but it is hoped sufficiently at length to secure the above-named object.

It is believed that numerous church members even, have but very imperfect information on a subject of vital interest to them. Such a state of things is incompatible with their happiness and usefulness. We live at a time, when all the disciples of Christ should be eminent in their Christian profession.

While we are particularly desirous to reach church members generally, it is hoped our effort will not prove unacceptable to pastors and deacons, who will find here what they need to enable them to act promptly and intelligently in ordinary church matters.

It is hoped, also, it will be found a convenient medium of information for those who are inquiring for the truth, anxious to know where among numerous denominations it lies. The author has seen the time when he would have deemed invaluable a single volume, which he could place in the hands of those needing "much in a little," who could hardly be expected to seek through many volumes, pamphlets, and papers, what is here embraced. It is no exaggeration to say, that the cases are numerous in which persons of other churches, and those who have not become members of any church, are looking towards Baptists for a home. They desire facts, and only need them to make a decision. Here they are. It is worthy of remark that a reliable man, who is distinguished for his accumulation of facts, has said: "the number of members received into the Baptist churches for some years past, from other denominations, exceeds 2000 annually; and that the number of ministers, so received, by change of conviction, is equal to one for every week in the year." This is a church emigration unheard of except in this direction.

It is a pleasing fact of the times, that the primitive state of religion is attracting attention. The nearer we approach the Son of God, His will, the more sure we may be of correctness and success. This volume has originated in a desire to aid, in some humble manner, such a result. If any suppose it leads too decidedly in a Baptist direction for such a profession, or to be of general interest, we have only to say, we believe it to be the result of the force of truth, and have presumed that others have no more regard for a mere sect than ourselves, and are as willing to receive the truth, wherever it may be found.

Philadelphia, Jan., 1856. D. C. H.

CONTENTS.

PART I.

THE ORIGIN AND HISTORY OF THE BAPTIST CRURCH, AND ITS IDENTITY WITH THE PRIMITIVE CHURCH.

CHAPTER I.

CHAPTER II.

CHAPTER III.

CHAPTER IV.

CHAPTER V.

PART II.

DOCTRINES AND ORDINANCES OF THE BAPTIST CHURCH.

CHAPTER I.

CHAPTER II.

CHAPTER III.

PART IV.

BAPTIST MARTYRS AND PERSECUTIONS, FOR THE FOREGOING PRINCIPLES.

CHAPTER III.

CHAPTER IV.

CHAPTER. V.

CHAPTER VI.

CHAPTER VII.

CHAPTER VIII.

CHAPTER IX.

PART V.

FACTS AND STATISTICS OF BAPTIST MISSIONARY INSTITUTIONS, SCHOOLS OF LEARNING, PERIODICALS AND CHURCHES, AND CONCLUDING CHAPTERS ON THE INDEBTEDNESS OF THE WORLD TO BAPTISTS, AND THEIR DUTY TO THE WORLD.

CHAPTER I.

CHAPTER II.

CHAPTER III.

INTRODUCTION.

Nothing is of greater importance to all who would make themselves familiar with the history and peculiarities of religious denominations, than a correct understanding of their *first principles*—those fundamental truths which lie at the foundation of their system of faith aud practice. Much of the asperity and unfairness which have characterized the polemics of religion, has arisen from a misunderstanding or misstatement of the belief of the parties in controversy and from ignorance of the fundamental principles, lying at the foundation of that belief, and giving rise to the distinctive peculiarities of each.

Whenever a doctrine or a practice is held, as the legitimate result of a principle, the proper course for a fair opponent is —not to brand with hard names, or charge with false conclusions—but candidly to examine the principle, and then the connection between that and the doctrine or practice based upon it. If he can show that the fundamental principle is unscriptural and unsound, of course he overturns the conclusions that are derived from it; just as a superstructure must fall when the foundation is knocked from under it. If the principle be admitted as true, then he must show that the doctrine or practice cannot be logically deduced from it. If he can do neither of these,—if he can neither prove the unsoundness of the principle, nor that the conclusion drawn from it is a *non sequitur*—then, as an honest man, he is bound to submit to the truth. The least he can do is to cease his opposition, and to "refrain from these men, and let them alone."

Alas! that the history of religious controversy shows how many there are, who are maddened rather than subdued by the impregnability of truth, and for lack of hard arguments, resort to hard names, and thus tread in the steps of the ancient accuser of the Apostle Paul, the orator Tertullus, who, conscious of his inability to answer his arguments, took the easier course of branding him as "a pestilent fellow, and a mover of sedition."* And thus it has come to pass that men who have found the task too difficult to undermine the principles, or to confute the reasoning of Baptists, have contented themselves with branding them as "mad men of Munster"—"movers of sedition"—and "Anabaptists" or Rebaptizers; epithets, which a knowledge of their principles and history—as faithfully exhibited in the following work—proves to be as inapplicable to them as to any denomination of evangelical Christians.

Much of the odium which, in earlier times, has been cast upon Baptists, and occasional instances of which are seen even at the present day, has arisen from an inadequate or mistaken view of the great fundamental principles which underlie their system of faith and practice. We hold that it is unfair to assail a doctrine or usage of a denomination, till the demolition of the principle upon which such doctrine or usage is based.

To illustrate our meaning:—The Episcopalian believes that no one can be a true minister of Christ unless episcopally ordained in the line of apostolical succession, and he therefore excludes from his pulpit his Methodist, or Presbyterian, or Baptist brother. Now, what we maintain is, that it would be unfair to attribute this seeming exclusiveness to bigotry or

* Acts xxiv. 5.

uncharitableness. The practice is a necessary result of the principle. If he really believes in the necessity of apostolical succession in order to a valid ministry, he is not to be blamed, because he refuses to be guilty of the inconsistency of violating this principle. Nor can we expect that such an one should admit us into his pulpit till he shall be as firmly convinced as we are, that this whole claim of apostolical succession is baseless, unscriptural and absurd. Just so, the Baptist believes that immersion only is valid baptism; and in common with all other denominations, he believes that baptism—whatever it is—must precede communion. How unjust, then, the odium cast upon Baptists, for what is termed their strict communion; when, in this matter, they stand, as the following work proves, upon precisely the same ground with their accusers, viz.: valid, scripture baptism a prerequisite to communion! Till the principle from which this practice necessarily follows is disproved, viz.: that immersion only is true baptism, no fair opponent will censure them, or excite prejudice against them for a practice which consistency with their principles imperatively enjoins.

That which we cheerfully concede to others, we have a right to demand for ourselves. We are firm believers in a principle that lies at the basis of the Baptist faith, viz.: that THE BIBLE IS THE ONLY AND SUFFICIENT RULE OF FAITH AND PRACTICE. We do not believe in the Romish or the Oxford doctrine, as expressed by Dr. Newman, a few years ago, before he had finished his voyage towards Rome—and which he still believes, now he has reached his haven, viz.: that "these two things, the Bible and the Catholic tradition—form *together* a united rule of faith." We cannot admit with the Papist at Trent, that the written books and "unwritten traditions" are to be received "with equal piety and veneration."*

* "Pari pietatis affectu ac reverentia suscipit et veneratur." See the decree of the Council of Trent on Tradition.

The reader of the work to which these remarks are prefixed, will find abundant proof, that the Baptist admits not of tradition as a joint authority with the word of God; but clings with unyielding tenacity to the Bible, and the Bible only as authority, in all matters of faith. Whatever we find in the Bible, that we receive as of paramount authority; whatever is not there, we reject, as of nothing worth. We care nothing for tradition; we have little regard for "the fathers," unless they confirm the declarations of the written word. Every true doctrine is as old as the apostles. If *they* knew nothing of it, no matter to us whether it be discovered in the musty folio of some visionary of the third or fourth century, or dug up from the charnelhouse of rottenness and oblivion to which the good sense of the people had consigned it fifteen hundred years ago, or whether it spring from the fertile brain of some visionary of the nineteenth century; if it is not in the Bible, it has not the slightest claim to our regard as an article of religious belief. Nay, more, we will add, that though Augustine, or Jerome, or even Tertullian or Irenæus, were to arise from the dead, and teach some new doctrine, we would simply ask—"Is it to be found in the inspired record?" and if truth should compel them to answer "No"—then we would esteem it of no greater worth, as matter of religious faith, than the vagaries of Emanuel Swedenborg, Joseph Smith, or Andrew Jackson Davis. With such principles, we ask—Is infant baptism to be found in the Bible? What says Schleiermacher, himself a Pedobaptist? "All traces of infant baptism, which one will find in the New Testament, must first be put into it." What says the Episcopal Dr. Hook, the celebrated champion of the Oxford theology, in a recent sermon in defence of tradition? "You know, my hearers," says he, "that the Bible says *nothing whatever* of the baptism of infants; if, then, you reject the authority of tradition, how can you account for infant baptism? With what consistency can you receive this doctrine, as you do, without a question, and reject other doctrines which are established upon precisely the same foundation?"

Now the only way in which a Pedobaptist can possibly meet this argument, is either to deny the Baptist principle—*the Bible only the rule of faith*—and take the Romish rules of *Scripture and tradition united*, or else to prove what the above Pedobaptist writers, and many others, flatly deny, viz.: that the baptism of infants is plainly commanded in the Bible; a task which never has been, and, we are very sure, never can be accomplished. The reader will not be surprised, therefore, to find it asserted, and we think conclusively proved, in the present work, that Baptists, who reject every doctrine based only upon tradition, can alone consistently oppose the errors of Rome.

From this fundamental principle *of the Bible only*, springs another principle, ever dear to Baptists, viz.: the personal right of every man to judge for himself what that Bible reveals—individual responsibility, intellectual freedom, and what Roger Williams so well named "soul liberty." No one can read the present volume, without being convinced that the world owes a mighty debt to the great Baptist family for their labors and sufferings as the martyrs and champions of religious liberty—"freedom to worship God."

The Baptist considers it an invasion of this individual and personal responsibility, to administer a so-called ordinance to an unconscious babe, with the expectation that he shall make that act his own, and be bound by it, when he arrives at maturity; and, to us, there appears both force and propriety in the question once put by a young man convinced of the duty of believers' immersion, when his parents endeavored to dissuade him from his purpose, by reminding him that he had been sprinkled in his infancy—"was it right, dear parents, to deprive me of the liberty of choice?" It will be seen, therefore, that the practice of infant baptism is in direct opposition to these two great principles of the Baptist faith—

the sufficiency of the Bible only, and *individual and personal responsibility before God.*

While we thus avoid most scrupulously any invasion of individual freedom; there is danger, on the other hand, lest Baptists should fall into an opposite error, and neglect the early instruction of their families in their peculiar and scriptural views. Religious instruction is a duty imperative upon every Christian parent, and no over-scrupulous fear of infringing upon the province of private judgment should prevent the performance of so plain a duty. This religious instruction of our children should include a statement of our principles, history, doctrines, and polity as Baptists. We believe that a great reform is needed here in Baptist families. If our principles are worth holding, they are worth disseminating, worthy of being taught to our children, worthy of being studied and understood by all. And they must be so taught and studied, if we would succeed in retaining the children of Baptists in Baptist churches and congregations. These principles have a history—a history of labors and sufferings, of "struggles and triumphs"—a history which is worthy of being *popularized,* that it may be read, and pondered, and treasured up by all Baptists and the children of Baptists. The names and achievements of Williams and Delaune, of Bunyan and Keach, of Gill and Booth, of Hall and Rayland, and Fuller and Ivimey—of Backus and Stillman, and Baldwin and Staughton, and scores of other Baptist worthies, both in the Old World and the New, should be familiar to us and our children as household words, and the precious truths for which they toiled and suffered, the doctrines, the polity, and government of the churches planted and nurtured by their labors, should be made in all Baptist families, the subjects of frequent reading, conversation, and instruction.

I cannot but esteem the present work of my valued friend and brother, the Rev. D. C. Haynes, as a successful attempt to popularize the knowledge of Baptist principles, history, doctrines, and polity of which I have spoken; and I am sure the volume, besides being a comprehensive and convenient manual for constant reference by every intelligent Christian, and especially by every Baptist, will prove a most important auxiliary to domestic religious instruction in every Baptist family into which it may be introduced.

JOHN DOWLING.

Philadelphia, March, 1856.

PART I.

THE ORIGIN AND HISTORY OF THE BAPTIST CHURCH, AND ITS IDENTITY WITH THE PRIMITIVE CHURCH.

CHAPTER I.

The importance of investigations in Church History. 2. Misrepresentations of Baptists by Historians—Prof. Hase and his translators—Statistics. 3. The Argument stated.

1. No honest, intelligent man can, on the least reflection, be disinterested in the question, is any one of the denominations now in being essentially the primitive church? If so, which is it? Put the question in a different form, and it is the same thing. Has any one denomination any more claim to this distinction than another? If so, which is it? Let the truth appear. No matter where the light flashes its rays. Let us have light. This is a subject of legitimate inquiry, and is as capable of investigation and fair decision as any other. If it is involved in difficulty, it is at the same time of no ordinary interest, and no pains should be spared to arrive at the truth. If the least important historical questions are deserving of examination, how much more those relating to the Church of God! Surely Christians should not be outdone in research, or interest, in such matters, by men of the world.

2. The obligation of Baptists, particularly, to such investigations, is amply illustrated in all church history, and in none

more than in the most recent works on the subject. Their church, though occupying by far the largest space in true church history, has no fair place in any, but those written by Baptists; and the recent one by Prof. Hase affords them no relief. Some are inclined to doubt the existence of Baptists in distant times, subsequent to the apostolic, because historians either pass them over in silence, or with contempt, or some very equivocal compliment. But Prof. Hase in this late day has done the same thing, and there are really no Baptists now, of any consideration, in any country, if to such men their history is to be trusted. Witness his false representations of Baptists in Germany. "In Germany persons sometimes become Baptists from pietistic scruples, or from some religious extravagancies (!); and a few small congregations have here and there been baptized by the *English Missionary* Oncken, of Hamburg" (since 1834). Prof. Hase dates modern missions from the "London Missionary Society" of 1796, when it is now well known that the English Baptist Mission bears date 1792. The American translators of Prof. Hase's book, who have prepared for it by his permission, an account of religion in this country, have treated the Baptists of America but a little, if any, better than historians treated the Anabaptists of Germany, and if we are to be ashamed of them on account of their history, written by enemies, we must be ashamed of ourselves, and acknowledge that Baptists have no desirable existence in America at the present time. A writer in the Christian Review says of this account—"within the brief compass of twenty lines, we detect eight or ten erroneous representations, and in the parts which are true in fact, there is no regard to the true proportions or proper coloring." Take a single statement from this American prepared account of Baptists in the United States. "The Baptists follow next (to the Congregationalists) in the order of time (1639), and if we include under the appellation all who deny the validity of Baptism except by immersion and on the professed faith of the subject, they must be regarded as the most numerous denomination but one in the United States." If these gentlemen had consulted as common a book as "Mitchell's School Atlas," they would have seen that the associated Baptists alone, are three times as numerous as any other denomination, excepting the Methodists; and that without reckoning several sects included in their estimate of Baptists. The Baptist *population* of the United States is larger than the Methodist. "Mitchell's School Atlas" is not a Baptist work, of course, and puts down the Methodist population, including six different sects, at 4,700,000; and the Baptist population, including seven different sects, at 5,200,000. All authorities unite in making the Baptist *church membership* a little less than the Methodist, and the *population* a little more.

It is supposing such historians dishonest to the last degree, to charge them with intentional misrepresentations so gross. It is the dictate of charity to attribute them to ignorance of Baptist history. It should be—it must be—the work of Baptists to give them the facts in so plain a manner, that they cannot misrepresent them for want of information. Indeed, it seems incredible now, that those making any pretensions to historical learning, should be ignorant of so palpable a history as is theirs.

3. The argument stated.

The Baptist church is the primitive church—that is, it originated in the primitive church—it has ever been essentially like it—there has never been a time when it was not in being—it is now, as it was in its origin, and has been in its history in all ages of Christianity, essentially the same. The bond of union among Baptists is a scriptural faith in Christ, manifested in a scriptural baptism, to be followed by an adherence to all of Jehovah's provisions for his church. Tradition is without authority, and ever has been among Baptists. It has never been Baptistical to require every man to be just like every other one, to give him a claim to be of us. It is an agreement essentially, in cardinal points, upon which we insist. A bond of union framed for another purpose is here as nowhere else appropriate. "In essentials, unity; in non-essentials liberty; in all things charity." In this manner the Baptist church has existed since the Saviour said, "upon this rock will I build my church, and the gates of hell shall not prevail against it."

CHAPTER II.

The probability of the truth of the position that the Baptist church is the primitive church, from the opinions of intelligent men, Baptists and others, who have paid particular attention to the subject. 1. Orchard —2. Dr. Brown—3. Prof. Duncan—4. Drs. Ypeig and Dermont—5. Writers in the Christian Review.

SUCH only as have paid particular attention to this subject are competent to express an opinion on it. The position may appear extravagant to some, for no other reason than that they have never investigated it. That we may not be deemed presumptuous in the position, and for the benefit of those having no time or facilities for such investigation, we give the following testimony.

Uneducated men, especially, are indebted to the labors of others having had better opportunities than themselves, for much they believe. In the nature of things it must be so. Reliable testimony is therefore valuable. It is only an exchange of work, for the educated are equally dependent upon them for other things, no less important.

1. Rev. G. H. Orchard published a book on this subject in London, in 1838. If we mistake not, others have a similar experience with his, in the circumstances which led to his work. He says—"While on a visit to Somersetshire, in 1823, a min-

ister of the Independent persuasion panegyrized Dr. Carey, as the individual who raised the Baptists out of obscurity, and further remarked that they had no existence before the days of the commonwealth. The respectability and age of the minister, did not allow me, a young man, and unacquainted as I was with history, to negative his assertion only by a relieving hint, 'that from the days of John the Baptist until now,' I believed they had had an existence. I was resolved to be satisfied on this subject."

Mr. Orchard calls his book: "A concise history of foreign Baptists, taken from the New Testament, the first fathers, early writers, and historians of all ages, chronologically arranged, exhibiting their distinct communities, with their orders in various kingdoms, under several discriminative appellations from the establishment of Christianity to the present age," &c. In summing up the result of his researches, which any one must be satisfied on reading the book are ample, he says, "it is stated in the most satisfactory manner, that all Christian communities during the first three centuries were of the Baptist denomination in constitution and practice. In the middle of the third century the Novation Baptists established separate and independent societies, which continued until the end of the sixth age, when these communities were succeeded by the Paterines, which continued until the Reformation (1517). The Oriental Baptist churches, with their successors, the Paulicians, continued in their purity until the tenth century, when they visited France, resuscitating and extending the Christian profession in Languedoc, where they flourished till the crusading army scattered or drowned in blood, one million of unoffending professors. The Baptists in Piedmont and Germany are exhibited as existing under different names down to the Reformation. These churches, with their genuine successors, the Mennonites of Holland, are connectedly and chronologically detailed to the present period (1838)." We only, in addition, remark of this work, and the opinion of its author, no one will contemn either, who will examine their claim to honesty, industry and research.

2. Rev. J. Newton Brown, D. D., Editorial Secretary of the American Baptist Publication Society, and author of the Encyclopedia of Religious Knowledge, who has given much attention to church history, says: "the Baptists have no difficulty whatever in tracing up their principles and churches to the apostolic age. It has often been said by our enemies that we originated in the German city of Munster, in 1534. Lamentable must be the weakness and ignorance of such an assertion, come from whom it may. It were easy to recite eminent Paedobaptist historians to refute this calumny—especially Limbroch and Mosheim, of the last century."

3. Rev. William Cecil Duncan, Professor of the Greek and Latin Languages, and Literature, in the University of Louisiana, in a recent history of the Baptists, says: "Baptists do not, as do most Protestant denominations, date their origin from the Reformation of 1520. By means of that great religious movement, indeed, they were brought forth from comparative obscurity into prominent notice, and through it a new and powerful impulse was given to their principles and practices in all those countries which had renounced allegiance to the Pope of Rome. They did not, however, originate with the Reformation; for long before Luther lived, nay, long before the Roman Catholic church herself was known, Baptists and Baptist churches existed and flourished in Europe, in Asia, and in Africa."

4. Not to multiply testimony, the most remarkable and conclusive is that of Dr. Ypeig, Professor of Theology at the University of Groningen; and Dr. J. J. Dermont, Chaplain to the King of Holland. These gentlemen are not Baptists, but learned and pious members of the Dutch Reformed church, and wrote a history of Dutch Baptists at the request of their sovereign. Here is their testimony:

"The Mennonites are descended from the tolerably pure

evangelical Waldenses, who were driven by persecution into various countries; and who, during the latter part of the twelfth century, fled into Flanders, and into the provinces of Holland and Zealand, where they lived simple and exemplary lives—in the villages as farmers, in the towns by trades—free from the charge of any gross immoralities, and professing the most pure and simple principles, which they exemplified in a holy conversation. *They were therefore in existence long before the Reformed church of the Netherlands.*" Again: "We have now seen that the Baptists, who were formerly called Anabaptists, and in later times Mennonites, were the original Waldenses; and who have long in the history of the church received the honor of that origin. ON THIS ACCOUNT THE BAPTISTS MAY BE CONSIDERED AS THE ONLY CHRISTIAN COMMUNITY WHICH HAS STOOD SINCE THE DAYS OF THE APOSTLES; AND AS A CHRISTIAN SOCIETY WHICH HAS PRESERVED PURE THE DOCTRINES OF THE GOSPEL THROUGH ALL AGES. The perfectly correct external and internal economy of the Baptist denomination, tends to confirm the truth, disputed by the Romish church, that the Reformation brought about in the sixteenth century, was in the highest degree necessary; and at the same time goes to refute the erroneous notion of the Catholics, that their communion is the most ancient."

This testimony has been styled: "a confession of the rarest candor," as coming from members of anothor denomination. But we see not how *honest* men, after having carefully examined the history of the church, could say any less. *Christians* deserve no praise for admitting the truth of each other: *they* can do no less.

5. Writers in the Christian Review.

A writer in the Christian Review of Jan., 1855, undoubtedly a Baptist, makes the following singular remark for a Baptist, or an ordinarily intelligent scholar: "Though Baptists, and attached for the time in which we live to this division of our Lord's followers, we must yet say that we know of no assumption more arrogant, and more destitute of proper historic support, than that which claims to be able to trace the distiuct and unbroken existence of a church substantially Baptist, from the time of the Apostles down to our own." How does this statement look in connection with the testimony just given? We freely, however, forgive the author of it, for the rebuke of his position which it has called out in the October number of the same Review: "But if he means, what his words seem properly to denote, taken in their whole connection, that no traces can be found of churches substantially Baptist throughout the centuries which connect Cyprian of Carthage with Martin Luther—then we must be permitted to take issue with him. Who is he, or what is the extent of his knowledge, that he should be qualified to speak on such a question in the style of oracular authority? Men who have gone deeper than any others into the investigation—for instance, Robinson of Cambridge—reached a very different conclusion. We hold in our possession at this moment a letter received from one of the most distinguished scholars of our denomination—one too that has filled the chair of Ecclesiastical History—who thus freely and forcibly expresses his views of the opinion advanced by the Reviewer: 'The language is exaggerated and offensive, and far more 'arrogant' than the assumption to which it is applied. I can see nothing resembling arrogance in the supposition that a body of Christian disciples, holding substantially the views of the Baptist churches of the present day, may be *historically* traced from the times of the Apostles. They may have taken different names, at different periods. The mere *name* amounts to little or nothing in such a historical view, and it is puerile to hang an objection on such a shadow. The thing itself would constitute the object of historical investigation. On the ground that the Baptist churches conform substantially in their doctrines and practice to the Apostolic churches' (which the Reviewer of course admits), 'we must either suppose that there has been a Christian people existing in every age from the Apostolic to the present, characterized by the same doctrines and practice; or that there were periods in the intervening history when Apostolic faith and practice *had absolutely no representative on the face of the earth.* Are we prepared to take the latter alternative? Have there been such hiatuses in the history of Christianity? No church, no Christian people, to uphold the standard of a pure Gospel, and bear witness to the truth as it is in Jesus amid a perverse and crooked generation? What then becomes of the Saviour's promise? Reasoning à priori, we must infer, I think, that there must be a continuous line of witnesses for the truth, not only as individuals, but as organized bodies, keeping the faith as originally delivered to the saints, and practicing the ordinances as instituted by the great Head. It cannot then be 'arrogant'—nay, it is a duty we owe to the truth, to go into a careful and thorough investigation of historical sources, to find out, if possible, such an uninterrupted line of witnesses.'" We beg leave to ask, if the "continuous line of witnesses" from the Apostles to the Reformation were *not Baptists, what were they?* Surely no one of the present sects having no earlier an origin than the Reformation, will claim them. Were they then Latins, Greeks, or Baptists?

We are now prepared to suppose it *probable* that the Baptist church can be traced directly to the primitive church. This testimony (which might be greatly increased) can be accounted for on no other supposition.

CHAPTER III.

The argument for the primitive character of the Baptist church from the history of baptism. 1. The origin of the church and the history of Baptism for the first century; testimony of the learned as to the mode and subjects of baptism during this period. 2. The history of baptism from the first century onward beyond the times when Baptist churches, subsequent to New Testament Baptists, arose; the mode of baptism; Prof. Stewart on the early fathers; Dr. Sears on Chrysostom and Winner; the time and origin of sprinkling; the subjects of baptism; Pedobaptist materials for Baptist arguments; Dr. Woods on infant baptism; Chevalier Bunson and Hypolytus and his age; Prof. Knowles on the origin of infant baptism; the time when it was introduced.

1. THE origin of the church and the history of baptism for the first century. "In those days came John the Baptist, preaching in the wilderness of Judea, saying, Repent ye, for the kingdom of heaven is at hand. For this is He that was spoken of by the prophet Isaiah, saying, The voice of one crying in the wilderness, Prepare ye the way of the Lord, and make his paths straight. * * * And then went out to Him Jerusalem, and all Judea, and all the region round about Jordan, and were baptized of him in Jordan, confessing their sins."

We see not how any one can deny that here we have the germ of the Baptist church; and of no other. "Then went out to Him Jerusalem, and all Judea, and all the region round about Jordan, *and were baptized of Him in Jordan, confessing their sins.*" Here is no sprinkling; no infant baptism. The "baptism in Jordan" is not sprinkling. The baptism of those "confessing their sins," could not have been of infants.

Whether John's baptism was precisely Christian baptism or not, does not affect this question. Though some differences may be made out between the two, there is none as it respects the mode and subjects of them.

The New Testament embraces the first century, the last

work of the Apostle John, bearing date, A. D. 96. He probably died, the last of the Apostles, four years later, A. D. 100.

It is safe to assert that in the New Testament there is no sprinkling and no infant baptism, for the most learned Pedobaptist scholars affirm it. It is suitable here, only to introduce a specimen of the testimony, with the remark that volumes are at hand for those who wish them.

The mode of baptism in New Testament times.

The Right Rev. Dr. Trevan, a high dignitary of the Church of Rome, in an argument with the Church of England, says: "But without going any farther, show us, my Lords, the validity of your baptism, 'by Scripture alone.' Jesus Christ there ordains that it shall be conferred, not by pouring water on the heads of believers, but by believers being plunged into the water. The word baptizo, employed by the Evangelists, strictly conveys this signification, as the learned are agreed."

Rev. Mr. Love, formerly missionary to Greece, has translated a standard work of the Greek church, in whose language the New Testament is written, from which we make the following selections: "We say that the baptism of the Latins" (the Roman Catholics, which is not immersion), "is baptism falsely named. Observe that we do not say that we rebaptize the Latins; but that we baptize them, since their baptism is a lie in its very name. It is not baptism at all, but bare sprinkling." If the New Testament contained anything but immersion for baptism, surely the Greeks would have discovered it; but they have never admitted anything of the kind in theory or practice.

"In a work recently re-published by C. Scribner, from the English edition, entitled 'Life and Epistles of St. Paul,' by Rev. W. J. Connybeare, and Rev. J. S. Howson, both ministers of the Episcopal church, we find the following: 'It is needless to add, that baptism was (unless in exceptional cases) administered by immersion, the convert being plunged beneath the surface of the water, to represent his death to the life of sin, and then raised from this momentary burial to represent his resurrection to the life of righteousness. It must be a subject of regret that the general discontinuance of this original form of baptism (though perhaps necessary to our Northern climate), has rendered obscure to popular apprehension some very important passages of Scripture.' The same authors, in a note respecting the 4th verse of Romans, 6th chapter, say: 'This passage cannot be understood, unless it be borne in mind that the primitive baptism was by immersion.' They translate the 4th verse thus: 'With Him therefore we were buried by the baptism wherein we shared His death (when we sank beneath the waters: and were raised from under them), that even as Christ was raised up from the dead by the glory of the Father, so we likewise might walk in newness of life.'

"In the July number of the London Quarterly Review, page 27, of Leonard Scott's reprint, we have the following statement: 'There can be no question that the original form of baptism—the very meaning of the word—was complete immersion in the deep baptismal waters; and that for at least four centuries any other form was either unknown, or regarded as an exceptional, almost a monstrous case.' "

There is no better scholar in the Congregational church, than Rev. Prof. Stewart, of the Andover Theological Seminary. Here is his testimony: "Bapto and baptizo, mean to dip, plunge, or immerge into any thing liquid. All lexicographers and critics of any note are agreed in this."

The well known Rev. Dr. Chalmers, of the Presbyterian church, says: "The original meaning of the word baptism is immersion. We do not doubt that the prevalent style of the administration in the Apostles' days was immersion."

The subjects of baptism in New Testament times. Infant baptism not in the New Testament.

An article in the North British Review, the organ of Presbyterianism in Scotland, attributed to Rev. Dr. Hanna, has the following: "Scripture knows nothing of the baptism of infants. There is absolutely not a single trace of it to be found in the New Testament." The same Review says: "That the recognized baptism of the ancient church was that of adults, of those whom the church only received into her fold after a long course of systematic, catechetical instruction, cannot indeed admit of any doubt."

Rev. Prof. Stewart says: "there are no commands, or plain and certain examples, in the New Testament, relative to infant baptism."

Rev. Dr. Woods, of the same school of theology as Prof. Stewart, says: "We have no express precept or example for infant baptism in all our holy writings."

Rev. Dr. Hodge, of the Princeton (Presbyterian) Theological Seminary, says: "When Christ came, the commonwealth (Jewish) was abolished, and there was nothing put in its place. The church remained. There was no external covenant, nor promise of external blessings, on conditions of external rites and subjection. There was a spiritual society, with spiritual promises, on the condition of faith in Christ. In no part of the New Testament is any other condition of membership in the church prescribed than that contained in the answer of Philip to the eunuch who desired baptism: 'if thou believest with all thy heart, thou mayest. And he answered and said, I believe that Jesus Christ is the Son of God.' The church, therefore, is in its essential nature a company of believers."

So much for the best possible testimony of the silence of the New Testament in regard to sprinkling and infant baptism, and consequently of the entire absence of both in the history of the church for the first century. It were superfluous, after this, for us to consume our pages with an examination of this period of the history of the church. These witnesses are too learned to be mistaken; and too partial to Pedobaptism, to bear so decided testimony against it without absolute necessity.

If it is asked why they do not renounce the doctrines they declare unscriptural, we answer, that is their affair. Our work here is historical, not controversial. We may say, however, in a word, that they attempt to sustain themselves upon other than Scriptural grounds, which, to say the least, is an abandonment of the Protestant maxim that: "the Bible is the only rule of faith and practice." We cannot see, nor can we understand how they can, the difference, in principle, between abandoning the Bible in one thing and in all things: why they are not, on their own showing, encouraging disorders in the church; and exposing themselves to the anathemas of Revelations xxii., 18, 19.

2. The history of Baptism, from the first century onward beyond the times when Baptist churches, subsequent to the New Testament Baptists, arose.

The mode of baptism during this period.

We deem the admissions of Rev. Prof. Stewart, in relation to the practice of the church for centuries immediately following New Testament times, abundantly reliable, both on account of his acknowledged learning and intimacy with the works of the fathers, and his aversion to Baptist sentiments. Interrogated in 1832, when in his prime, by missionaries and others, as to the "mode of baptism in early times," he prepares and publishes a work on the subject. This work is republished, 1855, by Baptists. From the eighth section of this edition we make the following selections: "In the writings of the Apostolic fathers, so called, that is, the writers of the first century, or at least those who lived in part during this century, scarcely anything of a definite nature occurs respecting baptism, either in a doctrinal or ritual respect. It is, indeed, frequently alluded to; but this is usually in a general way only. We can easily gather from these allusions that the rite was practiced in the church; but we are not able to determine, with precision, either the manner of the right or the stress laid upon it."

It should be observed in relation to this passage, that, for the first century, we have better testimony than that of the Apostolic fathers, namely, the Apostles themselves. The New Testament is all we need, as far as it carries the history, which is through the first century. We have seen, and any one may read for himself, what the New Testament teaches of the first century.

It should also be remarked of this period, and of the centuries immediately following, that there was no necessity or occasion for much to be said upon the mode and subjects of baptism, for there was but one opinion. When individuals and churches began to recede from the original Baptist position, then the remonstrances began to arise, and the testimony becomes most ample.

Passing into the second century, Prof. Stewart finds in the Pastor of Hermas (A. D. 116), Justin Martyr (A. D. 140), Tertullian (A. D. 200), ample evidence of Baptists. Of what he finds in Justin Martyr, he says: "I am persuaded that this passage, as a whole, most naturally refers to immersion; for why on any other ground should the convert to be initiated go out to a place where there is water? There could be no need of this, if mere sprinkling, or partial effusion only, was customary in the time of Justin."

Of what he finds in Tertullian (A. D. 200), he says: "I do not see how any doubt can well remain, that in Tertullian's time, the practice of the African church, to say the least, must have been that of trine immersion."

He then takes his reader through the works of Gregory Nyssen (A. D. 370), and Chrysostom (A. D. 398), and sums the whole up in that remarkable passage: "But enough. It is," says Augusti, "a thing made out, namely, the ancient practice of immersion. So, indeed, all the writers, who have thoroughly investigated this subject, conclude. I know of no one usage of ancient times which seems to be more clearly made out. I cannot see how it is possible for any candid man who examines the subject, to deny this."

"The passages which refer to immersion, are so numerous in the fathers that it would take a little volume merely to recite them."

"F. Brenner," continues Prof. Stewart, "a Roman Catholic writer, has recently published a learned work, which contains a copious history of usages in respect to the baptismal rite, namely, 'Geschichtliche Danstellungder Verrichtung der Taufe, etc., 1818.' I have not seen the work; but it is spoken of highly, on account of the diligence and learning which the author has exhibited in his historical details. The result of them respecting the point before us I present: 'Thirteen hundred years was baptism generally and ordinarily performed by the immersion of a man under water.

"'In the work of John Floyer, on cold bathing, it is mentioned that the English church practiced immersion down to the beginning of the seventeenth century, when a change to the method of sprinkling gradually took place.'

"We have," continues Prof. Stewart, "collected facts enough, to authorize us now to come to the following general conclusion, respecting the practice of the Christian church in general, with regard to the mode of baptism, viz., that from the earliest ages of which we have any account, subsequent to the Apostolic age, and downward for several centuries, the churches did generally practice immersion."

Chrysostom, who was made Patriarch of Constantinople in A. D. 398, and who died A. D. 407, was a voluminous writer. By means of his writings we have a history of baptism for the first four centuries. Dr. Sears says of him: "Chrysostom, who in innumerable instances, in thirteen folio volumes, speaks of baptism, never alludes to sprinkling, but on the contrary defines it to be plunging into the water, and raising out of it." Dr. Sears also remarks: "Winer, in his lectures on Archæology, in manuscript, says effusion was first applied only to the sick; but was gradually introduced for others after the seventh century; and in the thirteenth became the prevailing practice in the west."

We have seen that in New Testament times, the first century, the practice was exclusively immersion, as scholars of all persuasions admit. The same is true, as is generally admitted, of the first four centuries, or Chrysostom's voluminous writings would have some allusion to a different custom. Now, according to Winer, sprinkling soon began to be introduced for the sick, and was confined to them until the seventh century, when it gradually was used for others, and in the thirteenth century became a common custom. The Montanist Baptists (See Part I., chap. iv.) arose A. D. 150. They form the second link in our chain of Baptists, so that if sprinkling had been in use in the second century, instead of not until the fourth, our chain would be complete.

We may remark, in passing, upon the history of sprinkling, as baptism, that it originated not with Christians, but with the heathen. The earliest allusions to it are by the Apostolic fathers. "Justin Martyr says," according to Mosheim, "that it was an invention of demons, in imitation of the true baptism * * * that their votaries might also have their pretended purifications by water." Tertullian says: "the heathens did adopt a religious rite, particularly in the mysteries of Apollo and Ceres, whose persons were baptized for their regeneration and pardon of their perjuries. Here we see the aim of the Devil imitating the things of God." In process of time, the corrupted church adopted this more convenient baptism, so called; but Baptist churches have never been wanting to protest against it, as an unholy innovation.

The subjects of baptism during this period.

It is worthy of remark, that the works of Pedobaptists furnish abundant material in favor of Baptist positions. Works written to refute Baptist arguments furnish confirmation of them, just as numerous instances are on record of persons who have resorted to investigation to confirm Pedobaptist opinions, only to abandon them entirely, as in the case of Dr. Judson and wife, and others too numerous to mention.

The work of Rev. Dr. Woods, Professor in the Theological Seminary at Andover, on infant baptism, is an illustration in point. In the preface to his first edition, he gives notice that he declines a controversy on the subject with Baptists. In the preface to the second edition, he refers to answers to his first, from different Baptists, which have induced him "to give the subject a new examination," in which he says: "I have requested the aid of my beloved colleague, the Rev. Prof. Stewart, who, as the public know, is very familiar with this kind of investigation. In compliance with my request, he has given particular attention to the subject, and has carefully examined those passages in the Christian fathers on which the historical argument for infant baptism rests, together with the writings of Wall, Gale, Robinson and others; and has allowed me the privilege of making what use I please of his notes." He says also: "I take pleasure in acknowledging that the strictures of my Baptist brethren have been of real use to me, and have led me to correct some mistakes, to give to some of my expressions and arguments a more unexceptionable form, and to establish my positions by some new considerations."

We claim that, under these circumstances, we have in the work of Dr. Woods the best thing which could be done for infant baptism. What then is the surprise of the reader to find so poor an argument, such want of connection between facts given and conclusions drawn, and so many direct admissions of the Baptist position.

The doctor commences with a concession which is ruinous to his entire argument: "Whatever may have been the precepts of Christ, or his Apostles, to those who enjoyed their personal instructions, it is plain that there is no express precept respecting infant baptism in our sacred writings. The proof then, that infant baptism is a divine institution, must be made out in another way." If the "sacred writings" are silent on the subject, anything else is as soon thought of for infants as baptism. The argument, now abandoned by numerous Pedobaptist scholars, that it takes the place of circumcision, is ridiculous, because there is no resemblance between the two. Besides, when circumcision was abolished in the council of the Apostles, nothing was put in its place. It were as reasonable, in the silence of the "sacred writings," to say that anything else took the place of circumcision as that infant baptism did; or to fasten thus upon the church any other dogma of Romanism. The silence of the sacred writings admitted, and the first age of the history of the church so summarily disposed of, for us, we turn with no little interest to our author, to see how early in subsequent times he places infant baptism.

He thus disposes of Justin Martyr's testimony, who, he says, wrote about the middle of the second century, while he inconsistently claims him against his own showing: "Yet as the phrase ἐκ παιδων, from their infancy, or childhood, may relate to children who have come to years of understanding, as well as to infants, I am satisfied, on a review of the testimony of Justin, that it cannot well be urged as conclusive in favor of Pedobaptism." He treats the testimony of Irenæus (A. D. 178) in a similar manner. Tertullian (A. D. 206) he claims. With what reason it is curious to see. He quotes extensively from him, and because he remarks that infants should not be baptized, he infers that infant baptism was a common affair. He finds no positive evidence of it in the sacred writings; or in the fathers until the time of Origen (A. D. 230); and yet, because Tertullian speaks of adult baptism, he infers that infant baptism was in use. We may well ask, could an ordinance, so called, upon which the "sacred writings are silent," be fastened upon the church without opposition or controversy? or without appearing in the writings of the day, until it became a common practice?

It is sufficient to say of Dr. Woods' work, that he does not profess to find positive evidence of infant baptism until he gets well into the third century, namely, the time when Origen wrote (A. D. 230). He then has failed to show infant baptism an ordinance of the early church. We think Dr. Woods' work might well be republished by Baptists, as has Prof. Stewart's been. Not that they do not somewhat ably contend for Pedobaptism, but that their admissions are so numerous for our position, and their arguments of a nature abandoning all moral certainty for their opinions on the baptismal controversy.

A recent work of Chevalier Bunsen leaves us nothing to desire in regard to the time when infant baptism was introduced. This gentleman is a Pedobaptist scholar and Christian of distinction. He was for many years Prussian ambassador at Rome, and now (1855) holds the same office at London. Rev. Dr. Chase, of Boston, who has met him in Rome, speaks of his Christian and literary character in high terms, particularly of his "ample studies in ecclesiastical history." Bunsen's work is entitled "Hippolytus and his age; or, the doctrine and practice of the Church of Rome under Commodus and Alexander Severus" (Roman Emperors, the one late in the second century, and the other early in the third), "and ancient and modern divinity compared."

It is an old Greek manuscript, of a Roman Bishop, of the period of A. D. 198–236, in which are quoted a series of fifteen *preceding* authors. We are enabled thus to go back, in near proximity to the first century, where the New Testament leaves the history of the church. Bunsen reaches the following conclusions from the work he publishes: "The church adhered rigidly to the principle (as constituting the true purport of the baptism ordained by Christ), that no one can be a member of the communion of saints but by *his own* solemn vow, made in the presence of the church. It was with this understanding that the candidate for baptism was *im-*

mersed in water, and admitted as a brother upon *his* confession of the Father, Son, and Holy Ghost."

Hippolytus is represented by Bunsen as saying: "We, in our day, never defended the baptism of children. It had only began to be practiced (236) in some regions, unless it were an exception and an innovation." A reviewer, in the North British Review, of Bunsen's work, also a Pedobaptist, entirely approves of his conclusions.

The lamented Rev. Professor Knowles, who died while occupying a professor's chair in the Newton Theological Institution, gives the following reliable history of the origin of infant baptism: "Infant baptism was probably introduced into the church about the commencement of the third century, in connection with other corruptions, which even then began to prepare the way for popery. A superstitious idea respecting the necessity of baptism to salvation, led to the baptism of sick persons, and finally to the baptism of infants. Sponsors, holy water, anointing with oil, the sign of the cross, and a multitude of similar ceremonies, equally unauthorized by the Scriptures, were soon introduced. The church lost her simplicity and purity, her ministers became ambitious, and the darkness gradually deepened into the long and dismal night of papal despotism."

Infant baptism, introduced in A. D. 230, taking Dr. Woods' period, which is about the period in which all critics agree, its course was onward. But long before this, namely, (A. D. 150,) the Montanists arose, who, as is shown in our account of them, were Baptists, and form the second link in the Baptist chain of history. The New Testament period being the first, consequently, whatever its history from this point, it does not affect our position, that Baptists have ever existed, as infant baptism has ever found in them opponents.

CHAPTER IV.

The argument for the primitive character of the Baptist church, from the history of the church, being brief sketches of history, showing the chain of connection from the earliest period of the Christian church until the present time. 1. New Testament Baptists from A. D. 1 to 100. 2. The Montanists from 150 to 500. 3. The Novatians from 251 to 600. 4. The Donatists from 311 to 750. 5. The Paulicians from 653 to 1017. 6. The Paterines from 330 to 1250. 7. The Waldenses from 150 to 1523; Luther's appearance and the rise of evangelical Pedobaptism. 8. The Anabaptists of Germany from 1524 to 1674. 9. The Baptists of England, &c., from 100 to 1855. 10. The American Baptists from 1639 to 1855. 11. Other Baptist sects.

An extensive, thorough, critical work upon this subject is a desideratum. Our limits and plan admit of only brief sketches of history, which, however, we trust may be sufficient to show that the light of the Baptist church has never entirely gone out since it first appeared, when, "in those days came John the Baptist, preaching in the wilderness of Judea."

We do not profess to find a succession of Baptist churches, that is to say, one church terminating in another indefinitely. Baptist churches are independent of each other, and may exist without each other's knowledge. But we do find them in being in all ages, the periods, so to speak, lapping over each other. If they have sometimes died out in one place, it has not been until others have sprung up, so that no period of the world, since the introduction of Christianity, has been without them.

BRIEF SKETCHES OF BAPTISTS, FROM THE COMMENCEMENT OF THE CHRISTIAN ERA TO THE PRESENT TIME.

1. *New Testament Baptists*—from A. D. 1 to 100.

We have seen that in New Testament times, that is, the first century, baptism was exclusively immersion, administered only to believers. This is now generally admitted by the learned of our opponents, and needs no further proof than any one can obtain by resort to the New Testament. See also preceding chap. on history of baptism.

2. *Montanists*—from A. D. 150 to 500.

The second century dawns upon the world, and in proportion as it recedes from New Testament times, errors in doctrine and practice creep into the church. According to Mosheim, "about the middle of the second century, Montanus, the first dissenter entitled to notice, undertook a mission to restore Christianity to its native simplicity. He was successful, his doctrines spreading through Asia, Africa, and some portions of Europe." Numerous converts to his theory were made, and "amongst several others of no mean rank, two opulent women." "This sect continued to flourish down to the fifth century, and the list of its members was ennobled by not a few names distinguished both for learning and genius."

That the Montanists were Baptists, is evident from the fact that Tertullian joined them, and became eminent among them. Neander calls him "the Montanist Tertullian;" and speaks of him as "assuming a more important place," in Montanism, than its founder, on account of the superiority of his intellectual character. Mosheim gives Tertullian the same relation to Montanism as does Neander. His writings abound in Baptist sentiments, as we have seen in the chapter on the history of baptism. It is this distinguished writer who says of the mode of baptism in his time: "they were let down into the water, and dipped, between the utterance of a few words." When the Donatists arose (and we shall shortly see that they were Baptists), they were often called Montanists, from their resemblance to this more ancient sect.

It should be remarked that in forming the connection between the New Testament Baptists and the Montanists, a period of only fifty years is unprovided for, as the Montanists appear "about the middle of the second century." This is the only defect in the chain, if, indeed, this can be called one.

The New Testament history leaves the churches in a favorable condition, and fifty years is not a long period for the innovations to have reached a point requiring dissent.

Chevalier Bunsen's work (see preceding chapter on the history of baptism) supplies amply this slight defect. Commencing with the period A. D. 198, some time after Montanus arose, and quoting fifteen different preceding works, we are carried back in near proximity to the close of the first century. We have seen how favorable this work is to Baptist positions. It settles the question of the Baptist character of Christians in the times immediately following the Apostolic.

3. *Novatians*—from A. D. 251 to 600.

So called from their founder, Novatian, an Elder in the Church of Rome, of excellent intellectual and moral character. After protesting against the errors creeping into the church, he abandoned her and commenced a reform. The Novatian churches are spoken of by the ordinary authorities as "introducing their views into France as early as A. D. 254." They were planted all over the "Roman empire, and were numerous at Alexandria, Constantinople, and in Phrygia." Though greatly persecuted, the Novatians are found in a prosperous condition as late as the middle of the fifth century; and Robinson says, "a succession of them continued until the Reformation."

Were the Novatians Baptists? In the attack upon them of Pacianus, Bishop of Barcelona, (A. D. 380,) he says: "likewise you say that the church is a body of men regenerated by water and the Holy Spirit, who have not denied the name of Christ, which is the temple and house of God, the pillar and ground of truth." When an attempt was made to harmonize different factions, the Novatians stood aloof and would not adopt "children's baptism and communion."

If Novatian himself was "poured" for baptism, let it be remembered that it was on a sick bed, and was before his views had matured, and forms an exception to their general rule. It is suitable to remark here, that we do not deem it necessary to prove that in the different periods there were no exceptions to the general rule, though ordinarily any exception cannot be proved.

As to the charge here of baptismal regeneration, it should be observed that Baptists are now, and ever have been accused of it, though more than all others repudiating the sentiment as unscriptural. This grows out of their insisting upon the importance of baptism in the case of every believer, and that the only baptism is that provided in the New Testament. But it is as the outward manifestation of the inward change, for they never baptize any until they are satisfied of their conversion.

4. *Donatists*—from A. D. 311 to 750.

Donatus appears, another witness for the truth, about A. D. 311, and becomes the founder of a church of Christ. Jones remarks of them in A. D. 362: "there was scarcely a town in Africa in which there were not Donatist churches." Not until the middle of the eighth century did the Donatists cease to exist as a distinct people. Here let it be borne in mind that they were often called Montanists. And now it is remarked: "The Donatists aud Novatians very nearly resemble each other in doctrine and discipline." Indeed they are charged by Crispin, a French historian, "with holding together in the following things: First, for purity of church members, by asserting that none ought to be admitted into the church but such as are visibly true believers and real saints; Secondly, for purity of church discipline; Thirdly, for the independence of each church; and Fourthly, they baptized again those whose first baptism they had reason to doubt. They were consequently termed re-baptizers, and Anabaptists." Osiander says, "our modern Anabaptists were the same with the Donatists of old." Fuller, the English church historian, asserts that "the Baptists in England, in his days, were the Donatists, new dipped;" and Robinson declares "they were Trinitarian Anabaptists."

It should be remarked of the Donatists, that any practice unbaptistical can be accounted for only as exceptions to a general rule. Such views as we have quoted, which numerous authorities ascribe to them, can only be accounted for on such a supposition. We do not deny exceptions to the general rule among them, nor is it necessary to our position.

5. *Paulicians*—from A. D. 653 to 1017.

This sect appeared about A. D. 653, in Greece. In A. D. 1017, they appear in Europe, at Orleans. They derived their name from their fondness for the writings of Paul, while they were ever distinguished for their adherence to the entire New Testament. Though persecuted by church and state, they became, and were for centuries, a mighty people in numbers and influence.

Of the Baptist element in this people there can be no doubt. "It is evident," says Mosheim, "they rejected the baptism of infants. They were not charged with any error concerning baptism." "They, with the Manacheans, were Anabaptists, or rejectors of infant baptism," says Dr. Allix, "and were consequently often reproached with that term." "They were simply scriptural in the use of the sacrament," says Milner, "they were orthodox in the doctrine of the Trinity, they knew no other mediator than the Lord Jesus Christ."

6. *Paterines*—from A. D. 330 to 1250.

This term means sufferers or martyrs, and was applied to a people appearing as early, according to Socrates, as A. D. 330. By means of the Paterines, Dr. Allix says, the truth was preserved in A. D. 517. Falling and rising, as persecution became more or less severe, but never entirely disappearing, "the Paterines in the middle of the thirteenth century had exceedingly increased." They now disappear under the influence of augmenting persecution, but it is impossible for one aware of their self-denying, determined opposition to the dominant religion for so many centuries, to doubt the conclusion, to which so many have come, that so far from ceasing to be, they were simply scattered, to form churches of other names, or coalesce with kindred brethren. "It is highly creditable, and there are some reasons to believe, that the Paterines did continue dispersed in Italy, till the Reformation in Germany" (A. D. 1517). In confirmation of this opinion, observe that Reiner says of them, A. D. 1245–50, less than three hundred years before that Reformation broke out: "they had four thousand members in the perfect class; but those called disciples were an innumerable multitude." "And notwithstanding the persecutions to which they were exposed, they maintained themselves in Italy, and kept up a regular correspondence with their brethren in other countries. They had public schools, where their sons were educated, and these were supported by contributions from churches of the same faith in Bohemiah and Poland." It is incredible that such a people could cease to be in less than three hundred years, and no doubt they disappear in other churches, of the same faith and order.

The only question to be settled in relation to the Paterines, is, were they Baptists? I have only space to quote of their sentiments extracts of what relates to this topic. "They said a Christian church ought to consist of *only* good people." "That *faith alone* could save a man." "The church ought not to *persecute.*" "The Catholics of those times immersed, hence the Paterines made no complaint of the action of baptism, but they objected vehemently against the baptism of infants."

7. *The Waldenses*—from A. D. 150 to 1533.

We now approach the time of the Reformation, A. D. 1517, when the Waldenses were in being in great numbers. D'Aughbigne, in his account of the state of religion just prior to the Reformation, remarks: "The Waldenses, far superior to the Mystics in purity of doctrine, compose a long line of witnesses for the truth. Men more unfettered than the rest of the church, seem from the most distant times to have inhabited the summits of the Piedmontese Alps. Their number was augmented, and their doctrine purified by the discipline of

Valdo. From their mountain heights they protested during a long series of ages against the superstitions of Rome."

Four things seem settled in regard to the Waldenses. First, they derive their name from their valleys. Second, they existed in early times, long before some of the churches we have named rose. Third, they rejected sprinkling and infant baptism until Luther's appearance. And fourth, that shortly after that important event, many of these churches were merged in the Lutheran church.

We come now to the rise of evangelical Pedobaptism, and Luther's appearance. Thus far sprinkling and infant baptism, as far as any considerable organization for them is concerned, have been confined to the Roman Catholic church, and Baptists have had only to contend with those unscriptural in numerous other particulars. From this point they have had earnestly to contend for the faith once delivered to the saints, not only with this ancient and formidable enemy of the truth, but with others.

It is a curious, and at the same time serious task, to trace the rise of evangelical Pedobaptism. Luther seems at first to have appreciated the Baptists, who appeared in great numbers simultaneously, when the good news of his appearance and success became known. He seems, at first, to have embraced their views of baptism. It is said that Muncer was at one time called, on account of the attachment between them, Luther's Absalom. Luther's translation of the New Testament, gave to the Baptists great hope, as may well be supposed, when it is remarked that he translated Matt. iii., 1: "In those days came John the dipper." "It cannot," said Luther, "be proved by the Scripture, that infant baptism was instituted by Christ, or began by the first Christians after the Apostles."

But quite early in his Christian career, he decides against Baptists; and, singular enough, is left to persecute them. What was the cause of this change in his policy, which has resulted in so serious consequences? I have given this question all the attention I am able to, and must concur in the opinion of others, to whom, I presume, it was as painful as to myself, that Luther's ambition to be the originator and leader of the Reformation was the cause. The transition is soon told: "When the news reached Luther of Carolstadt re-baptizing; that Muncer had won the hearts of the people; and that the Reformation was going on in his absence; he, on the 6th of March, 1522, flew like lightning from his confinement, at the hazard of his life, and without the advice of his patron, to put a stop to Carolstadt's proceedings. On his return to Wittemburg, he banished Carolstadt, Pelargus, More, Dydymus, and others, and only received Melancthon again." In confirmation of this view of Luther, see Maclean in Mosheim, Ivimy, Bobinson, Neal, M'Crie's Italy, &c. But charity forbids us to linger about this frailty of a truly great and good man.

8. *German Anabaptists*—from 1524 to 1674.

"We have now," to use the language of Benedict, in relation to this people, "arrived at a wide, open, and interesting field, so far as the history of Baptists is concerned, where we shall not have to feel our way amidst the obscure and equivocal statements of both friends and foes; we have now entered the land of the ancient dippers, who may justly claim their descent from the Waldenses, Wickliffites, Hussites, Henrecians, Petrobrussians, and other ancient sects; and to the country where the old and perpetually repudiated name of Anabaptists was applied to our brethren in early times, where their sufferings were long and severe, and their triumphs were distinguished; and from which they have at different times swarmed out in multitudes into all the surrounding nations."

It is of the German Anabaptists that Mosheim says: "The true origin of that sect which acquired the denomination of Anabaptists, by their administering anew the rite of baptism to those who came over to their communion, and derived that of Mennonites from the famous man to whom they owe the greatest part of their present felicity, is hid in the remote depth of antiquity, and is, of consequence, extremely difficult to be ascertained. This uncertainty will not appear surprising when it is considered that this sect started up all of a sudden, in several countries, at the same point of time, under leaders of different talents and different intentions; and at the very period when the first contests of the Reformers with the Roman pontiffs, drew the attention of the world, and employed the pens of the learned, in such a manner as to render all other objects and incidents almost matters of indifference."

This testimony of the "great historian," Mosheim, who was not a Baptist, is valuable in establishing the antiquity of the German Baptists, and their number at the time of the Reformation. So far from its being true that they originated in the Reformation, they existed at the time in great numbers, in numerous localities, and were only emboldened by what the Reformers were permitted to accomplish, to recommence with new energy the contest for the faith once delivered to the saints. They suffered incredible hardships during the Reformation, being persecuted for their sentiments by fines, imprisonment, banishment, and death itself. Would that the Reformers were innocent in relation to this matter; but truth requires us to say, that they were anything but "fathers" to the Baptists, ever contending against their peculiarities, and attempting to crush by the strong arm of persecution, what they could not by argument. But "the blood of the martyrs was the seed of the church."

Mr. Benedict says: "I have followed the history of the German Anabaptists from 1524 till towards the close of the seventeenth century, a period of about one hundred and fifty years—have noticed every kind of impeachment which was brought against them by their enemies, and am happy in being able to state that they were never accused of any personal misconduct. They continually challenged their accusers for proof of any thing immoral or injurious in their conduct, but nothing of the kind was ever attempted."

It should be remarked of the Anabaptists of this period, that they suffered greatly from the application of the term to all kinds of dissenters. Men were called Anabaptists, for the reason that they opposed the prevailing faith, often when they bore little resemblance to the genuine party, to whom the term was applied. The affair at Munster, for instance, has been charged to the Anabaptists, when the fact is, that it originated with "one Bernard Rotman, a Pedobaptist minister, of the Lutheran persuasion." Some real Anabaptists, undoubtedly, ultimately had a part in this fanatical affair, and "this conduct of a handful of Anabaptists, with others, drew upon the whole body" odium. "Casiander, a papist, declares that many Anabaptists in Germany did resist and oppose the opinions and practices of those at Munster."

In a similar manner, undoubtedly, we may account for the fact, for fact it is, that there were those "in the period of the Reformation," who did not immerse in their rebaptisms. But that the genuine Anabaptists did immerse, is too obvious a historical fact to admit of dispute.

The Anabaptists were numerous prior to and during the time of Luther. Mosheim says of them, in A. D. 1536: "An innumerable multitude of Baptists preferred death in its worst forms, to a retraction of their sentiments." They came out of the persecution of that period multiplied and strengthened in numerous countries. In A. D. 1540, it is said: "Shoals of Baptists who had hitherto resided in Germany, now left their native country, and passed into Holland and the Netherlands, to enjoy their religious privileges." In A. D. 1606, "Some of the Mennonites," as the Anabaptists were sometimes called, "introduced pouring, and pleaded that it virtually contained baptism, while the greater part retained dipping and were called immergenten." Whatever, in fine, may be said of this people as to their sentiments, character, and ultimate deterioration, they constitute an important link in the Baptist chain, reaching far into the past and into the future beyond the history of Baptists now existing in different countries.

We have now traced the Baptists through the period of the Reformation. It remains for us, in leaving the period thus comprehended, to remark, first, that it is not claimed that the churches considered, were in every particular like the Baptist churches of the present time. It is sufficient that they were evangelical, and distinguished for their mode and subjects of baptism, as are Baptists now. Second, it may be remarked, that, while they undoubtedly had peculiarities which cannot be defended, they had more excellencies; and are indebted for many of the extravagances attributed to them to the misrepresentations of enemies. Third, it is impossible to study their character without admiring it, and feeling assured that they were instrumentally the preservers of the church of Christ, through its long, dark night.

9. *Baptists of England, Wales, Scotland and Ireland*—from A. D. 100 to 1855.

Our brethren in England, in their "Jubilee Memorial," say: "England undoubtedly received the Gospel in the days of the Apostles; and its ecclesiastical history plainly proves that thousands were baptized according to the primitive model. About the same time, or soon after, Wales was visited by Christian teachers; and when Austin visited this country, about the A. D. 600, he found a society of Christians at Bangor, consisting of twenty-one hundred, who were afterwards destroyed at the command of the Pope, because they would not baptize infants." According to Ivimy, Crosby, and Dutch Martyrology, as early as A. D. 1575, a company of German Anabaptists, flying from persecution, had settled in London, to experience the same treatment as at home. An article attributed to Rev. Dr. Williams, has the following item of English Baptist history: "to the Baptists then, the age of

Baxter" (A. D. 1615–1691) "is a memorable one. The period of the Commonwealth and the Protectorate was the season in which our distinguished sentiments became the property of the people. Through many years, they had been held in deep retirement, and at the peril of their lives; now they began rapidly working their way, and openly into the masses of society." It is sufficient to add, that of the present Baptist churches in England, at least seven of them date back to the period to which Dr. Williams alludes. They are, 1. Little Prescot St. Ch., constituted 1633; 2. Devonshire Square, 1638; 3. Red Cross St., 1644; 4. Commercial Road, 1657; 5. Milford, 1664; 6. Little Wild St., 1691; 7. Maze Pond, 1692. This brings their history down to the present time. It is sufficient to remark of Wales, Scotland, and Ireland, on account of their proximity and connection with England, that from early times until now, they have had their Baptist churches.

10. *American Baptists*—from A. D. 1639 to 1855.

The oldest Baptist church in Britain, continuing to the present time, bears date A. D. 1633. The two oldest Baptist churches in the United States, namely, first Providence and first Newport, R. I., who still dispute the honor of being the older, bear date, the former A. D. 1639, and the latter A. D. 1644. The chain of Baptist history thus crosses the Atlantic ocean, connecting the two countries.

The first permanent settlement of the Pilgrim Fathers was in Plymouth, Mass., A. D. 1620, about nineteen years before the two oldest Baptist churches still existing were constituted. During this period, Baptists appeared in Massachusetts, denying the union of church and state, and infant baptism, to suffer reproach, which they bore with Christian patience and firmness, their opponents becoming more and more bold. Roger Williams flies from Salem, persecuted by the Pilgrim Fathers, and after a short sojourn with the Indians in their native forest, founds the State of Rhode Island and the City of

Providence, A. D. 1636. He was accused before leaving Salem, of "preaching doctrines tending to Anabaptistry." He was then a Presbyterian, and pastor of a Presbyterian church. In March, 1638–9, he was baptized, and was honored with being the apostle of the Baptists in America. As Baptist sentiments have ever been wont to, from the days of John the Baptist, so in America they prevailed in spite of oppressive persecution. In the following order they appear in the different United States. Rhode Island, 1638–56; Massachusetts, 1663–6; Pennsylvania, 1711–46; New Jersey, 1712–47; New York, 1724–48; Connecticut, 1726–50; South Carolina, 1738–45; and thus onward to the present time.

The progress of regular Baptists in the United States is on this wise: "In 1792 there were 70,017 communicants; in 1812, 189,345; in 1832, 384,859; in 1852, 770,839. In 1853, there were of regular Baptists in the United States, 500 associations; 10,131 churches; 6,475 ordained ministers; 60,820 baptisms in the year; 808,754 communicants; 45 Baptist periodicals; 25 colleges; 10 theological institutions; and 8 national missionary associations." Our church then has existed since the dawn of the Christian era; and is still in all the vigor of youth. Though she has had to contend through poverty and reproach, with every kind of enemy, she has never yielded to despondency; and promises now, more than at any period of her history, to stand and flourish, until time shall be no more.

Undoubtedly, the Baptist church may be traced, for the most part, by other channels, from the commencement up to the time of the Anabaptists. We have selected this channel, because on the whole we have preferred it, and not because it is the only one. Orchard's is somewhat different from ours, but I presume not easily shown incorrect. We only ask that those who doubt the correctness of this channel will examine the subject and show us where we are wrong.

11. There are several minor sects of Baptists having no

more connection with the regular Baptists than have denominations not bearing the name. They harmonize with the regular Baptists in baptism, and most of them are evangelical, and like other denominations hold several doctrines in common with them. They all have peculiarities of which the regular Baptists do not partake. The more important of these are the Sabbatarians or Seventh-day Baptists; the General Baptists of England and the Free-will Baptists of America; the Six principle Baptists; the German Baptists or Tunkers (Dippers); the Church of God Baptists; the Mennonite Baptists; the Disciples or Campbelite Baptists; and the Old School or Anti-Mission or Anti-Effort Baptists. All of these, excepting the two last, have a very early origin, and all of them have members of good character. Their names generally designate their peculiarities. They all belong, in some sense, to the great Baptist family; and it is by no means improbable, will some day be merged in "the Baptist denomination." The reader is referred to the statistics of churches, in the latter part of this book, for the present condition of these different sects.

CHAPTER V.

The argument for the primitive character of the Baptist church from its identity with the primitive church; the identity wanting in the case of the Roman Catholic, the Greek, and the Protestant churches. 1. If the Baptist church is the primitive church, there should be an identity, and there is. 2. There is none between the Roman Catholic and primitive church; D'Aubigne on the rise and fall of Romanism; Gavazzi's demolition of Romanism. 3. The Greek church originating in the Roman. 4. Church of England no claim to primitive resemblance. 5. The other evangelical churches primitive only in part.

1. If the foregoing testimony is reliable, their should be a sameness between the primitive church and the Baptist church,

in fundamental points. It is not to be supposed that Jehovah gave the world a church, which in process of time was to be so changed by men, as to bear but little resemblance to its former self. Churches, therefore, now fundamentally unlike the Apostolic, either never were like it, or have departed from the Divine model, and which is their greater condemnation it may be difficult to tell; but either supposition must condemn them with thinking persons.

2. It is unaccountable presumption for the Roman Catholic church to claim any resemblance to the Apostolic church, for it has none. If it commenced in the original church at Rome, it very soon degenerated into its present worldly form. The following from D'Aubigne's history of the Reformation, is probably a reliable account of the rise and fall of the church of Rome:

"Paul of Tarsus, one of the greatest Apostles of the new religion, had arrived at Rome, the capital of the empire, and of the world, preaching in bondage the salvation which cometh from God. A church was formed beside the throne of the Cæsars. Composed at first of a few converted Jews, and Greeks, and Roman citizens, it was rendered famous by the teaching and the death of the Apostle of the Gentiles. For a time it shone out brightly as a beacon upon a hill. Its faith was everywhere celebrated, but ere long it declined from its primitive condition. It was by small beginnings that both imperial and Christian Rome advanced to the usurped dominion of the world.

"If Rome is the queen of cities, why should not her pastor be the king of bishops? Why should not the Roman church be the mother of Christendom? Why should not all nations be her children, and her authority their sovereign law? It was easy for the ambitious heart of man to reason thus. Ambitious Rome did so. Thus when Pagan Rome fell, she bequeathed to the humble ministers of the God of peace, sitting in the midst of her ruins, the proud titles which her invincible sword had won from the nations of the earth.

"No sooner was the erroneous notion of the necessity for a visible unity of the church established, than another appeared—the necessity of an outward representation of that union. Although we find no traces in the Gospel of Peter's superiority over the other Apostles, although the very idea of a primacy is opposed to the fraternal relations which united the brethren, and even to the spirit of the Gospel dispensation, which, on the contrary, requires all the children of the Father, to 'minister one to another,' acknowledging only one teacher and one master; although Christ had strongly rebuked his disciples whenever ambitious desires of pre-eminence were conceived in their carnal hearts; the primacy of St. Peter was invented and supported by texts wrongly interpreted; and men next acknowledged in this Apostle, and in his self-styled successors at Rome, the visible representatives of visible unity—the heads of the universal church.

"New and more powerful friends than all the rest soon came to her assistance. Ignorance and superstition took possession of the church, and delivered it, fettered and blindfold, into the hands of Rome."

I will also quote on this subject the eloquent Italian convert from Romanism, Gavazzi, who, in a few burning sentences, places in its true light the claim of Romanism to Apostolic origin or resemblance:

"Christianity was founded by Christ; it was then a simple, pure, spiritual church. After some centuries it received the patronage of emperors; then it was corrupted into a haughty, material, and profane system. Constantine, emperor of Rome, a Pagan, embraced Christianity; other emperors countenanced and adopted it, and became its guardians—a bad guardianship; for, warped by their political aims, they sought to please Christian and Pagan; the priests of the faith, warped by private aims, were content to please the emperors; an evil contiguity resulted in an incongruous, absurd, profane medley; and Paganism, wedded to a vitiated, debased, false Christianity, became the parent of the church of Rome. Almost all the forms of Paganism are found in the Roman church. The Pagans had their Pontifex Maximus, Rome has her supreme pontiff; Paganism had its purgatory with material fire, Rome has the same; Paganism had expiations for the dead, so has Rome; Paganism had its vestal virgins, Rome has her nuns; Paganism had its processions and sacred images, Rome abounds in hers; Paganism had its penates, Rome has her peculiar saints; Paganism had its sanctuaries, holy water, pilgrimages, votive tables, and Rome has all these too; Paganism had the perpetual fire of vesta, and Rome has the perpetual sacrifice of the mass. The sacrifice of the mass, then, is an inheritance from the heathen. The word of God is expressly contrary to it.

"Is that which Catholics believe and practice, founded on the Holy Scriptures? No! I have looked into history, and I can point to the date when errors were introduced into the Roman church; intruded upon the true church of Christ; masses, transubstantiation, infallibility, purgatory, absolution, indulgences, worship of images, relics of saints, invocation of saints, works of supererogation, celibacy of the clergy, monasteries, church processions, holy water and holy wafers, are all found in history—none of them in the Bible—and therefore does the Pope prohibit the reading of the Bible. More and more: such a system of Pagan and coarse intrusions, which is called the *spiritual* power, is supported by another iron, muddy machinery, called the *temporal* power, which both constitute that sacred political drama, called the Romish church. And both are unscriptural and anti-scriptural."

It is a waste of time to prove any farther, the absence of all identity between the Roman Catholic and the Christian church. Not only has the former all Gavazzi names, and much more, which the latter never had, but she is wanting in numerous internal and external vitalities which characterize the church of Christ.

It is not denied that the church of Rome has had individual members of a high order of piety; but these have been too few to characterize her; and even these have been so unlike primitive Christians, as to be able to live and die in a church claiming to be the only church of Christ; and yet not only wanting in, but denying most of the inward and outward characteristics of that church.

3. The Greek church is in a similar condemnation, in respect to any identity with the primitive church. It has its origin in the political partition of the Roman empire into the Oriental or Greek, and the Occidental or Latin, in A. D. 381. The formal separation of the church did not take place until A. D. 482. The Greek church, originating in the Roman Catholic, and superior to it in some particulars, yet too greatly resembles it to give it any considerable preference. Its liturgy, its tradition, its confession and penance, its extreme unction, its superstition, its abandonment of spirituality in outward forms, and its connection with the state, &c., &c., annihilate any claim it may make to identity with the church of Christ.

4. Of the Protestant churches, that of England claims identity with the primitive churches with least reason. Where in the New Testament, the history of the primitive church, do we find the alliance between the church and state which exists between the church of England and the crown? Nowhere. On the contrary, the New Testament directly prohibits that alliance in such passages as: "My kingdom is not of this world." Where in the New Testament do we find anything like the superior order of clergy; and the worldly secular character of the clergy, of the church of England? Nowhere; while the entire system is annihilated by such passages as: "Be ye not called Rabbi, for one is your Master even Christ, and all ye are brethren." Where in the New Testament is there anything approaching the liturgy of the church of England, her

forms and prayers for public worship? Nowhere; for remarkable is the simplicity of the Divine plan; and the only defence of the Episcopal is, that it is an improvement of the Divine, which is as insulting to God as it is contrary to fact. The principal difference between the Roman and Greek church, and the English church, in this respect, is, that the latter has not carried so far the innovations; but far enough to destroy its claim to resemblance to the church of Christ.

5. The position of the other evangelical churches is very different from that of the church of England. Though they have all rejected the primitive form and subjects of baptism, they acknowledge and imitate its simplicity of worship, and its spiritual character. They all agree with the Baptist church in the following great doctrines of Christianity: "Man's native sinfulness—the purity and obligation of the law of God—the true and proper divinity of our Lord Jesus Christ—the necessity and reality of His atonement and sacrifice—the efficiency of the Holy Spirit in the work of renovation—the free and full offers of the Gospel, and the duty of man to accept it—the necessity of personal holiness, and a state of rewards and punishments beyond the grave."

On this account the evangelical churches are considered, in a general sense, the church of Christ. Nevertheless, excepting the Baptist church, they all differ essentially from the primitive church, in the subjects and mode of baptism; and, therefore, cannot claim the same identity with that church.

We claim for the Baptist church a remarkable identity with the primitive. We ask for the difference between the two. We place the New Testament in the hands of those who doubt, and invite a comparison. Nor is this boasting, if our claims are well founded. The language of Baptists is that of Paul: "God forbid that I should glory, save in the cross of our Lord Jesus Christ." We claim not perfection of spirit, but of laws. The primitive church was imperfect in spirit. All churches are. Imperfection is stamped upon everything in this world

We claim, however, what other churches have in harmony with the primitive; and in addition what others have not, the primitive subjects and mode of baptism.

We refer our readers to the chapters in this book upon the different topics for the evidence of the correctness of our position, with the remark, that, admitting its correctness, there can be no doubt as to the origin of the Baptist church. Let none, however, imagine that we have nothing to attain. The spirituality of all is greatly beneath what it should be. It is due to the Saviour, to the church, to the world, that we "grow in grace, and in the knowledge of our Lord and Saviour Jesus Christ." O how sadly deficient are Christians in these respects, and how it becomes them to "covet earnestly the best gifts," and still "behold a more excellent way," than that to which they have attained! Particularly is this obligatory upon Baptists, claiming such identity with the primitive church.

PART II.

DOCTRINES AND ORDINANCES OF THE BAPTIST CHURCH.

Reader! pass not over this part of our book, on the ground that it is nothing new. We admit your plea; but deny that on this account you should pass it entirely, or with a hasty perusal. You should be familiar with the doctrines and ordinances of the church, particularly of your own church, what they are and the reasons for them. Are you familiar with them? Could you teach to others, or give even a moderate account of them? Unless you are better informed than the masses of even church members, you must acknowledge your deficiency in this important matter. Here are the doctrines and ordinances of the church, and the reasons for them, in a convenient, condensed form. Read and reflect.

CHAPTER I.

Articles of Faith. 1. Harmony in the midst of variety. 2. Articles of Faith, with proof texts. 3. Church Covenant.

1. Baptist churches generally have their articles of faith, being a compendium of their belief, with proof passages. In addition to the insertion of a copy of these in this chapter, I shall insert able articles upon their distinguishing peculiarities.

It is remarkable that so great harmony should prevail on so many topics, among the multitudinous churches of the denomination in their articles of faith, when it is remembered that the churches are independent of each other. Rev. Dr. Church, one of the editors of the New York Chronicle, says:

"Henry B. Dawson, Esq., Secretary of the Baptist Historical Society of this city, is in possession of a Confession of Faith, which was drawn up and subscribed to by the members of seven Baptist churches in London, more than two hundred years ago. It is the oldest document of the kind in the English language, not excepting the one found in Dr. Neal's historical work from Crosby's. It consists of an interesting preface, and fifty-two articles, to all of which we can subscribe as heartily as to any document, of the same length, ancient or modern. In fact, we have seen nothing, in our estimation, that equals the articles on the independence of our churches, the ordinance of baptism, the officers of churches, and discipline of members."

The principal difference in Baptist Articles of Faith, is in the phraseology or style of them, not in the doctrines. In some of the older ones obnoxious terms are used, without any gain to the sentiment it is designed to express. This might have been intentional, for it must be confessed that our fathers were not anxious to conciliate a giddy world, by endeavoring to make the truth palatable to the human heart. They may have carried this feeling too far. We may carry the opposite one too far. The true ground is, as usual, the medium. The great effort should be to give the mind of the Holy Spirit, as nearly as possible.

The harmony among the Baptists on these points, can only be accounted for in that with them the only rule of faith and practice is the Bible. As they all resort to the same source of knowledge, they harmonize in a most remarkable manner. Almost every church has its Articles of Faith, differing in numerous unessential particulars, but agreeing in substance.

2. Among the numerous Confessions of Faith in use in the denomination, we have been not a little perplexed in making a selection. We have finally decided to adopt that prepared by Rev. J. Newton Brown, D. D., Editorial Secretary of the American Baptist Publication Society. These articles of

6

faith were prepared several years ago, and are now in very general use.

DECLARATION OF FAITH.

I. OF THE SCRIPTURES.—We believe that the Holy Bible was written by men divinely inspired, and is a perfect treasure of heavenly instruction;[1] that it has God for its author, salvation for its end,[2] and truth without any mixture of error for its matter;[3] that it reveals the principles by which God will judge us;[4] and therefore is, and shall remain to the end of the world, the true centre of Christian union,[5] and the supreme standard by which all human conduct, creeds, and opinions should be tried.[6]

Places in the Bible where taught.

[1] 2 Tim. iii. 16, 17. All scripture is given by inspiration of God, and is profitable for doctrine, for reproof, for correction, for instruction in righteousness; that the man of God may be perfect, thoroughly furnished unto all good works. Also, 2 Pet. i. 21. 2 Sam. xxiii. 2. Acts i. 16; iii. 21. John x. 35. Luke xvi. 29–31. Ps. cxix. 111. Rom. iii. 1, 2.

[2] 2 Tim. iii. 15. Able to make thee wise unto salvation. Also, 1 Pet. i. 10–12. Acts xi. 14. Rom. i. 16. Mark xvi. 16. John v. 38–39.

[3] Proverbs xxx. 5, 6. Every word of God is pure.—Add thou not unto his words, lest he reprove thee, and thou be found a liar. Also, John xvii. 17. Rev. xxii. 18, 19. Rom. iii. 4.

[4] Rom. ii. 12. As many as have sinned in the law, shall be judged by the law. John xii. 47, 48. If any man hear my words—the word that I have spoken, the same shall judge him in the last day. Also, 1 Cor. iv. 3, 4. Luke x. 10–16. xii. 47, 48.

[5] Phil. iii. 16. Let us walk by the same rule; let us mind the same thing. Also Ephes. iv. 3–6. Phil. ii. 1, 2. 1 Cor. i. 10. 1 Pet. iv. 11.

[6] 1 John iv. 1. Beloved, believe not every spirit, but try the spirits whether they are of God. Isaiah viii. 20. To the law and to the testimony; if they speak not according to this word, it is because there is no light in them. 1 Thess. v. 21. Prove all things. 2 Cor. xiii. 5. Prove your own selves. Also, Acts xvii. 11. 1 John iv. 6. Jude 3d. v. Ephes. vi. 17. Ps. cxix. 59, 60. Phil. i. 9–11.

II. OF THE TRUE GOD.—We believe that there is one, and only one, living and true God, an infinite, intelligent Spirit, whose name is JEHOVAH, the Maker and Supreme Ruler of Heaven and Earth;[1] inexpressibly glorious in holiness,[2] and worthy of all possible honor, confidence and love;[3] that in the unity of the Godhead there are three persons, the Father, the Son, and the Holy Ghost;[4] equal in every divine perfection,[5] and executing distinct but harmonious offices in the great work of redemption.[6]

Places in the Bible where taught.

John iv. 24. God is a spirit. Ps. cxlvii. 5. His understanding is infinite. Ps. lxxxiii. 18. Thou whose name alone is JEHOVAH, art the Most High over all the earth. Heb. iii. 4. Rom. i. 20. Jer. x. 10.

[2] Ex. xv. 11. Who is like unto Thee—glorious in holiness? Isa. vi. 3. 1 Pet. i. 15, 16. Rev. iv. 6–8.

[3] Mark xii. 30. Thou shalt love the Lord thy God with all thy heart, and with all thy soul, and with all thy mind, and with all thy strength. Rev. iv. 11. Thou art worthy, O Lord, to receive glory, and honor, and power: for thou hast created all things, and for thy pleasure they are and were created. Matt. x. 37. Jer. ii. 12, 13.

[4] Matt. xxviii. 19. Go ye therefore and teach all nations, baptizing them in the name of the Father, and of the Son, and of the Holy Ghost. John xv. 26. When the comforter is come, whom I will send you from the Father, even the Spirit of Truth, which proceedeth from the Father, he shall testify of me. 1 Cor. xii. 4–6. 1 John v. 7.

[5] John x. 30. I and my Father are one. John v. 17; xiv. 23; xvii. 5, 10. Acts v. 3, 4. 1 Cor. ii. 10, 11. Phil. ii. 5, 6.

[6] Ephes. ii. 18. For through Him [the Son] we both have an access by one Spirit unto the Father. 2 Cor. xiii. 14. The grace of our Lord Jesus Christ, and the love of God, and the communion of the Holy Ghost, be with you all. Rev. i. 4, 5. Comp. ii. 7.

III. Of the Fall of Man.—We believe that man was created in holiness, under the law of his Maker;[1] but by voluntary transgression fell from that holy and happy state;[2] in consequence of which all mankind are now sinners,[3] not by constraint but choice;[4] being by nature utterly void of that holiness required by the law of God, positively inclined to evil; and therefore under just condemnation to eternal ruin,[5] without defence or excuse.[6]

Places in the Bible where taught.

[1] Gen. i. 27. God created man in his own image. Gen. i. 31. And God saw everything that he had made, and behold, it was very good. Eccles. vii. 29. Acts xvii. 26. Gen. ii. 16.

[2] Gen. iii. 6–24. And when the woman saw that the tree was good for food, and that it was pleasant to the eyes, and a tree to be desired to make one wise; she took of the fruit thereof, and did eat; and gave also unto her husband with her, and he did eat.—Therefore the Lord God drove out the man; and he placed at the east of the garden of Eden, Cherubims, and a flaming sword which turned every way to keep the way of the tree of life. Rom. v. 12.

[3] Rom. v. 19. By one man's disobedience many were made sinners. John iii. 6. Ps. li. 5. Rom. v. 15–19; viii. 7.

[4] Isa. liii. 6. We have turned, every one to his own way. Gen. vi. 12. Rom. iii. 9–18.

[5] Eph. ii. 1–3. Among whom also we all had our conversation in times past in the lusts of our flesh, fulfilling the desires of the flesh and of the mind; and were by nature the children of wrath even as others. Rom. i. 18. For the wrath of God is revealed from heaven against all ungodliness and unrighteousness of men, who hold the truth in unrighteousness. Rom. i. 32; ii. 1–16. Gal. iii. 10. Matt. xx. 15.

[6] Ex. xviii. 19, 20. Yet say ye, Why? doth not the son bear the iniquity of the father?—The soul that sinneth it shall die. The son shall not bear the iniquity of the father, neither shall the father bear the iniquity of the son; the righteousness of the righteous shall be upon him, and the wickedness of the wicked shall be upon him. Rom. i. 20. So that they are without excuse. Rom. iii. 19. That every mouth may be stopped and all the world may become guilty before God. Gal. iii. 22.

IV. Of the Way of Salvation.—We believe that the salvation of sinners is wholly of grace;[1] through the mediatorial offices of the Son of God;[2] who by the appointment of the Father, freely took upon Him our nature, yet without sin;[3] honored the Divine law by his personal obedience;[4] and by his death made a full atonement for our sins;[5] that having risen from the dead, He is now enthroned in Heaven;[6] and uniting in His wonderful person the tenderest sympathies with divine perfections, He is every way qualified to be a suitable, a compassionate, and an all-sufficient Saviour.[7]

Places in the Bible where taught.

[1] Eph. ii. 5. By grace ye are saved. Matt. xviii. 11. 1 John iv. 10. 1 Cor. iii. 5–7. Acts xv. 11.

[2] John iii. 16. For God so loved the world, that he gave his only begotten Son, that whosoever believeth in him should not perish but have everlasting life. John i. 1–14. Heb. iv. 14; xii. 24.

[3] Phil. ii. 6, 7. Who being in the form of God, thought it not robbery to be equal with God; but made himself of no reputation, and took upon him the form of a servant, and was made in the likeness of men. Heb. ii. 9; ii. 14. 2 Cor. v. 21.

[4] Isa. xlii. 21. The Lord is well pleased for his righteousness' sake; he will magnify the law and make it honorable. Phil. ii. 8. Gal. iv. 4, 5. Rom. iii. 21.

[5] Isa. liii. 4, 5. He was wounded for our transgressions, he was bruised for our iniquities; the chastisement of our peace was upon him; and with his stripes we are healed. Matt. xx. 28. Rom. iv. 25; iii. 21–26. 1 John iv. 10; ii. 2. 1 Cor. xv. 1–3. Heb. ix. 13–15.

[6] Heb. i. 8. Unto the Son he saith, Thy throne, O God, is forever and ever. Heb. i. 3; viii. 1. Col. iii. 1–4.

[7] Heb. vii. 25. Wherefore he is able also to save them to the utmost that come unto God by him, seeing he ever liveth to make intercession for them.

Col. ii. 9. For in him dwelleth all the fullness of the Godhead bodily. Heb. ii. 18. In that he himself hath suffered, being tempted, he is able to succor them that are tempted. Heb. vii. 26. Ps. lxxxix. 19. Ps. xlv.

V. Of Justification.—We believe that the great Gospel blessing which Christ[1] secures to such as believe in Him, is Justification;[2] that Justification includes the pardon of sin,[3] and the promise of eternal life on principles of righteousness;[4] that it is bestowed, not in consideration of any works of righteousness which we have done, but solely through faith in the Redeemer's blood;[5] by virtue of which faith His perfect righteousness is freely imputed to us of God;[6] that it brings us into a state of most blessed peace and favor with God, and secures every other blessing needful for time and eternity.[7]

Places in the Bible where taught.

[1] John i. 16. Of his fullness have all we received. Eph. iii. 8.

[2] Acts xiii. 39. By him all that believe are justified from all things. Isa. iii. 11, 12. Rom. viii. 1.

[3] Rom. v. 9. Being justified by his blood, we shall be saved from wrath through him. Zech. xiii. 1. Matt. ix. 6. Acts x. 43.

[4] Rom. v. 17. They which receive the abundance of grace and of the gift of righteousness shall reign in life by one, Jesus Christ. Titus iii. 5, 6. 1 Pet. iii. 7. 1 John ii. 25. Rom. v. 21.

[5] Rom. iv. 4, 5. Now to him that worketh is the reward not reckoned of grace, but of debt. But to him that worketh not, but believeth on Him that justifieth the ungodly, his faith is counted for righteousness. Rom. v. 21; vi. 23. Phil. iii. 7–9.

[6] Rom. v. 19. By the obedience of one shall many be made righteous. Rom. iii. 24–26; iv. 23–25. 1 John ii. 12.

[7] Rom. v. 1, 2. Being justified by faith, we have peace with God, through our Lord Jesus Christ; by whom also we have access by faith into this grace wherein we stand, and rejoice in hope of the glory of God. Rom. v. 3. We glory in tribulations also. Rom. v. 11. We also joy in God. 1 Cor. i. 30, 31. Matt. vi. 33. 1 Tim. iv. 8.

VI. Of the Freeness of Salvation.—We believe that the blessings of salvation are made free to all by the Gospel;[1] that it is the immediate duty of all to accept them by a cordial, penitent and obedient faith;[2] and that nothing prevents the salvation of the greatest sinner on earth, but his own determined depravity and voluntary rejection of the Gospel;[3] which rejection involves him in an aggravated condemnation.[4]

Places in the Bible where taught.

[1] Isa. lv. 1. Ho, every one that thirsteth, come ye to the waters. Rev. xxii. 17. Whosoever will, let him take the water of life freely. Luke xiv. 17.

[2] Rom. xvi. 26. The Gospel according to the commandment of the everlasting God, made known to all nations for the obedience of faith. Mark i. 15. Rom. i. 15–17.

[3] John v. 40. Ye will not come to me, that ye might have life. Matt. xxiii. 37. Rom. ix. 32. Prov. i. 24. Acts xiii. 46.

[4] John iii. 19. And this is the condemnation, that light is come into the world, and men loved darkness rather than light, because their deeds were evil. Matt. xi. 20. Luke xix. 27. 2 Thess. i. 8.

VII. Of Grace in Regeneration.—We believe that in order to be saved, sinners must be regenerated, or born again;[1] that regeneration consists in giving a holy disposition to the mind;[2] that it is effected in a manner above our comprehension, by the power of the Holy Spirit, in connection with Divine truth,[3] so as to secure our voluntary obedience to the Gospel;[4] and that its proper evidence appears in the holy fruits of repentance, and faith, and newness of life.[5]

Places in the Bible where taught.

[1] John iii. 3. Verily, verily, I say unto thee, Except a man be born again, he cannot see the kingdom of God. John iii. 6. 7. 1 Cor. i. 14. Rev. viii. 7–9. Rev. xxi. 27.

[2] 2 Cor. v. 17. If any man be in Christ, he is a new creature. Ez. xxxvi. 26. Deut. xxx. 6. Rom. ii. 28, 29; v. 5. 1 John iv. 7.

[3] John iii. 8. The wind bloweth where it listeth, and thou hearest the sound thereof, but canst not tell whence it cometh, and whither it goeth; so is every one that is born of the Spirit. John i. 13. Which were born not of blood, nor of the will of the flesh, nor of the will of man, but of God. James i. 16–18. Of his own will begat he us with the word of truth. 1 Cor. i. 30. Phil. ii. 13.

[4] 1 Pet. i. 22–25. Ye have purified your souls by obeying the truth through the Spirit. 1 John v. 1. Whosoever believeth that Jesus is the Christ, is born of God. Eph. iv. 20–24. Col. iii. 9–11.

[5] Eph. v. 9. The fruit of the Spirit is in all goodness, and righteousness, and truth. Rom. viii. 9. Gal. v. 16–23. Eph. iii. 14–21. Matt. iii. 8–10; vii. 20. 1 John v. 4, 18.

VIII. Of Repentance and Faith.—We believe that Repentance and Faith are sacred duties, and also inseparable graces, wrought in our souls by the regenerating Spirit of

God;[1] whereby being deeply convinced of our guilt, danger and helplessness, and of the way of salvation by Christ,[2] we turn to God with unfeigned contrition, confession, and supplication for mercy;[3] at the same time heartily receiving the Lord Jesus Christ as our Prophet, Priest and King, and relying on Him alone as the only and all-sufficient Saviour.[4]

Places in the Bible where taught.

[1] Mark i. 15. Repent ye, and believe the Gospel. Acts xi. 18. Then hath God also to the Gentiles granted repentance unto life. Ephes. ii. 8. By grace ye are saved, through faith; and that not of yourselves; it is the gift of God. 1 John v. 1. Whosoever believeth that Jesus is the Christ, is born of God.

[2] John xvi. 8. He will reprove the world of sin, and of righteousness, and of judgment. Acts ii. 37, 38. They were pricked in their heart, and said—Men and brethren, what shall we do? Then Peter said unto them, Repent, and be baptized every one of you in the name of Jesus Christ for the remission of your sins. Acts xvi. 30, 31.

[3] Luke xviii. 13. And the publican smote upon his breast, saying, God be merciful to me a sinner. Luke xv. 18–21. James iv. 7–10. 2 Cor. vii. 11. Rom. x. 12, 13. Ps. li.

[4] Rom. x. 9–11. If thou shalt confess with thy mouth the Lord Jesus, and shalt believe in thy heart that God hath raised him from the dead, thou shalt be saved. Acts iii. 22, 23. Heb. iv. 14. Ps. ii. 6. Heb. i. 8; viii. 25. 2 Tim. i. 12.

IX. Of God's Purpose of Grace.—We believe that Election is the eternal purpose of God, according to which He graciously regenerates, sanctifies, and saves sinners;[1] that being perfectly consistent with the free agency of man, it comprehends all the means in connection with the end;[2] that it is a most glorious display of God's sovereign goodness, being infinitely free, wise, holy and unchangeable;[3] that it utterly excludes boasting, and promotes humility, love, prayer, praise, trust in God, and active imitation of his free mercy;[4] that it encourages the use of means in the highest degree;[5] that it may be ascertained by its effects in all who truly believe the Gospel;[6] that it is the foundation of Christian assurance;[7] and that to ascertain it with regard to ourselves demands and deserves the utmost diligence.[8]

Places in the Bible where taught.

[1] 2 Tim. i. 8, 9. Be not thou therefore ashamed of the testimony of our Lord, nor of me his prisoner; but be thou partaker of the afflictions of the

Gospel, according to the power of God; who hath saved us and called us with an holy calling, not according to our works, but according to his own purpose and grace, which was given us in Christ Jesus before the world began. Eph. i. 3–14. 1 Pet. i. 1, 2. Rom. xi. 5, 6. John xv. 16. 1 John iv. 19. Hos. xii. 9.

[2] 2 Thess. ii. 13, 14. But we are bound to give thanks always to God for you, brethren beloved of the Lord, because God hath from the beginning chosen you to salvation, through sanctification of the Spirit and belief of the truth; whereunto he called you by our Gospel, to the obtaining of the glory of our Lord Jesus Christ. Acts xiii. 48. John x. 16. Matt. xx. 16. Acts xv. 14.

[3] Ex. xxxiii. 18, 19. And Moses said, I beseech thee, show me thy glory. And He said, I will cause all my goodness to pass before thee, and I will proclaim the name of the Lord before thee, and will be gracious to whom I will be gracious, and will show mercy on whom I will show mercy. Matt. xx. 15. Is it not lawful for me to do what I will with my own? Is thine eye evil, because I am good? Eph. i. 11. Rom. ix. 23, 24. Jer. xxxi. 3. Rom. xi. 28, 29. Jam. i. 17, 18. 2 Tim. i. 9. Rom. xi. 32–36.

[4] 1 Cor. iv. 7. For who maketh thee to differ from another? and what hast thou that thou didst not receive? Now if thou didst receive it, why dost thou glory as if thou hadst not received it? 1 Cor. i. 26–31. Rom. iii. 27; iv. 16. Col. iii. 12. 1 Cor. iii. 5–7; xv. 10. 1 Pet. v. 10. Acts i. 24. 1 Thess. ii. 13. 1 Pet. ii. 9. Luke xviii. 7. John xv. 16. Eph. i. 16. 1 Thess. ii. 12.

[5] 2 Tim. ii. 10. Therefore I endure all things for the elects' sake, that they also may obtain the salvation which is in Christ Jesus with eternal glory. 1 Cor. ix. 22. I am made all things to all men, that I might by all means save some. Rom. viii. 28–30. John vi. 37–40. 2 Pet. i. 10.

[6] 1 Thess. i. 4–10. Knowing, brethren beloved, your election of God; for our Gospel came unto you, not in word only, but in power, and in the Holy Ghost, and in much assurance, &c.

[7] Rom. viii. 28–30. Moreover, whom he did predestinate, them he also called, and whom he called, them he also justified, and whom he justified them he also glorified. What shall we then say to these things? If God be for us, who can be against us? Isa. xlii. 16. Rom. xi. 29.

[8] 2 Pet. i. 10, 11. Wherefore the rather, brethren, give diligence to make your calling and election sure; for if ye do these things, ye shall never fall; for so an entrance shall be ministered unto you abundantly into the everlasting Kingdom of our Lord and Saviour Jesus Christ. Phil. iii. 12. Heb. vi. 11.

X. Of Sanctification.—We believe that Sanctification is the process by which, according to the will of God, we are made partakers of his holiness;[1] that it is a progressive work;[2] that it is begun in regeneration;[3] and that it is carried on in the hearts of believers by the presence and power of the Holy Spirit, the Sealer and Comforter, in the continual use of the appointed means—especially, the word of God, self-examination, self-denial, watchfulness and prayer.[4]

Places in the Bible where taught.

[1] 1 Thess. iv. 3. For this is the will of God, even your sanctification. 1 Thess. v. 23. And the very God of peace sanctify you wholly. 2 Cor. vii. 1; xiii. 9. Epis. i. 4.

[2] Prov. iv. 18. The path of the just is as the shining light, which shineth more and more, unto the perfect day. 2 Cor. iii. 18. Heb. vi. 1. 2 Pet. i. 5–8. Phil. iii. 12–16.

[3] John ii. 29. If ye know that he [God] is righteous, ye know that every one that doeth righteousness is born of him. Rom. viii. 5. They that are after the flesh, do mind the things of the flesh; but they that are after the Spirit, the things of the Spirit. John iii. 6. Phil. i. 9–11. Ephes. i. 13, 14.

[4] Phil. ii. 12, 13. Work out your own salvation with fear and trembling, for it is God which worketh in you both to will and to do, of his good pleasure. Ephes. iv. 11, 12. 1 Pet. ii. 2. 2 Pet. iii. 18. 2 Cor. xiii. 5. Luke xi. 35; ix. 23. Matt. xxvi. 41. Ephes. vi. 18; iv. 30.

XI. Of the Perseverance of Saints.—We believe that such only are real believers as endure unto the end;[1] that their persevering attachment to Christ is the grand mark which distinguishes them from superficial professors;[2] that a special Providence watches over their welfare;[3] and they are kept by the power of God through faith unto salvation.[4]

Places in the Bible where taught.

[1] John viii. 31. Then said Jesus—If ye continue in my word, then are ye my disciples indeed. 1 John ii. 27, 28; iii. 9; v. 18.

[2] 1 John ii. 19. They went out from us, but they were not of us; for if they had been of us, they would no doubt have continued with us; but they went out that it might be made manifest that they were not all of us. John xiii. 18. Matt. xiii. 20, 21. John vi. 66–69. Job xvii. 9.

[3] Rom. viii. 28. And we know that all things work together for good unto them that love God, to them who are the called according to his purpose. Matt. vi, 30–33. Jer. xxxii. 40. Ps. cxxi. 3; xci. 11, 12.

[4] Phil. i. 6. He who hath begun a good work in you, will perform it until the day of Jesus Christ. Phil. ii. 12, 13. Jude 24, 25. Heb. i. 14. 2 Kings vi. 16. Heb. xiii. 5. 1 John iv. 4.

XII. Of the Harmony of the Law and the Gospel.—We believe that the Law of God is the eternal and unchangeable rule of His moral government;[1] that it is holy, just, and good;[2] and that the inability which the Scriptures ascribe to fallen men to fulfill its precepts, arises entirely from their love of sin :[3] to deliver them from which, and to restore them through a Mediator to unfeigned obedience to the holy Law, is one great end of the Gospel, and of the Means of Grace connected with the establishment of the visible church.[4]

Places in the Bible where taught.

[1] Rom. iii. 31. Do we make void the law through faith? God forbid. Yea, we establish the law. Matt. v. 17. Luke xvi. 17. Rom. iii. 20; iv. 15.

[2] Rom. vii. 12. The law is holy, and the commandment holy, and just, and good. Rom. vii. 7, 14, 22. Gal. iii. 21. Ps. cxix.

[3] Rom. viii. 7, 8. The carnal mind is enmity against God: for it is not subject to the law of God, neither indeed can be. So then they that are in the flesh cannot please God. Josh. xxiv. 19. Jer. xiii. 23. John vi. 44; v. 44.

[4] Rom. viii. 2, 4. For the law of the Spirit of Life in Christ Jesus hath made me free from the law of sin and death. For what the law could not do, in that it was weak through the flesh, God sending his own Son in the likeness of sinful flesh, and for sin, condemned sin in the flesh; that the righteousness of the law might be fulfilled in us, who walk not after the flesh, but after the Spirit. Rom. x. 4. 1 Tim. i. 5. Heb. viii. 10. Jude 20, 21. Heb. xii. 14. Matt. xvi. 17, 18. 1 Cor. xii. 28.

XIII. Of a Gospel Church.—We believe that a visible church of Christ is a congregation of baptized believers,[1] associated by covenant in the faith and fellowship of the Gospel;[2] observing the ordinances of Christ;[3] governed by His laws;[4] and exercising the gifts, rights, and privileges invested in them by his word;[5] that its only scriptural officers are Bishops or Pastors, and Deacons,[6] whose qualifications, claims, and duties are defined in the Epistles to Timothy and Titus.

Places in the Bible where taught.

[1] 1 Cor. i. 1–13. Paul—unto the church of God which is at Corinth.—Is Christ divided? Was Paul crucified for you? Or were ye baptized in the name of Paul? Matt. xviii. 17. Acts v. 11; viii. 1; xi. 31. 1 Cor. iv. 17; xiv. 23. 3 John 9. 1 Tim. iii. 5.

[2] Acts ii. 41, 42. Then they that gladly received his word were baptized; and the same day there were added to them about three thousand souls. 2 Cor. viii. 5. They first gave their ownselves to the Lord, and unto us by the will of God. Acts ii. 47. 1 Cor. v. 12, 13.

[3] 1 Cor. xi. 2. Now I praise you, brethren, that ye remember me in all things, and keep the ordinances as I delivered them unto you. 2 Thess. iii. 6. Rom. xvi. 17–20. 1 Cor. xi. 23. Matt. xviii. 15–20. 1 Cor. v., vi. 2 Cor. ii., vii. 1 Cor. iv. 17.

[4] Matt. xxviii. 20. Teaching them to observe all things whatsoever I have commanded you. John xiv. 15; xv. 12. 1 John iv. 21. John xiv. 21. 1 Thess. iv. 2. 2 John 6. Gal. vi. 2. All the Epistles.

[5] Ephes. iv. 7. Unto every one of us is given grace according to the measure of the gift of Christ. 1 Cor. xiv. 12. Seek that ye may excel to the edifying of the church. Phil. i. 27. That I may hear of your affairs, that ye stand fast in one spirit, with one mind, striving together for the faith of the Gospel. 1 Cor. xii., xiv.

[6] Phil i. 1. With the Bishops and Deacons. Acts xiv. 23; xv. 22. 1 Tim. iii. Titus i.

XIV. Of Baptism and the Lord's Supper.—We believe that Christian Baptism is the immersion in water of a believer,[1] in the name of the Father, and Son, and Holy Ghost;[2] to show forth in a solemn and beautiful emblem, our faith in the crucified, buried, and risen Saviour, with its effect, in our death to sin and resurrection to a new life;[3] that it is pre-requisite to the privileges of a church relation; and to the Lord's Supper,[4] in which the members of the church by the sacred use of bread and wine, are to commemorate together the dying love of Christ;[5] preceded always by solemn self-examination.[6]

Places in the Bible where taught.

[1] Acts viii. 36–39. And the eunuch said, See, here is water; what doth hinder me to be baptized? And Philip said, If thou believest with all thy heart thou mayest.—And they went down into the water, both Philip and the eunuch, and he baptized him. Matt. iii. 5, 6. John iii. 22, 23; iv. 1, 2. Matt. xxviii. 19. Mark xvi. 16. Acts ii. 38; viii. 12; xvi. 32–34; xviii. 8.

[2] Matt. xxviii. 19. Baptizing them in the name of the Father, and of the Son, and of the Holy Ghost. Acts x. 47, 48. Gal. iii. 27, 28.

[3] Rom. vi. 4. Therefore we are buried with him by baptism into death; that like as Christ was raised from the dead by the glory of the Father, even so we also, should walk in newness of life. Col. ii. 12. 1 Pet. iii. 20, 21. Acts xxii. 16.

[4] Acts ii. 41, 42. Then they that gladly received his word were baptized, and there were added to them, the same day, about three thousand souls. And they continued steadfastly in the Apostles' doctrine and fellowship, and in breaking of bread, and in prayers. Matt. xxviii. 19, 20. Acts, and Epistles.

[5] 1 Cor. xi. 26. As often as ye eat this bread and drink this cup, ye do show the Lord's death till he come. Matt. xxvi. 26–29. Mark xiv. 22–25. Luke xxii. 14–20.

[6] 1 Cor. xi. 28. But let a man examine himself, and so let him eat of that bread and drink of that cup. 1 Cor. v. 1, 8; x. 3–32; xi. 17–32. John vi. 26–71.

XV. Of the Christian Sabbath.—We believe that the first day of the week is the Lord's Day, or Christian Sabbath;[1] and is to be kept sacred to religious purposes,[2] by abstaining from all secular labor and sinful recreations;[3] by the devout observance of all the means of grace, both private[4] and public;[5] and by preparation for that rest that remaineth for the people of God.[6]

Places in the Bible where taught.

Acts xx. 7. On the first day of the week, when the disciples came together to break bread, Paul preached to them. Gen. ii. 3. Col. ii. 16, 17. Mark ii. 27. John xx. 19. 1 Cor. xvi. 1, 2.

[2] Ex. xx. 8. Remember the Sabbath day, to keep it holy. Rev. i. 10. I was in the Spirit on the Lord's day. Ps. cxviii. 24. This is the day which the Lord hath made; we will rejoice and be glad in it.

[3] Isa. lviii. 13, 14. If thou turn away thy foot from the Sabbath, from doing thy pleasure on my holy day; and call the Sabbath a delight, the holy of the lord honorable; and shalt honor him, not doing thine own ways, nor finding thine own pleasure, nor speaking thine own words; then shalt thou delight thyself in the Lord, and I will cause thee to ride upon the high places of the earth, and feed thee with the heritage of Jacob. Isa. lvi. 2–8.

[4] Ps. cxviii. 15. The voice of rejoicing and salvation is in the tabernacles of the righteous.

[5] Heb. x. 24. 25. Not forsaking the assembling of yourselves together, as the manner of some is. Acts xi. 26. A whole year they assembled themselves with the church, and taught much people. Acts xiii. 44. The next Sabbath-day came almost the whole city together to hear the word of God. Lev. xix. 30. Ex. xlvi. 3. Luke iv. 16. Acts xvii. 2, 3. Ps. xxvi. 8; lxxxvii. 3.

[6] Heb. iv. 3–11. Let us labor therefore to enter into that rest.

XVI. Of Civil Government.—We believe that Civil Government is of Divine appointment, for the interests and good order of human society;[1] and that magistrates are to be prayed for, conscientiously honored, and obeyed;[2] except only in things opposed to the will of our Lord Jesus Christ,[3] who is the only Lord of the conscience, and the Prince of the kings of the earth.[4]

Places in the Bible where taught.

[1] Rom. xiii. 1–7. The powers that be are ordained of God. For rulers are not a terror to good works, but to the evil. Deut. xvi. 18. 2 Sam. xxiii. 3. Ex. xviii. 23. Jer. xxx. 21.

[2] Matt. xxii. 21. Render therefore unto Cæsar the things that are Cæsar's, and unto God the things that are God's. Titus iii. 1. 1 Pet. ii. 13. 1 Tim. ii. 1–8.

[3] Acts v. 29. We ought to obey God rather than man. Matt. x. 28. Fear not them which kill the body, but are not able to kill the soul. Dan. iii. 15–18; vi. 7–10. Acts iv. 18–20.

[4] Matt. xxiii. 10. Ye have one Master, even Christ. Rom. xiv. 4. Who art thou that judgest another man's servant? Rev. xix. 16. And he hath on his vesture and on his thigh a name written, KING OF KINGS, AND LORD OF LORDS. Ps. lxxii. 11. Ps. ii. Rom. xiv. 9–13.

XVII. Of the Righteous and the Wicked.—We believe that there is a radical and essential difference between the righteous and the wicked:[1] that such only as through faith are justified in the name of the Lord Jesus, and sanctified by the Spirit of our God, are truly righteous in His esteem;[2] while all such as continue in impenitence and unbelief are in his sight wicked, and under the curse;[3] and this distinction holds among men both in and after death.[4]

Places in the Bible where taught.

[1] Mal. iii. 18. Ye shall discern between the righteous and the wicked; between him that serveth God and him that serveth him not. Prov. xii. 26. Isa. v. 20. Gen. xviii. 23. Jer. xv. 19. Acts x. 34, 35. Rom. vi. 16.

[2] Rom. i. 17. The just shall live by faith. Rom. vii. 6. We are delivered from the law, that being dead wherein we were held, that we should serve in newness of spirit, and not in the oldness of the letter. 1 John ii. 29. If ye know that he is righteous, ye know that every one that doeth righteousness is born of him. 1 John iii. 7. Rom. vi. 18, 22. 1 Cor. xi. 32. Prov. xi. 31. 1 Pet. iv. 17, 18.

[3] 1 John v. 19. And we know that we are of God, and the whole world lieth in wickedness. Gal. iii. 10. As many as are of the works of the law, are under the curse. John iii. 36. Isa. lvii. 21. Ps. x. 4. Isa. lv. 6, 7.

[4] Prov. xiv. 32. The wicked is driven away in his wickedness, but the righteous hath hope in his death. See, also, the example of the rich man and Lazarus. Luke xvi. 25. Thou in thy lifetime receivedst thy good things, and likewise Lazarus evil things: but now he is comforted, and thou art tormented. John viii. 21–24. Prov. x. 24. Luke xii. 4, 5; ix. 23–26. John xii. 25, 26. Eccl. iii. 17. Matt. vii. 13, 14.

XVIII. Of the World to Come.—We believe that the end of this world is approaching;[1] that at the Last Day, Christ will descend from heaven;[2] and raise the dead from the grave to final retribution;[3] that a solemn separation will then take place;[4] that the wicked will be adjudged to endless punishment, and the righteous to endless joy;[5] and that this judgment will fix forever the final state of men in heaven or hell, on principles of righteousness.[6]

Places in the Bible where taught.

[1] 1 Pet. iv. 7. But the end of all things is at hand; be ye therefore sober, and watch unto prayer. 1 Cor. vii. 29–31. Heb. i. 10–12. Matt. xxiv. 35. 1 John ii. 17. Matt. xxviii. 20; xiii. 39, 40. 2 Pet. iii. 3–13.

[2] Acts i. 11. This same Jesus which is taken up from you into heaven, shall so come in like manner as ye have seen him go into heaven. Rev. i. 7. Heb. ix. 28. Acts iii. 21. 1 Thess. iv. 13–18; v. 1–11.

[3] Acts xxiv, 15. There shall be a resurrection of the dead, both of the

just and unjust. 1 Cor. xv. 12–59. Luke xiv. 14. Dan. xii. 2. John v. 28, 29; vi. 40; xi. 25, 26. 2 Tim. i. 10. Acts x. 42.

[4] Matt. xiii. 49. The angels shall come forth, and sever the wicked from among the just. Matt. xiii. 37–43; xxiv. 30, 31; xxv. 31–33.

[5] Matt. xxv. 35–41. And these shall go away into everlasting punishment, but the righteous into life eternal. Rev. xxii. 11. He that is unjust, let him be unjust still; and he which is filthy, let him be filthy still; and he that is righteous, let him be righteous still; and he that is holy, let him be holy still. 1 Cor. vi. 9, 10. Mark ix. 43–48. 2 Pet. ii. 9. Jude 7. Phi. iii. 19. Rom. vi. 22. 2 Cor. v. 10, 11. John iv. 36. 2 Cor. iv. 18.

[6] Rom. iii. 5, 6. Is God unrighteous, who taketh vengeance? (I speak as a man.) God forbid; for how then shall God judge the world? 2 Thess. i. 6–12. Seeing it is a righteous thing with God to recompense tribulation to them who trouble you, and to you who are troubled, rest with us—when he shall come to be glorified in his saints, and to be admired in all them that believe. Heb. vi. 1, 2. 1 Cor. iv. 5. Acts xvii. 31. Rom. ii. 2–16. Rev. xx. 11, 12. 1 John ii. 28; iv. 17.

Seeing then that all these things shall be dissolved, what manner of persons ought ye to be in all holy conversation and godliness, looking for and hasting unto the coming of the day of God? 2 Peter iii. 11, 12.

3. *Church Covenant.*

In addition to articles of faith, Baptist churches generally have a Covenant to which the members agree. It is read on the reception of new members, for their edification and acquiescence. In some of the churches, the covenant is read at each communion, for the benefit of all the members. This is a good practice, and should prevail in all churches.

Baptist Church Covenants, like the Articles of Faith, are very numerous, differing in unessential particulars, but agreeing substantially. They are generally productions of distinguished piety and beauty, and worthy of attention and imitation. We insert the following as a fair specimen of numerous covenants, and as suitable for use in any church:

COVENANT.

Having been, as we trust, brought by Divine Grace, to embrace the Lord Jesus Christ, and to give ourselves up wholly to him, we do now solemnly and joyfully covenant with each other, to walk together in Him with brotherly love to His glory as our common Lord. And to the end that we may stand perfect and complete in all the will of God, and that the glory of Christ may be manifested in the salvation of men, it is our solemn purpose, as God shall give us strength, to exercise a mutual care, as members one of another, to promote the growth of the whole body in Christian knowledge and true holiness, and to let our light shine before the world; particularly to uphold the public worship of God and the ordinances of his house, by a regular attendance thereon, to search diligently the sacred Scriptures, to train our children, and those under our care, with a view to the service of Christ and the enjoyment of Heaven, to contribute cheerfully of our property for the support of the poor, for the maintenance of a faithful ministry of the Gospel among us, and for the spread of the Gospel in all the earth; to exhort, and, if occasion require, to admonish one another in the spirit of meekness, considering ourselves lest we also be tempted; to cheerfully submit to, and conscientiously enforce, the wholesome discipline of the church—keeping ever the unity of the Spirit in the bonds of peace; and to endeavor by example and precept, to teach transgressors the ways of that God whose we are, and whom we serve, remembering that as in baptism we have been buried with Christ and raised again, so there is on us a special obligation henceforth to walk in newness of life; and may the God of peace, who brought again from the dead our Lord Jesus, that Great Shepherd of the sheep, make us perfect in every good work, to do his will, working in us that which is well pleasing in his sight, through Jesus Christ, to whom be glory forever and ever. Amen.

CHAPTER II.

Baptist Catechism. 1. The object of it. 2. Keach's Catechism.

1. We insert here a Baptist Catechism for three purposes. In harmony with this chapter, it serves to illustrate the doc-

trines, principles, and practice of the church. It shows also their views of the early training of children. While they reject the baptism of children, until they can and do believe for themselves in the Lord Jesus Christ, they insist on their early religious education in the family and the Sabbath School. We hope also the insertion of a catechism well known and approved, may be the means of promoting the suitable training of the young and rising generation. Of several catechisms in use in Baptist families and Sabbath Schools, I select the following as most full, and in most common use. It is published by the American Baptist Publication Society, 118 Arch St., Philadelphia.

In the year 1677, a Confession of Faith was published by the Baptists, in London and vicinity. This Confession of Faith was reprinted in the year 1689, having been approved and recommended by the ministers and messengers of above an hundred congregations in England and Wales—signed by Hanserd Knollys, Wm. Kiffin, Benjamin Keach, and others.

THE BAPTIST CATECHISM:

COMMONLY CALLED KEACH'S CATECHISM.

Q. 1. Who is the First and Best of beings?

A. God is the First and Best of beings.

Isaiah xliv. 6. Psalm viii. 1, 2.

Q. 2. Ought every one to believe there is a God?

A. Every one ought to believe there is a God, and it is their great sin and folly who do not.

Hebrews xi. 6. Psalm xiv. 1.

Q. 3. How may we know there is a God?

A. The light of nature in man and the works of God, plainly declare there is a God: but his Word and Spirit only do it fully and effectually for the salvation of sinners.

Psalm xix. 1, 2. 1 Cor. i. 21. 1 Cor. ii. 14.

Q. 4. What is the Word of God?

A. The holy scriptures of the Old and New Testaments are

the word of God, and the only certain rule of faith and obedience.

2 Timothy iii. 15, 16, 17. Isaiah viii. 20.

Q. 5. May all men make use of the holy scriptures?

A. All men are not only permitted, but commanded and exhorted to read, hear, and understand the holy scriptures.

Q. 6. What things are chiefly contained in the holy scriptures?

A. The holy scriptures chiefly contain what man ought to believe concerning God, and what duty God requires of man.

Q. 7. What is God?

A. God is a Spirit, infinite, eternal, and unchangeable, in his being, wisdom, power, holiness, justice, goodness and truth.

Q. 8. Are there more gods than one?

A. There is but one only, the living and true God.

Q. 9. How many persons are there in the Godhead?

A. There are three persons in the Godhead—the Father, the Son, and Holy Spirit, and these three are one God, the same in essence, equal in power and glory.

Q. 10. What are the decrees of God?

A. The decrees of God are his eternal purpose, according to the counsel of his will, whereby for his own glory he hath foreordained whatsoever comes to pass.

Q. 11. How does God execute his decrees?

A. God executes his decrees in the works of creation and providence.

Q. 12. What is the work of creation?

A. The work of creation is God's making all things of nothing, by the word of his power, in the space of six days, and all very good.

Q. 13. How did God create man?

A. God created man, male and female, after his own image, in knowledge, righteousness, and holiness, with dominion over the creatures.

Q. 14. What are God's works of providence?

A. God's works of providence are his most holy, wise, and

powerful preserving and governing all his creatures, and all their actions.

Q. 15. What special act of providence did God exercise towards man, in the state wherein he was created?

A. When God had created man, he entered into a covenant of life with him, upon condition of perfect obedience, forbidding him to eat of the tree of knowledge of good and evil, upon pain of death.

Q. 16. Did our first parents continue in that state wherein they were created?

A. Our first parents, being left to the freedom of their own will, fell from the state wherein they were created, by sinning against God.

Q. 17. What is sin?

A. Sin is any want of conformity unto, or transgression of, the law of God.

Q. 18. What was the sin whereby our first parents fell from the state wherein they were created?

A. The sin whereby our first parents fell from the state wherein they were created, was their eating the forbidden fruit.

Q. 19. Did all mankind fall in Adam's first transgression?

A. The covenant being made with Adam, not only for himself but for his posterity, all mankind, descending from him by ordinary generation, sinned in him, and fell with him in his first transgression.

Q. 20. Into what state did the fall bring mankind?

A. The fall brought mankind into a state of sin and misery.

Q. 21. Wherein consists the sinfulness of that state whereinto man fell?

A. The sinfulness of that state whereinto man fell, consists in the guilt of Adam's first sin, the want of original righteousness, and the corruption of his whole nature, which is commonly called original sin, together with all actual transgressions which proceed from it.

Q. 22. What is the misery of that state whereinto man fell?

A. All mankind, by their fall, lost communion with God, are under his wrath and curse, and so made liable to all the miseries in this life, to death itself, and to the pains of hell forever.

Q. 23. Did God leave all mankind to perish in the state of sin and misery?

A. God having, out of his mere good pleasure, from all eternity, elected some to everlasting life, did enter into a covenant of grace, to deliver them out of the state of sin and misery, and to bring them into a state of salvation, by a Redeemer.

Q. 24. Who is the Redeemer of God's elect?

A. The only Redeemer of God's elect is the Lord Jesus Christ, who being the eternal Son of God, became man, and so was and continues to be God and man, in two distinct natures, and one person, forever.

Q. 25. How did Christ, being the Son of God, become man?

A. Christ, the Son of God, became man by taking to himself a true body, and a reasonable soul, being conceived by the power of the Holy Spirit, in the womb of the Virgin Mary, and born of her, yet without sin.

Q. 26. What offices does Christ execute as our Redeemer?

A. Christ, as our Redeemer, executes the offices of a prophet, of a priest, and of a king, both in his state of humiliation and exaltation.

Q. 27. How does Christ execute the office of a prophet?

A. Christ executes the office of a prophet, in revealing to us, by his word and Spirit, the will of God for our salvation.

Q. 28. How does Christ execute the office of a priest?

A. Christ executes the office of a priest, in his once offering up of himself a sacrifice to satisfy divine justice, and to reconcile us to God, and in making continual intercession for us.

Q. 29. How does Christ execute the office of a king?

A. Christ executes the office of a king, in subduing us to

himself, in ruling and defending us, and in restraining and conquering all his and our enemies.

Q. 30. Wherein did Christ's humiliation consist?

A. Christ's humiliation consisted in his being born, and that in a low condition, made under the law, undergoing the miseries of this life, the wrath of God, and the cursed death of the cross; in being buried, and continuing under the power of death for a time.

Q. 31. Wherein consists Christ's exaltation?

A. Christ's exaltation consists in his rising again from the dead on the third day, in ascending up into heaven, in sitting at the right hand of God the Father, and in coming to judge the world at the last day.

Q. 32. How are we made partakers of the redemption purchased by Christ?

A. We are made partakers of the redemption purchased by Christ, by the effectual application of it to us, by his Holy Spirit.

Q. 33. How does the Spirit apply to us the redemption purchased by Christ?

A. The Spirit applies to us the redemption purchased by Christ, by working faith in us, and thereby uniting us to Christ in our effectual calling.

Q. 34. What is effectual calling?

A. Effectual calling is the work of God's Spirit, whereby, convincing us of our sin and misery, enlightening our minds in the knowledge of Christ, and renewing our wills, he doth persuade and enable us to embrace Jesus Christ, freely offered to us in the Gospel.

Q. 35. What benefits do they that are effectually called, partake of in this life?

A. They that are effectually called, do in this life partake of justification, adoption, sanctification, and the several benefits which in this life do either accompany or flow from them.

Q. 36. What is justification?

A. Justification is an act of God's free grace, wherein he pardoneth all our sins, and accepts us as righteous in his sight, only for the righteousness of Christ imputed to us, and received by faith alone.

Q. 37. What is adoption?

A. Adoption is an act of God's free grace, whereby we are received into the number, and have a right to all the privileges, of the sons of God.

Q. 38. What is sanctification?

A. Sanctification is the work of God's free grace, whereby we are renewed in the whole man after the image of God, and are enabled more and more to die unto sin, and live unto righteousness.

Q. 39. What are the benefits which in this life do accompany or flow from justification, adoption, and sanctification?

A. The benefits which in this life do accompany or flow from justification, adoption, and sanctification, are, assurance of God's love, peace of conscience, joy in the Holy Spirit, increase of grace, and perseverance therein to the end.

Q. 40. What benefits do believers receive from Christ at their death?

A. The souls of believers are at their death made perfect in holiness, and do immediately pass into glory, and their bodies, being still united to Christ, do rest in their graves till the resurrection.

Q. 41. What benefits do believers receive from Christ at the resurrection?

A. At the resurrection, believers being raised up in glory, shall be openly acknowledged and acquitted in the day of judgment, and made perfectly blessed both in soul and body, in the full enjoyment of God to all eternity.

Q. 42. But what shall be done to the wicked at their death?

A. The souls of the wicked shall at their death be cast into the torments of hell, and their bodies lie in their graves till the resurrection and judgment of the great day.

Q. 43. What shall be done to the wicked at the day of judgment?

A. At the day of judgment, the bodies of the wicked, being raised out of their graves, shall be sentenced, together with their souls, to unspeakable torments with the devil and his angels forever.

Q. 44. What is the duty which God requires of man?

A. The duty which God requires of man, is obedience to his revealed will.

Q. 45. What did God at first reveal to man for the rule of his obedience?

A. The rule which God at first revealed to man for his obedience, was the moral law.

Q. 46. Where is the moral law summarily comprehended?

A. The moral law is summarily comprehended in the ten commandments.

Q. 47. What is the sum of the ten commandments?

A. The sum of the ten commandments is, to love the Lord our God, with all our heart, with all our soul, with all our strength, and with all our mind; and our neighbor as ourselves.

Q. 48. What is the preface to the ten commandments?

A. The preface to the ten commandments is in these words, "I am the Lord thy God, which have brought thee out of the land of Egypt, out of the house of bondage."

Q. 49. What does the preface to the ten commandments teach us?

A. The preface to the ten commandments teaches us, that because God is the Lord, and our God and Redeemer, therefore we are bound to keep all his commandments.

Q. 50. Which is the first commandment?

A. The first commandment is, "Thou shalt have no other gods before me."

Q. 51. What is required in the first commandment?

A. The first commandment requires us to know and acknowledge God to be the only true God, and our God, and to worship and glorify him accordingly.

Q. 52. What is forbidden in the first commandment?

A. The first commandment forbids the denying, or not worshipping and glorifying the true God, as God and our God; and the giving that worship and glory to any other, which is due unto him alone.

Q. 53. What are we especially taught by these words, "before me," in the first commandment?

A. These words, "before me," in the first commandment, teach us, that God, who sees all things, takes notice of, and is much displeased with, the sin of having any other God.

Q. 54. Which is the second commandment?

A. The second commandment is, "Thou shalt not make unto thee any graven image, or any likeness of any thing that is in heaven above, or that is in the earth beneath, or that is in the water under the earth. Thou shalt not bow down thyself to them, nor serve them; for I the Lord thy God am a jealous God, visiting the iniquity of the fathers upon the children, unto the third and fourth generations of them that hate me: and showing mercy unto thousands of them that love me and keep my commandments."

Q. 55. What is required in the second commandment?

A. The second commandment requires the receiving, observing, and keeping pure and entire, all such religious worship and ordinances, as God has appointed in his word.

Q. 56. What is forbidden in the second commandment?

A. The second commandment forbids the worshipping of God by images, or any other way not appointed in his word.

Q. 57. What are the reasons annexed to the second commandment?

A. The reasons annexed to the second commandment, are,

God's sovereignty over us, his property in us, and the zeal he has for his own worship.

Q. 58. Which is the third commandment?

A. The third commandment is, "Thou shalt not take the name of the Lord thy God in vain: for the Lord will not hold him guiltless that taketh his name in vain."

Q. 59. What is required in the third commandment?

A. The third commandment requires the holy and reverend use of God's names, titles, attributes, ordinances, word, and works.

Q. 60. What is forbidden in the third commandment?

A. The third commandment forbids all profaning and abusing of any thing whereby God makes himself known.

Q. 61. What is the reason annexed to the third commandment?

A. The reason annexed to the third commandment is, that however the breakers of this commandment may escape punishment from men, yet the Lord our God will not suffer them to escape his righteous judgment.

Q. 62. Which is the fourth commandment?

A. The fourth commandment is, "Remember the Sabbath day to keep it holy. Six days shalt thou labor and do all thy work: but the seventh day is the Sabbath of the Lord thy God: in it thou shalt not do any work, thou, nor thy son, nor thy daughter, thy man-servant, nor thy maid-servant, nor thy cattle, nor the stranger that is within thy gates; for in six days the Lord made heaven and earth, the sea, and all that in them is, and rested the seventh day: wherefore the Lord blessed the Sabbath day and hallowed it."

Q. 63. What is required in the fourth commandment?

A. The fourth commandment requires the keeping holy to God one whole day in seven, to be a Sabbath to himself.

Q. 64. Which day of the seven hath God appointed to be the weekly Sabbath?

A. Before the resurrection of Christ, God appointed the

seventh day of the week to be the weekly Sabbath, and the first day of the week, ever since, to continue to the end of the world, which is the Christian Sabbath.

Q. 65. How is the Sabbath to be sanctified?

A. The Sabbath is to be sanctified by a holy resting all that day, even from such worldly employments and recreations as are lawful on other days, and spending the whole time in the public and private exercises of God's worship, except so much as is to be taken up in the works of necessity and mercy.

Q. 66. What is forbidden in the fourth commandment?

A. The fourth commandment forbids the omission or careless performance of the duties required, and the profaning the day by idleness, or doing that which is in itself sinful, or by unnecessary thoughts, words, or works about worldly employments or recreation.

Q. 67. What are the reasons annexed to the fourth commandment?

A. The reasons annexed to the fourth commandment, are, God's allowing us six days of the week for our own lawful employments, his challenging a special property in the seventh, his own example, and his blessing the Sabbath day.

Q. 68. Which is the fifth commandment?

A. The fifth commandment is, "Honor thy father and thy mother, that thy days may be long upon the land which the Lord thy God giveth thee."

Q. 69. What is required in the fifth commandment?

A. The fifth commandment requires the preserving the honor, and performing the duties, belonging to every one in their several places and relations, as superiors, inferiors, or equals.

Q. 70. What is forbidden in the fifth commandment?

A. The fifth commandment forbids the neglecting of, or doing any thing against the honor or duty which belongeth to every one in their several places and relations.

Q. 71 What is the reason annexed to the fifth commandment?

A. The reason annexed to the fifth commandment is, a promise of long life and prosperity, (as far as it shall serve for God's glory and their own good,) to all such as keep this commandment.

Q. 72. Which is the sixth commandment?

A. The sixth commandment is, "Thou shalt not kill."

Q. 73. What is required in the sixth commandment?

A. The sixth commandment requires all lawful endeavors to preserve our own life and the life of others.

Q. 74. What is forbidden in the sixth commandment?

A. The sixth commandment absolutely forbids the taking away our own life, or the life of our neighbor unjustly, or whatsoever tendeth thereto.

Q. 75. Which is the seventh commandment?

A. The seventh commandment is, "Thou shalt not commit adultery."

Q. 76. What is required in the seventh commandment?

A. The seventh commandment requires the preservation of our own and our neighbor's chastity, in heart, speech, and behavior.

Q. 77. What is forbidden in the seventh commandment?

A. The seventh commandment forbids all unchaste thoughts, words, and actions.

Q. 78. Which is the eighth commandment?

A. The eighth commandment is, "Thou shalt not steal."

Q. 79. What is required in the eighth commandment?

A. The eighth commandment requires the lawful procuring and furthering the wealth and outward state of ourselves and others.

Q. 80. What is forbidden in the eighth commandment?

A. The eighth commandment forbids whatsoever does or may unjustly hinder our own or our neighbor's wealth or outward state.

Q. 81. Which is the ninth commandment?

A. The ninth commandment is, "Thou shalt not bear false witness against thy neighbor."

Q. 82. What is required in the ninth commandment?

A. The ninth commandment requires the maintaining and promoting of truth between man and man, and of our own and our neighbor's good name, especially in witness-bearing.

Q. 83. What is forbidden in the ninth commandment?

A. The ninth commandment forbids whatsoever is prejudicial to truth, or injurious to our own, or our neighbor's good name.

Q. 84. Which is the tenth commandment?

A. The tenth commandment is, "Thou shalt not covet thy neighbor's house, thou shalt not covet thy neighbor's wife, nor his man-servant, nor his maid-servant, nor his ox, nor his ass, nor any thing that is thy neighbor's."

Q. 85. What is required in the tenth commandment?

A. The tenth commandment requires full contentment with our own condition, with a right and charitable frame of spirit towards our neighbor, and all that is his.

Q. 86. What is forbidden in the tenth commandment?

A. The tenth commandment forbids all discontentment with our own state, envying or grieving at the good of our neighbor, and all inordinate motions and affections to any thing that is his.

Q. 87. Is any man able perfectly to keep the commandments of God?

A. No mere man, since the fall, is able in this life perfectly to keep the commandments of God, but doth daily break them in thought, word, or deed.

Q. 88. Are all transgressions of the law equally heinous?

A. Some sins in themselves, and by reason of several aggravations, are more heinous in the sight of God than others.

Q. 89. What does every sin deserve?

A. Every sin deserves God's wrath and curse, both in this life and in that which is to come.

Q. 90. What does God require of us, that we may escape his wrath and curse, due to us for sin?

A. To escape the wrath and curse of God due to us for sin, God requires of us faith in Jesus Christ, repentance unto life, with the diligent use of all the outward means whereby Christ communicates to us the benefits of redemption.

Q. 91. What is faith in Jesus Christ?

A. Faith in Jesus Christ is a saving grace, whereby we receive and rest upon him alone for salvation, as he is revealed as the free gift of God to us, in the Gospel.

Q. 92. What is repentance unto life?

A. Repentance unto life is a saving grace, whereby a sinner, out of a true sense of his sins, and apprehension of the mercy of God in Christ, does, with grief and hatred of his sin, turn from it unto God, with full purpose of, and endeavor after, new obedience.

Q. 93. What are the outward means whereby Christ communicates to us the benefits of redemption?

A. The outward and ordinary means whereby Christ communicates to us the benefits of redemption, are his Ordinances, especially the Word, Baptism, the Lord's Supper, and Prayer; all which means are made effectual to the elect, through faith, for salvation.

Q. 94. How is the Word made effectual to salvation?

A. The Spirit of God makes the reading, but especially the preaching of the word, an effectual means of convincing and converting sinners, and of building them up in holiness and comfort, through faith, unto salvation.

Q. 95. How is the word to be read and heard?

A. We must attend thereunto with diligence, preparation, and prayer, receive it with faith and love, lay it up in our hearts, and practise it in our lives.

Q. 96. What is Baptism?

A. Baptism is an ordinance of the New Testament, instituted by Jesus Christ, to be unto the party baptized a sign of his fellowship with him, in his death, and burial, and resurrection, of his being ingrafted into him, of remission of sins, and of his giving up himself unto God, through Jesus Christ, to live and walk in newness of life.

Q. 97. To whom is baptism to be administered?

A. Baptism is to be administered to all those who actually profess repentance towards God, faith in, and obedience to, our Lord Jesus Christ; and to none other.

Q. 98. Are the infants of such as are professing believers to be baptized?

A. The infants of such as are professing believers are not to be baptized: because there is neither command nor example in the holy scriptures, or certain consequence from them, to baptize such.

Q. 99. How is baptism rightly administered?

A. Baptism is rightly administered by immersion, or dipping the whole body of the person in water, in the name of the Father, and of the Son, and of the Holy Spirit, according to Christ's institution, and the practice of the Apostles, and not by sprinkling or pouring of water, or dipping some parts of the body, after the tradition of men.

Q. 100. What is the duty of such as are rightly baptized?

A. It is the duty of those who are rightly baptized, to give up themselves to some particular and orderly church of Jesus Christ, that they may walk in all the commandments and ordinances of the Lord blameless.

Q. 101. What is the Lord's Supper?

A. The Lord's Supper is an ordinance of the New Testament, instituted by Jesus Christ, wherein, by giving and receiving bread and wine, according to his appointment, his death is showed forth, and the worthy receivers are, not after a corporeal and carnal manner, but by faith, made partakers of his body and blood, with all his benefits, to their spiritual nourishment, and growth in grace.

Q. 102. Who are the proper subjects of this ordinance?

A. Godly persons who have been baptized upon a personal profession of their faith in Jesus Christ, and repentance from dead works.

Q. 103. What is required to the worthy receiving of the Lord's Supper?

A. It is required of them that would worthily (that is, suitably,) partake of the Lord's Supper, that they examine themselves, of their knowledge, to discern the Lord's body; of their faith, to feed upon him, of their repentance, love, and new obedience: lest, coming unworthily, they eat and drink judgment to themselves.

Q. 104. What is prayer?

A. Prayer is an offering up our desires to God, by the assistance of the Holy Spirit, for things agreeable to his will, in the name of Christ, believing; with confession of our sins, and thankful acknowledgment of his mercies.

Q. 105. What rule has God given for our direction in prayer?

A. The whole word of God is of use to direct us in prayer, but the special rule of direction is that prayer, which Christ taught his disciples, commonly called the Lord's Prayer.

Q. 106. What does the preface to the Lord's Prayer teach us.

A. The preface of the Lord's Prayer, which is, "Our Father, which art in heaven," teaches us to draw near to God with all holy reverence and confidence, as children to a father, able and ready to help us, and that we should pray with and for others.

Q. 107. What do we pray for in the first petition?

A. In the first petition, which is, "Hallowed by thy name," we pray, that God would enable us and others to glorify him in all that whereby he makes himself known, and that he would dispose all things to his own glory.

Q. 108. What do we pray for in the second petition?

A. In the second petition, which is, "Thy kingdom come," we pray that Satan's kingdom may be destroyed, and that the kingdom of grace may be advanced; ourselves and others brought into it, and kept in it; and that the kingdom of glory may be hastened.

Q. 109. What do we pray for in the third petition?

A. In the third petition, which is, "Thy will be done on earth as it is in heaven," we pray, that God by his grace, would make us able and willing to know, obey, and submit to his will in all things, as the angels do in heaven.

Q. 110. What do we pray for in the fourth petition?

A. In the fourth petition, which is, "Give us this day our daily bread," we pray, that of God's free gift, we may receive a competent portion of the good things of this life, and enjoy his blessing with them.

Q: 111. What do we pray for in the fifth petition?

A. In the fifth petition, which is, "And forgive us our debts, as we forgive our debtors," we pray, that God, for Christ's sake, would freely pardon all our sins; which we are the rather encouraged to ask, because by his grace we are enabled from the heart to forgive others.

Q. 112. What do we pray for in the sixth petition?

A. In the sixth petition, which is, "And lead us not into temptation, but deliver us from evil," we pray, that God would either keep us from being tempted to sin, or support and deliver us when we are tempted.

Q. 113. What does the conclusion of the Lord's Prayer teach us?

A. The conclusion of the Lord's Prayer, which is, "For thine is the kingdom, and the power, and the glory, forever. Amen," teaches us to take our encouragement in prayer from God only, and in our prayers to praise him, ascribing kingdom, power, and glory to him. And in testimony of our desire, and assurance to be heard, we say, AMEN.

THE LAW OF GOD, CONTAINED IN THE TEN COMMANDMENTS GIVEN BY GOD AT MOUNT SINAI.

EXODUS, CHAPTERS XIX. AND XX.

And it came to pass on the third day in the morning, that there were thunders, and lightnings, and a thick cloud upon the mount, and the voice of the trumpet exceeding loud: so that all the people that was in the camp trembled. And Moses brought forth the people out of the camp to meet with God; and they stood at the nether part of the mount. And Mount Sinai was altogether on a smoke, because the Lord descended upon it in fire; and the smoke thereof ascended as the smoke of a furnace, and the whole mount quaked greatly. And when the voice of the trumpet sounded long, and waxed louder and louder, Moses spake, and God answered him by a voice.

And God spake all these words, saying: I am the Lord thy God, which have brought thee out of the land of Egypt, out of the house of bondage.

I. Thou shalt have no other gods before ME.

II. Thou shalt not make unto thee any graven image, or any likeness of any thing that is in heaven above, or that is in the earth beneath, or that is in the water under the earth: Thou shalt not bow down thyself to them, nor serve them: for I THE LORD THY GOD am a jealous God, visiting the iniquity of the fathers upon the children unto the third and fourth generation of them that hate me; and showing mercy unto thousands of them that love me and keep my commandments.

III. Thou shalt not take the name of THE LORD THY GOD in vain; for the LORD will not hold him guiltless that taketh his name in vain.

IV. Remember the SABBATH-DAY, to keep it holy. Six days shalt thou labor, and do all thy work; but the seventh day is the SABBATH OF THE LORD THY GOD: in it thou shalt not do any work, thou, nor thy son, nor thy daughter, thy man-servant, nor thy maid-servant, nor thy cattle, nor thy stranger that is within thy gates: For in six days the LORD made heaven and earth, the sea, and all that in them is, and rested the seventh day; wherefore the LORD blessed the SABBATH-DAY and hallowed it.

V. Honor thy father and thy mother; that thy days may be long upon the land which THE LORD THY GOD giveth thee.

VI. Thou shalt not kill.

VII. Thou shalt not commit adultery.

VIII. Thou shalt not steal.

IX. Thou shalt not bear false witness against thy neighbor.

X. Thou shalt not covet thy neighbor's house, thou shalt not covet thy neighbor's wife, nor his man-servant, nor his maid-servant, nor his ox, nor his ass, nor anything that is thy neighbor's.

THE SPIRIT OF THE WHOLE LAW.

MATTHEW XXII. 36–40.

One of the Pharisees asked Jesus, saying, Master, which is the great commandment in the law?

Jesus said unto him, Thou shalt love THE LORD THY GOD with all thy heart, and with all thy soul, and with all thy mind. This is the first and great commandment.

And the second is like unto it, Thou shalt love thy neighbor as thyself.

On these two commandments hang all the law and the prophets.

OUR SAVIOUR'S NEW COMMANDMENT.

JOHN XIII. 34–35.

A new commandment I give unto you, That ye LOVE ONE ANOTHER: as I have loved you, that ye also love one another.

By this shall all men know that ye are my disciples, if ye have love one to another.

CHAPTER III.

Baptism—Pengilly's work all which is necessary. 1. The four Gospels. 2. John's Baptism. 3. The subjects, mode, and spiritual design of baptism. 4. The mode of John's baptism. 5. The baptism of Jesus. 6. Christ baptizing by his disciples. 7. John's last baptizing in Ænon. 8. References of Jesus to John, and his baptism and success. 9. Christ's sufferings under the figure of baptism. 10. The great commission. 11. Conclusion of the four Gospels. 12. The Acts of the Apostles. 13. The pentecostal baptism. 14. Philip baptizing at Samaria. 15. Mode of the Eunuch's baptism. 16. The baptism of Paul. 17. Of Cornelius and his friends. 18. Of Lydia and her household. 19. Of the jailor and his household. 20. Paul and household baptisms at Corinth. 21. Reflections upon household baptisms. 22. Baptisms at Ephesus. 23. Conclusion of the Acts. The Epistles. 24. Passages which contain express allusions to baptism. 25. Occasional mention of baptism. 26. Baptism illustrated by events in the Old Testament. 27. Conclusion of the New Testament.

It seems a work of supererogation to attempt to originate any thing upon the subject of baptism. So much has been written, so well, that the only task left us is that of selection for our pages.

It would require a volume to notice the numerous able works on the subject of baptism. Learned and practical men have furnished works on every phase of it; so that little, if any thing, remains to be desired, except that these works should be studied. Their study would produce a desirable harmony on the subject among Christians. I have selected so much of Pengilly's work as relates to "a faithful citation of all the passages in the New Testament on the subject of baptism, with the passages referred to in the Old Testament:"

1. *Passages in the Four Gospels.*

2. *The Mission, Preaching and Baptizing of John the Baptist.*

The first place of Scripture where the ordinance of baptism

is found, is in the account given of the ministry of John the Baptist, the forerunner of Christ. The surname of "Baptist" was most probably given him because he was "sent to baptize" by Divine authority, and was the first so authorized and employed. As all the four evangelists have given some account of John, I shall unite the testimony of the four, and present it to the reader in a continued relation.

Mark i. 1. The beginning of the Gospel of Jesus Christ, the Son of God.

John i. 6, 7. There was a man sent from God, whose name *was* John: the same came to bear witness of the Light, that all *men* through him might believe. Matt. iii. 3. For this is he that was spoken of by the prophet Esaias, saying, The voice of one crying in the wilderness, Prepare ye the way of the Lord, make his paths straight.

Luke i. 16, 17. And many of the children of Israel shall he turn to the Lord their God: And he shall go before him in the spirit and power of Elias, to turn the hearts of the fathers to the children, and the disobedient to the wisdom of the just; to make ready a people prepared for the Lord. iii. 1, 2. Now the word of God came unto John, the son of Zacharias, in the wilderness.

Matt. iii. 1. In those days came John the Baptist, preaching in the wilderness of Judea; Luke iii. 3. And he came into all the country about Jordan, preaching the baptism of repentance for the remission of sins; Matt. iii. 2. And saying, Repent ye, for the kingdom of heaven is at hand.

Acts xiii. 24. John preached the baptism of repentance to all the people of Israel; (xix. 4,) saying unto the people, that they should believe on HIM which should come after him, that is, on Christ Jesus.

John i. 19 to 31. And this is the record of John, when the Jews sent priests and Levites to ask him, Who art thou? He confessed, I am not the Christ. I *am* the voice of one crying in the wilderness, Make straight the way of the Lord. And they asked him, Why baptizest thou, if thou be not that Christ? John answered, I baptize with water: but there standeth one among you, who, coming after me, is preferred before me. That HE should be manifest to Israel, therefore am I come baptizing with water. 33. [For God] sent me to baptize with water.

Matt. iii. 5. Then went out to him Jerusalem and all Judea, and all the region round about Jordan, 6. And were baptized of him in Jordan, confessing their sins.

Mark i. 4. John did baptize in the wilderness, and preach the baptism of repentance for the remission of sins, 5. And there went out unto him all the land of Judea and they of Jerusalem, and were all baptized of him in the river of Jordan, confessing their sins.

Luke iii. 12. Then came also publicans to be baptized, and said unto him, Master, what shall we do? 13. And he said unto them, Exact no more than that which is appointed you.

Matt. iii. 7. But when he saw many of the Pharisees and Sadducees come to his baptism, he said unto them, O generation of vipers, who hath warned you to flee from the wrath to come? 8. Bring forth, therefore, fruits meet for repentance: 9. And think not to say within yourselves, We have Abraham to *our* father: for I say unto you, that God is able of these stones to raise up children unto Abraham. 11. I indeed baptize you with water unto repentance; but he that cometh after me is mightier than I, whose shoes I am not worthy to bear: he shall baptize you with the Holy Ghost and *with* fire: 12. Whose fan is in his hand, and he will thoroughly purge his floor, and gather his wheat into the garner; but he will burn up the chaff with unquenchable fire.

3. *The Subjects, Mode, and Spiritual Design of Baptism.*

There are three inquiries in relation to the ordinance of baptism, upon which, I shall imagine, you are desirous of obtaining satisfaction of mind, purely deduced from the Scriptures—namely:

I. Who are proper *subjects* of Christian baptism, according to the authority of Christ, and the practice of his harbinger and apostles?

II. By what *mode* should the ordinance be administered, according to the same authority and practice?

III. What is the *spiritual design* of Baptism, and in whom is that design realized?

These three inquiries will be kept constantly in view in the following pages. In the forgoing section of Scriptures you have a full account of John the Baptist, with reference to his practice, in which you may notice,—

His mission was divine. He was "sent from God." He was raised up by the special purpose and power of God, and employed in a work entirely his own; succeeding to no one who had gone before him, and followed by no one in the same office. His instructions for his work he obtained by Divine revelation:—"The word of God came unto John," and thus his entire work was of God's immediate appointment.

The great object of his ministry was to "prepare the way of the Lord;" i. e., of Christ, who was immediately to follow him, according to the prediction of the prophets; Isa. xl. 3. Mal. iii. 1. This great design John was to accomplish, 1. By *proclaiming repentance*—impressing on the minds of his hearers their *guilt* before God; the necessity of being sensible of it, and *confessing* it; and thus, with contrition of heart, "to turn to the Lord their God." 2. By *announcing the immediate approach of the long-promised* MESSIAH; assuring the Jews that his "kingdom was at hand;" and, 3. By seriously charging and exhorting them to "*Believe on him* who should come after him, that is, on Christ Jesus." By these labors attended with the blessing of heaven, he was "to make ready a people prepared for the Lord." And this was happily accomplished, inasmuch as the first disciples of Christ were previously disciples of John. John i. 35–47.

It does not appear, therefore, that the design of John's

mission could be realized in any but in *adult* persons, or persons come to the years of understanding; none else could repent of sin; none else could embrace the glad tidings of the coming Saviour, and thereby be "a people prepared" for the service of Christ; who, within one year, was to follow John, and receive the people so prepared.

His ministry was to be followed by the administration of the ordinance of baptism. His commission from heaven included this ordinance. Baptism as a divine institution was unknown in the church of God previous to the mission of John. But he informed his hearers, that the same God who sent him to prepare the way of the Lord, "sent him to baptize with water," (John i. 33,) and this too was preparatory to the ministry of Christ, as it was fitted and intended to teach *the guilt of sin*, and the penitent sinner's *purification* in the way which the gospel of Christ should bring more fully to light. Of that blessed work of purification baptism was an appropriate and impressive EMBLEM. In accordance with these remarks, we have the excellent

MATTHEW HENRY. "Baptism with water made way for the manifesting of Christ, as it supposed our corruption and filthiness, and signified our cleansing by him, who is the *Fountain opened.*" Of John's express commission from heaven for baptizing, Mr. Henry adds, "See what sure grounds John went upon in his ministry and baptism. He did not run without sending; God *sent him to baptize.* He had a warrant from heaven for what he did. . . God gave him both his mission and his message; both his credentials and instructions." *Expos. on John* i. 6–14, and 29–36.

The persons John baptized had received his ministry, and were professed penitents. One particular circumstance is expressly asserted by Matthew, and repeated again by Mark, descriptive of the persons whom John baptized, and by the latter it is asserted of "all" of them; namely, that they CONFESSED THEIR SINS. He had preached repentance—exhorted to repentance—and of the Pharisees and Sadducees demanded the "fruits of repentance;" while he peremptorily rejected every plea they might urge, particularly that, in which they generally gloried, *that they were the children of Abraham;* and hence, in accordance with *that repentance* which John thus *preached and demanded,* "they were all baptized of him, confessing their sins." Thus his baptism is expressly called by Mark i. 4, by Luke iii. 3, and twice by Paul, Acts xiii. 24, and xix. 4, "the baptism of repentance." This being admitted, it will follow, that the persons, yea, *all* the persons, whom John baptized, WERE THOSE WHO HAD RECEIVED AND BELIEVED HIS MINISTRY; and, as the "fruit" of their conviction, they openly professed repentance toward God, and faith in the approaching Saviour. Thus,

MR. ERSKINE. "John's baptism was termed the *baptism of repentance,* and baptism *to repentance;* because he required of ALL whom he admitted to baptism, a profession of repentance, and exhorted them to such a conduct as would demonstrate their repentance genuine." *In Booth's Pœdobap. Exam.* Vol. II. p. 241. Ed. 2.

MR. SCOTT. "It does not appear that any but adults were baptized by John. . . adult Jews, professing repentance and a disposition to become the Messiah's subjects, were the ONLY PERSONS whom John admitted to baptism." *Comment. on Matt.* iii. 5, 6.

MR. BURKITT. "John's baptism was the baptism of repentance, of which infants were incapable." *Expos. Notes on Matt.* xix. 13–15.

4. *Of the Mode of John's Baptism.*

My reader will, no doubt, be aware that the ordinance of baptism is administered THREE different ways, in different countries, and by different bodies of Christians; namely, by DIPPING—POURING—and SPRINKLING. He will also be aware, that in *whatever way* the water be employed, it cannot take away sin. No spiritual benefit can be conveyed by any one mode more than by another; but, notwithstanding this, it is a serious and interesting question, *which of these has* DIVINE AUTHORITY? How did the harbinger of Christ, having *God's command* upon the subject, administer the ordinance? *By which of these modes was* JESUS *baptized? and his disciples* by his sanction? There can be but ONE mode that has this DIVINE AUTHORITY; a deviation from this, is a deviation from the revealed will of God, and can be nothing better than a mere human invention. What is that ONE authorized mode? Will the Scriptures afford an inquiring mind satisfaction on this subject? No doubt; they were intended for that purpose, on this as well as on every other subject, in which our obedience to God is required.

Turn then your eye, reader, from the diversified and often varying practices of men, to that unerring and unchangeable source of information, which, in these pages, we propose to examine. Two inquiries here suggest themselves:

I. What does the *word* in the original language, employed by the Spirit of God to express this ordinance, signify? Does it express the action of *dipping, pouring,* or *sprinkling?*

II. What mode do the *circumstances* attending the ordinance most evidently favor?

I. To express *the action* by which this ordinance is to be administered, the word so chosen is Βαπτίζω; which our translators have not rendered into English by a verb of our own language expressive of the *same action,* but adopted the original Greek word, which with us is to *baptize.* To obtain therefore *the sense* of this word, we will tnrn to a Lexicon, where the word in question is explained.* The following is

* We might here call to our assistance lexicographers and other learned writers out of number; but I may with confidence affirm, that in citing *one,* we cite *every* competent authority on the subject; for in the *proper* and *primary* sense of the word *baptize,* learned men of all classes and countries are agreed, as I shall show in the Appendix.

[We may add to this note of Pengilly, that Robinson, a learned Pedobaptist, who has prepared a valuable Lexicon of the New Testament, does from the excellent Greek and English Lexicon of DR. JOHN JONES, which gives the plain sense of words without refining or accommodating:

"Βαπτω, *I dip;—I dye, stain.*

"Βαπτίζω, *I plunge; I plunge* in water, *dip, baptize; bury, overwhelm.*

"Βαπτιζομαι, *I am plunged; plunge myself in sorrow; submit to suffer.*

"Βαπτισμα, *immersion, baptism; plunging in affliction.*"

To the unlearned reader it may be proper to observe, that the *first* of these words is the *theme* or *root* of the three following, and gives the *primary idea* of all; the first sense of which is *to dip.* The *second* is the word chosen by inspiration, to express *the action* by which the ordinance is administered, *to baptize,* i. e., *to plunge.* The *third* is the same, in the *passive* form, used by our Lord respecting his sufferings, in Matt. xx. 22, 23, and Luke xii. 50. The last is the Scripture name of the ordinance, *baptism;* the first sense of which is *immersion.*

According to this authority, *to baptize,* is *to plunge, to plunge* in water, *to dip;* and then, figuratively, *to plunge,* or *overwhelm,* as in sorrow, suffering, or affliction; and also, that *baptism* is *immersion.* I refer my reader to the Appendix, at the end of this pamphlet (Part II.), for a confirmation of the sense here given; and requesting him to associate this sense with the words *baptize* and *baptism,* when they occur in future sections of Scripture, in order to observe whether that sense harmonizes with other statements connected with the ordinance, we pass on to notice

II. What mode do the *circumstances* attending the ordinance, as now administered by John, most evidently favor?

We should notice the *place* where John administered this ordinance. It was "the river Jordan." If, in reference to

not intimate that baptizo means to sprinkle. The same is true of Donnegan; and indeed of all modern lexicographers.]

the people of Jerusalem, a situation where water might be easily obtained for *sprinkling* or *pouring* was what John required, we read of our Lord at this place directing the man that was born blind to go and "wash in the pool of Siloam;" so we read of the "pool called Bethesda," and "the brook Cedron;" all *in* or *near* Jerusalem (and we read of others in the Old Testament); and, without doubt, at some of them the penitent Jews of that city and neighborhood might have received the ordinance, if *such* were the mode by which John administered it; and it cannot reasonably be imagined he would have required those persons to go the distance of several miles for the convenience of the river Jordan: more reasonable to suppose he would have baptized in every town and village where his ministry had its intended effect; and especially at or near the metropolis. This strongly favors the opinion, that IMMERSION was his mode. Thus,

MR. TOWERSON. "For what need would there have been of the Baptist's resorting to great confluxes of water, were it not that the baptism was to be performed by an immersion? A very little water, as we know it doth with us, sufficing for an effusion or sprinkling." *In Booth's Pædobap. Exam.* Vol. I. p. 209. Ed. 2.

It is moreover affirmed, that not only was *the river Jordan* chosen by John for his baptism, but Matthew states, the people "were baptized of him IN Jordan," and Mark adds, "IN the RIVER of Jordan." The idea of *going* INTO *the water of a river* for the purpose of baptizing IN it, by sprinkling on the face, or pouring on the head, is too absurd to be entertained.

John also states himself, "I indeed baptize you (ἐν ὑδατι,) that is, "IN water;" not "*with* water," as it is rendered in the English authorized version. The passage was translated *in water,* in some of the early versions of the New Testament into our language. It is *in water* in the Vulgate, Syriac, Arabic, and Ethiopic versions; it is so rendered by Montanus, and recently, in our own country, by that pre-eminent scholar, G.

Campbell, (Principal of Marischal College, Aberdeen,) whose judicious and, in my opinion, unanswerable note upon the place I will lay before my reader.

MR. CAMPBELL. "So inconsistent are the interpreters last mentioned [i. e., certain Protestant] that none of them have scrupled to render εν τω Ιορδανη, *in Jordan;* though nothing can be plainer than that, if there be any incongruity in the expression *in water*, this, *in Jordan*, must be equally incongruous. But they have seen that the preposition *in* could not be avoided there, without adopting a circumlocution—which would have made this deviation from the text too glaring. The word βαπτιζειν, both in sacred authors and in classical, signifies *to dip, to plunge, to immerse,* and was rendered by Tertullian, the oldest of the Latin fathers, *tingere;* the term used for dyeing cloth, which was by immersion. It is always construed suitably to this meaning; thus it is, εν ὑδατι, εν τω Ιορδανη," (that is, *in water, in the Jordan.*) "But I should not lay much stress on the preposition εν, which, answering to the Hebrew (beth), may denote *with,* as well as *in,* DID NOT THE WHOLE PHRASEOLOGY, in regard to this ceremony, CONCUR IN EVINCING THE SAME THING. Accordingly, the baptized are said *to arise, emerge,* or *ascend,* ver. 16, and Acts viii. 39, *from* or *out of the water.* When, therefore, the Greek word [baptizo] is adopted, rather than translated into modern languages, the mode of construction ought to be preserved so far as may conduce to suggest its original import." Let the reader seriously consider what follows. "It is to be regretted that we have so much evidence, that even good and learned men allow their judgments to be warped by the sentiments and customs of the sect which they prefer. *The true partisan, of whatever denomination,* ALWAYS INCLINES TO CORRECT THE DICTION OF THE SPIRIT BY THAT OF THE PARTY." *Four Gospels, Note on Matt.* iii. 11.

TERTULLIAN, who lived within a century after the Apostle John, mentions expressly the people (quos Joannes in Jordane tinxit) "whom John dipped in Jordan." *In Stennett's Answer to Russen*, p. 144.

Would it not be absurd to render the passage "John baptized *with* the Jordan?" and if, of necessity, it must be "in the Jordan," then it undeniably follows, it must be "in water;" and baptism *in water* or *in a river*, wherever so observed throughout the world, is baptism by *immersion*. But I hope to satisfy any candid inquirer on this subject in the Appendix.

MR. HERVEY, when contending that *εν* signifies *in*, adds, "I can prove it to have been in peaceable possession of this signification for more than *two thousand years*." "Every one knows," he observes in another place, that *with* "is not the native, obvious, and literal meaning; rather a meaning swayed, influenced, moulded by the preceding or following word." *Letters to Mr. Wesley*, Let. X. and II.

LIGHTFOOT AND ADAM CLARKE. "That the baptism of John was by *plunging* the body (after the same manner as the washing unclean persons was) seems to appear from those things which are related of him; namely, that he *baptized in Jordan*, that he baptized in *Enon, because there was much water there*," *&c.* *In A. Clarke's Commentary*, at the end of Mark.

Inference. If, then, I am a sincere inquirer after the will of God, and disposed to gather that will from what God has been pleased to reveal in his word for that purpose, I am constrained, from the foregoing Scriptures, to draw the following inference, namely, "that John baptized none but those who gave him satisfactory evidence of being *conscious of their sin* and guilt before God, and whom he exhorted to *repent* and to *believe* in Jesus; and as to the Mode, that he *immersed* them *in water, in the Jordan*."

5. *The Baptism of Jesus.*

Our Lord's baptism we next find immediately following the foregoing account of John. This place attaches to it infinite interest, by the infinite dignity of the Person baptized.

Matt. iii. 13. Then cometh Jesus from Galilee to Jordan unto John to be baptized of him. 14. But John forbade him, saying, I have need to be baptized of thee, and comest thou to me? 15. And Jesus answering, said unto him, Suffer *it to be so* now: for thus it becometh us to fulfil all righteousness. Then he suffered him. Mark i. 9. [Thus] Jesus came from Nazareth of Galilee, and was baptized of John in Jordan.

Matt. iii. 16. And Jesus, when he was baptized, went up straightway out of the water. Mark i. 10. And coming up out of the water, Luke iii. 21, and praying, the heaven was opened, 22, And the Holy Ghost descended in a bodily shape like a dove upon him, and a voice came from heaven, which said, Thou art my beloved Son; in thee I am well pleased. 23. And Jesus himself began to be about thirty years of age.

John i. 32. And John bare record, saying, I saw the Spirit descending from heaven like a dove, and it abode upon him. 29, 36. And looking upon Jesus as he walked, he saith, Behold the Lamb of God, which taketh away the sin of the world! 34. And I saw, and bare record that this is the Son of God. 28. These things were done in Bethabara, where John was baptizing.

What, my pious reader, shall we say of the PERSON baptized in *this* case! What an honor is hereby attached to the ordinance, and consequently to all that duly follow the example of the Redeemer in it!

Let the man who slights and contemns this sacred institution, calling it "an useless, unmeaning ceremony, incapable of washing away sin, or of effecting any good," let him read these verses, and view the immaculate SON OF GOD, who had "no sin" to wash away, proceeding from Galilee down to Jordan, "to be baptized." Let him see the "Wisdom of God" entering the streams, and bowing beneath them,

"The emblem of his future grave!"

This, we should suppose, would induce a different sentiment of the ordinance, and silence every objection to the practice of it.

And if a sight of CHRIST in Jordan had not that effect, let him *hear* and *see* the approbation of the FATHER and SPIRIT testified on this very occasion, and *immediately* upon his submission to this sacred rite. Never was an ordinance so honored! Here is a dignity given to it infinitely exceeding any of the rites of the Old Testament. Each PERSON of the sacred TRINITY is specially present, and each DIVINE PERSON gives it the testimony of his approbation! The blessed REDEEMER submits to be baptized; the FATHER, at the instant of his rising from the water, calls him *his beloved Son*, in whose conduct he was *well pleased;* and the DIVINE SPIRIT, at the same instant, descended upon him in a visible form! O, to have witnessed this scene, how overwhelming! Nothing since the commencement of time, has equalled in sublimity and glory this wonderful event.

Four things are to be noticed in this place. The *Reason* why Christ would be baptized; upon which, hear the celebrated and excellent

WITSIUS. "Our Lord would be baptized, that he might conciliate authority to the baptism of John—that, by his own example, he might commend and sanctify our baptism—that men might not be loath to come to *the baptism of the* LORD, seeing the Lord was not backward to come to the baptism of a *servant*—that, by his baptism, he might represent the future condition both of himself and his followers; first *humble*, then *glorious;* now mean and low, then glorious and exalted; *that* represented by IMMERSION, *this* by EMERSION—and finally, to declare by his voluntary submission to baptism, that he would not delay the delivering up of himself to be immersed in the torrents of hell, yet with a certain faith and hope of emerging." —*In Pœd. Exam.* Vol. I. page 147.

The *Time* chosen for fulfilling the promise of pouring forth the Spirit upon Christ. This is noticed and improved by the pious

DODDRIDGE. "Jesus had no sin to wash away, yet he was

baptized; and God owned that ordinance so far as to make it the season of pouring forth the Spirit upon him. And where can we expect this sacred effusion, but in a conscientious and humble attendance upon divine appointments?" *Fam. Expos.* Improv. of the place.

The *Language* of Christ, in answer to John; which is thus explained by an esteemed commentator:

MR. SCOTT. *Thus it becometh us, &c.* "We never find that Jesus spake of himself in the plural number; and it must therefore be allowed he meant John also, and ALL the servants of God, in a subordinate sense. It became Christ, as our surety and our example, perfectly to *fulfil all righteousness;* it becomes us to walk in all the commandments and ordinances of God, without exception, and to attend on every divine institution—as long as it continues in force. Thus far Christ's example is OBLIGATORY." *Commentary on Matt.* iii. 13–15.

The *Circumstance* immediately following his baptism, namely, his "*coming up* OUT OF *the water,*" which evidently implies that he went down *into* it, (as is expressly said of Philip and the eunuch, Acts viii. 38;) a circumstance required in no mode of baptism but immersion, and hence we infer that Jesus was *buried* or *immersed* in the water. To this mode of baptism our blessed Saviour plainly alludes, when referring to his overwhelming sufferings, in Luke xii. 50, which we shall come to presently.

CAMPBELL'S Translation. "Jesus, being baptized, no sooner rose out of the water, than heaven was opened to him." *Four Gospels*, Matt. iii. 16.

DODDRIDGE'S. "And after Jesus was baptized, as soon as he ascended out of the water, behold, the heavens were opened unto him." *In loco.*

MACKNIGHT. Jesus "submitted to be baptized, that is, buried under the water by John, and to be raised out of it again, as an emblem of his future death and resurrection." *Apostol. Epis. Note on Rom.* vi. 4.

Bishop Taylor. "The custom of the ancient churches was not sprinkling, but immersion; in pursuance of the sense of the word in the commandment, and the example of our blessed Saviour." *In Pœd. Exam.* Vol. I. p. 199.

I never, my reader, can think of the baptism of this glorious and divine Person—the Son of God—the Lord from heaven—the righteous Judge of the last day—the Author of our salvation, and the Giver of eternal life, but with feelings of the deepest interest. We observe him here proceeding on his long journey, (for Nazareth was three days journey from Jerusalem, and not less from Bethabara,) the object of which is, "to be baptized." We observe him admitting of no argument against his submission to that rite; and we ought never to forget how he associated *his people*, his followers, with himself, "thus it becometh us!" the *servant* as well as the Lord, the *members* as well as the Head, "to fulfil all" practical "righteousness;" all that God enjoins and requires. How strong is the obligation to realize what the Saviour here intended! Who will not concur in the pious decision of Mr. Polhill? "The pattern of Christ and the Apostles is more to me than all the human wisdom in the world." Nor can any one deny me the following

Inference. The Baptism of Jesus, as an *Example,* is fulfilled in the baptism of a Believer by *Immersion,* and in no other case.

6. *Christ Baptizing by his Disciples.*

This is the only mention of our Lord's baptizing, or of the disciples by his authority and direction, during his corporeal presence with them; and, consequently, it claims our very serious attention.

John iii. 22. After these things came Jesus and his disciples into the land of Judea; and there he tarried with them and baptized. 26. And they came unto John, and said unto him,

Rabbi, he that was with thee beyond Jordan, to whom thou bearest witness, behold, the same baptizeth, and all men come to him. 27. John answered and said, A man can receive nothing, except it be given him from heaven. 30. He must increase, but I *must* decrease.

Chap. iv. 1. When, therefore, the Lord knew how the Pharisees had heard that Jesus made and baptized more disciples than John, 2. (Though Jesus himself baptized not, but his disciples,) 3. He left Judea, and departed again into Galilee. x. 40. And [he] went away again beyond Jordan, into the place where John at first baptized;—42. And many believed on him there.

The import of this passage is simply this: "Jesus went into the land of Judea, and baptized certain disciples,—many hearing of him, and remembering what John had preached concerning him, flocked to him,—and soon it was generally known and said, as the happy fruit of his labors, '*That Jesus made and baptized more disciples than John;*' upon which the Saviour departed, and went into Galilee. He again, however, visited this interesting place, and many more believed on him there."

The only thing to be noticed here, and it is certainly of some importance as to our *first inquiry*, is this, that Christ MADE disciples *before* he baptized them. He did not begin by baptizing, and afterwards instructing; but he *first* taught them his gospel, and they, believing and embracing his word, are thereby "made his disciples;" and hence they are said to "come to him," to conform to his commandments, and then, *secondly*, he baptized them. As this is *all* the Evangelists have recorded respecting Christ baptizing, through the whole of his ministry, this is, consequently, ALL in which the *Practice* of Christ is given for the guide of his people. What we are to understand by "disciples," or "making disciples," is thus described by

MR. OWEN. "By the disciples of Christ, I intend them, and them only, who profess faith in his person and doctrine,

&c. This is the method of the gospel, that first men, by the preaching of it, be MADE DISCIPLES, or be brought unto faith in Christ, and then to be taught to do and observe whatever he commands." *In Pæd. Exam.* Vol. II. p. 275 and 287.

MR. BAXTER. "A disciple and a Christian are all one." *Ibid.* p. 288.

Our LORD, however, may be heard for himself, as to what is intended by *his disciples:* "Whosoever doth not bear his cross, and come after me, cannot be my disciple." Luke xiv. 27. Whatever, therefore, may be said in favor of infant baptism, it cannot be said that either CHRIST'S *Example or Practice* affords it any support; and we shall presently come to his *Command* on the subject. But, in passing from noticing the *Practice* of Jesus, let me cite the words of one of the most eminent Pædobaptist Commentators on the Bible England has ever witnessed:—

MR. SCOTT. "The baptism of Jesus was, doubtless, of adults alone." *Commentary* on John iii. 22–24.

7. *John's last baptizing in Ænon.*

The next passage we find on our subject, is contained in few words. It is, however, of powerful import relative to the MODE.

John iii. 23. And John also was baptizing in Ænon, near to Salim, because there was much water there; and they came and were baptized.

Of the *Persons* here alluded to as baptized by the Harbinger of the Redeemer, nothing is said descriptive of them, except that "they came" to John, as the penitent Jews had before done at Jordan, and, like them, "were baptized;" which fairly implies, that it was their own *voluntary act* thus to seek this holy rite; and if so, they must have been previously *instructed.*

But, in reference to our inquiry on the *Mode* of baptism, this passage is of great weight. We have here the REASON assigned, on account of which John chose the place where we now find him pursuing the object in which he is divinely employed. He is baptizing in Ænon, "because there was MUCH WATER there." No candid Christian, I think, can object to the following

Inference. If John chose a place for the purpose of baptizing, on account of one circumstance, necessary for that ordinance, namely, "because there was much water there," then his Mode of baptism required *much water.* But much water is not necessary for any Mode of baptism but *Immersion,* and hence, without doubt, *that* was his practice. The same inference was drawn, with as little doubt, by the illustrious Pedobaptists following :—

CALVIN. "From these words, John iii. 23, it may be inferred, that baptism was administered, by John and Christ, by plunging the whole body under water." *In Pœd. Exam.* Vol. I. p. 194.

WHITBY. "Οτι ὑδατα πολλα ην εκει; *Because there was much water there,* in which their whole bodies might be dipped; for in this manner *only* was the Jewish baptism performed, by a descent into the water, Acts. viii. 38, and an ascent out of it, ver. 39, and a burial in it. Rom vi. 3, 4. Colos. ii. 12." *Annot.* on the place. See Lightfoot and A. Clarke, at p. 16.

My readers scarcely need be told, that those who practice *sprinkling* never go to *rivers,* or places of *much water,* to administer the ordinance, and, if they should do so, *the great quantity* of the water could not be assigned as the reason for choosing such places ; because, in their Mode, a very *small quantity* only is required.—Not much candor is necessary to admit the truth so plainly conveyed as in this passage.*

* The answer that some have made that the words, "much water," should be "many waters," and refer to *many shallow streams,* is sufficiently answered by the learned Pedobaptist Expositor, who thus *renders* and *explains* the passage :

DODDRIDGE. "John was also at that time baptizing at Ænon; and he particularly chose that place, because there was a *great quantity* of water

8. *References of Jesus Christ to John, his baptism and success.*

As the passage in the preceding section contains the last record of John's baptizing, it appears proper to follow it by the testimony Jesus bore to his Harbinger and his labors.

Luke vii. 24. And when the messengers of John were departed, he began to speak unto the people concerning John. What went ye out into the wilderness for to see? 26. A prophet? Yea, I say unto you, and more than a prophet. Matt. xi. 10. For this is *he* of whom it is written, Behold, I send my messenger before thy face, which shall prepare thy way before thee. 11. Verily I say unto you, Among them that are born of women, there hath not arisen a greater than John the Baptist. John v. 35. He was a burning and a shining light.

Mark xi. 29. And Jesus answered and said unto them, I will also ask you one question. 30. The baptism of John, was it from heaven, or of men? answer me. 31. And they reasoned with themselves, saying, If we shall say, From heaven; he will say, Why then did ye not believe him? 32. But if we shall say, Of men: (all the people will stone us: Luke xx. 6,) they feared the people; for all men counted John that he was a prophet indeed. 33. And they answered and said unto Jesus, We cannot tell.

Luke vii. 29. And all the people that heard *him*, and the publicans, justified God, being baptized with the baptism of John. 30. But the Pharisees and lawyers rejected the counsel of God against themselves, being not baptized of him.

Here observe, 1. The Redeemer in the first of these passages, gives John a pre-eminence above all the servants of

there, which made it very convenient for his purpose." "Nothing surely can be more evident, than that [ὕδατα πολλα] *many waters,* signifies a *large quantity of water,* it being sometimes used for he Euphrates. Jer. li. 13. (*Septuagint.*) To which, I suppose, there may be an allusion, Rev. xvii. 1. Compare Ezek. xliii. 2., and Rev. i. 15; xiv. 2; xix. 6; where *the voice of many waters* does plainly signify the roaring of a high sea." *Fam. Expos.* Paraph., and Note on the Place.

God, of the former dispensation; not excepting Abraham, Moses, or Isaiah. His revelations were more signal; his preaching of more vital importance, and his success greater. Thus was he *more than a prophet.*

2. From the question which the Redeemer proposed to the Jews, Whether the baptism of John was from heaven or of men? in order to convict them of their guilt in treating John's labors as they had done, it will evidently follow that it was "From heaven." Had John's baptism been borrowed from *Jewish proselyte baptism*, it would have been *of men*, (for that is unknown in the word of God,) and then the question might have been answered without hesitation, and the design of our Lord, in that case, could not have been realized.

3. The common people, who heard John's ministry, (the Saviour adds,) "justified God," i. e., approved of the Divine conduct in John's ministry and baptism; and this they evinced in "being baptized with the baptism of John;" while classes of higher religious repute, "the Pharisees and lawyers," in contempt of this messenger of God, and his message too, "*rejected the counsel of God against themselves, being not baptized of him.*" Here our Lord plainly indicates that the ordinance of baptism was a part of "the counsel of God," i. e., his mind and will; and, as far as this rite is contemned, so far the counsel of God is "rejected;" and it is, emphatically, "against themselves" who thus opposed what God enjoins.

Inference. If John, who was but a man, is to be so highly regarded, and his baptism considered "the counsel of God;" so that neglect of it thus meets the marked disapprobation of our Redeemer;—how much more may the Divine indignation be expected on them who slight this sacred ordinance in that still more interesting form, in which we shall presently find it, —enjoined by HIM, whose name is written "KING of kings, and LORD of lords!" Surely I may add, "*If they escaped not who refused him that spake on earth, much more shall*

*10

not we escape, if we turn away from HIM *that speaketh from heaven!"* Heb. xii. 25.

9. *Christ represents his Sufferings under the Figure of Baptism.*

Matt. xx. 22. But Jesus answered and said, Ye know not what ye ask. Are ye able to drink of the cup that I shall drink of, and to be baptized with the baptism that I am baptized with? They say unto him, We are able. 23. And he said unto them, Ye shall drink indeed of my cup, and be baptized with the baptism that I am baptized with; but to sit on my right hand, and on my left, is not mine to give, but *it shall be given to them* for whom it is prepared of my Father.

Luke xii. 50. But I have a baptism to be baptized with; and how am I straitened till it be accomplished!

Our Lord, in these affecting and impressive passages, is referring to the greatness of his approaching sufferings,—and, by a metaphor, he calls them *"a Baptism."* An interesting question from hence arises in reference to our second inquiry, Does *sprinkling* a little water on the face, or being totally *immersed* and *overwhelmed* in a large quantity, most appropriately exhibit an image of the severity of the sufferings of Christ? The following extracts will, I have no doubt, contain my reader's opinion:

DODDRIDGE thus paraphrases the places: "Are you able to drink of the bitter cup of which I am now about to drink so deep, and to be baptized with the baptism, and *plunged* into that sea of sufferings with which I am shortly to be baptized, and, as it were, *overwhelmed* for a time!" "I have, indeed, a most dreadful baptism to be baptized with; and I know that I shall be shortly bathed, as it were, in blood, and *plunged* in the most *overwhelming* distress." *Fam. Expos.* on the places.

WITSIUS. "Immersion into the water is to be considered by us, as exhibiting that dreadful abyss of Divine justice, in which Christ, for our sins, was for a time, as it were, absorbed; as in

David, his type, he complains, Psalm lxix. 2, "*I am come into deep waters, where the floods overflow me.*" *Œcon. of the Cov.* L. IV. C. xvi. § 26.

Mr. James Hervey expresses himself, on this subject, with great energy. "He longed, (beneficent, blessed Being!) he longed for the fatal hour. He severely rebuked one of his disciples who would have dissuaded him from going as a volunteer to the cross. He was even *straitened*, under a kind of holy uneasiness, till the dreadful work was accomplished; till he was *baptized with the baptism of his sufferings*, bathed in blood, and *plunged* in death!" *Theron and Aspasio*, Vol. II. Let. 7.

"Sir H. Trelawney, under whose impressive ministry," says the late amiable Mr. Dore, of London, "my first religious feelings were invigorated, referring to those words of our Lord, exclaimed to this effect: 'Here, I must acknowledge, our Baptist brethren have the advantage: for our Redeemer's sufferings must not be compared to a few drops of water sprinkled on the face, for he was *plunged* into distress, and his soul was environed with sorrows.'" *Sermons on Baptism*, by J. Dore, p. 39.

Inference. If our Lord intended the ordinance of baptism to exhibit an image of the *overwhelming sorrows of his soul*, in the garden and on the cross, his intention is frustrated by the change of immersion into sprinkling! And if this be admitted, (and it cannot be denied,) what devout Christian can think of this change but with deep regret!

10. *The Commission which our Lord gave his Apostles about the time of his Ascension into Heaven, containing the formal Institution of Christian Baptism.*

We have already seen that Baptism, as a New Testament ordinance, was instituted of God, and enjoined upon John as the herald and precursor of Christ. It is evident, also, that John administered it upon an admitted or professed acknowledgment of faith "in him *who was to come* after him." Acts

xix. 4. But after our Redeemer *had come*, and finished his work, an alteration was necessary in this particular circumstance. None on earth, but Jesus, could make that alteration; and he, as HEAD and LORD of the church, now does it; requiring it to be administered from this hour, "In the name of the FATHER, and of the SON, and of the HOLY GHOST." This I consider as a RENEWED INSTITUTION of the same sacred rite, altered only in its reference to the coming of Christ, to set up his kingdom. And, what adds greatly to the solemnity of it in this renewed form, our Lord delayed its institution till his *last moments on earth*, and then united it with his final parting and solemn charge, given by Matthew and Mark in the verses following:

Matt. xxviii. 16. Then the eleven disciples went away into Galilee, into a mountain where Jesus had appointed them. 18. And Jesus came and spake unto them, saying, All power is given unto me in heaven and in earth. 19. Go ye, therefore, and teach all nations, baptizing them in the name of the Father, and of the Son, and of the Holy Ghost: 20. Teaching them to observe all things whatsoever I have commanded you: and, lo, I am with you always, *even* unto the end of the world. Amen.

Mark xvi. 15. And he said unto them, Go ye into all the world, and preach the gospel to every creature. 16. He that believeth, and is baptized, shall be saved; but he that believeth not, shall be damned. 19. So then, after the Lord had spoken unto them, he was received up into heaven, and sat on the right hand of God.

How solemn and interesting was this occasion! The Redeemer had undergone the baptism of his sufferings, last described—he had been bathed in blood in the garden!—he had sunk into death on the cross under floods of wrath, due to mankind! But now he is risen triumphant, and is about to ascend to his glory.

He had appointed his disciples to meet him on a mountain

of Galilee, where he was to give them his last most solemn and important charge contained in the verses above. The interesting hour is come; we may be sure the disciples are eager to catch every word from their ascending Lord, and that he would give them his directions in the *plainest language* possible.

He begins by encouraging their sorrowful minds, with a view of his supreme power in heaven and earth—*in heaven,* to give them the Holy Spirit; to employ the angels in their behalf; and, finally, to bestow the kingdom of heaven upon them. So he had all power *in earth,* to gather his church out of all nations; to subdue or restrain his enemies, and to reign over and dwell with his people, as Lord and King of Zion.

Hence the Saviour gives them the "COMMISSION" for preaching and baptizing, which you, my reader, cannot too attentively consider. If you conceive there is any obscurity in the one Evangelist, the other will explain him; and this explanation you will, no doubt, esteem preferable to ten thousand criticisms. By uniting the words of both, they may be thus disposed: "*Go ye, therefore, into all the world; teach all nations, and* "*preach the gospel to every creature: him that believeth bap-* "*tize, in the name of the Father, and of the Son, and of the* "*Holy Ghost, and he shall be saved; but he that believeth not* "*shall be damned.*"

Our great Legislator, who only has the right to enact laws for his church, to whom we must submit, and who will have nothing taken away from, or added to his word, Rev. xxii. 19, has here described to his apostles *the person* to whom they are to administer this his ordinance, namely, the BELIEVER; the person who shall cordially believe the gospel which they shall preach. And if we allow him to have expressed his mind clearly and fully, *he restricts the ordinance to the believer alone.* He has given no direction to admit any other to it, and who will dare to speak where HE is silent? Who shall enlarge or extend the limits HE has prescribed? or, who will dare to go beyond, or attempt to remove, the boundaries HE has fixed and established? Surely the mind of a true disciple recoils at the thought! Let us now hear the remarks of some eminent Pedobaptist writers on these passages:—

MR. ARCHIBALD HALL, predecessor of Mr. Waugh, of London. "How grand and awful is that weighty preface to the institution of Christian Baptism! Matt. xxviii. 18, 19. Who is that daring, insolent worm, that will presume to dispute the authority, or change the ordinances of HIM who is given to be head over all things to the church? The solemnity of this ordinance is complete: and all the purposes of its institution are secured by the authority and blessing of Christ. His laws are not subject to any of those imperfections which are attendants of the best contrived systems among men, and frequently need explanations, amendments, and corrections. It is most dangerous and presumptuous to add any ceremony, or to join any service, on any pretence, unto heaven's appointment." *Gospel Worship*, Vol. I. pp. 325, 326.

SAURIN. "In the primitive church, instruction preceded baptism, agreeable to the order of Jesus Christ, *Go, teach all nations, baptizing them*," &c. *In Pæd. Exam.* Vol. II. p. 274.

MR. BAXTER has a very forcible passage on the same place. "*Go, disciple me all nations, baptizing them.* As for those who say they are discipled by baptizing, and not before baptizing, they speak not the sense of the text; nor that which is true or rational; else, why should one be baptized more than another?—This is not like some occasional historical mention of baptism; but it is the very commission of Christ to his apostles, for preaching and baptizing; and purposely expresseth their several works in their several places and order. Their *first* task is, by teaching, to make disciples, which are, by Mark, called believers. The *second* work is, to baptize them, whereto is annexed the promise of their salvation. The *third* work is, to teach them all other things which are afterwards to be learned in the school of Christ. [Observe what follows.] To contemn this order, is to renounce all rules of order; for where can we expect to find it, if not here? I profess, my conscience is fully satisfied from this text, that it is one sort of faith, *even saving*, that MUST GO BEFORE BAPTISM; and the profession whereof the minister must expect." *In Pœd. Exam.* Vol. II. p. 270.

11. *Conclusion of the Four Gospels.*

The last Scriptures we cited close the information which the Four Gospels afford us on the subject of Baptism. Before we pass to the subsequent books, I beg to remind the reader, that we have had before us the practice of John; and the Example, Practice, and Command of our Lord Jesus Christ. As yet, we have not met with a single passage or word, which can fairly be interpreted as indicating that any persons should receive this ordinance, or are proper subjects for it, but those who have been first *taught the gospel*, and who *profess to believe it.*

But I am most anxious to impress on the attention of an inquirer the words of Jesus in the Commission, which we have just read. Remember, reader, that this Jesus is to be our JUDGE at the last great and awful day; and that He will not judge us according to the opinions or practices of men, but according to his own word. Upon this command of our Saviour, I would, therefore, beg briefly to add, and leave to the reader's deliberate meditations:—

I. That we have here *the enactment* of the DIVINE LAW, in reference to Baptism: and this Law we find delivered in language the most solemn, and in circumstances the most interesting and affecting.

II. That this Law of Jesus is not like human laws, which admit of *alterations* or *amendments.* None but Jesus has authority to alter: and, coming from the Fountain of heavenly Wisdom, who will presume to improve upon HIS appointment? And

III. This Law is as *delightful* to the mind of a Christian, as it is solemn. The words, "baptizing them *into* the name of the Father, Son, and Holy Spirit," imply a public recognition of the glorious change which has taken place in the spiritual circumstances of true converts, in their having passed from the family of sin and Satan, into the family of the TRIUNE GOD! A change, not of the *ordinance*, but of the power and grace of God.

We now pass on to the *Acts of the Apostles.* Here we have an historical relation of the labors of the Apostles, for above thirty years after the ascension of Christ; and here we shall find the baptism of *many thousands* of persons. If we have misunderstood the will of Christ on this subject, THE APOSTLES SURELY DID NOT, and their obedience to his command will correct our error; but if, on the contrary, we have rightly interpreted his will, their obedience will confirm our opinion.

12. *The Acts of the Apostles.*

"The penman of this Scripture," the Assembly of Divines, in the argument to it, assures us, "was Luke the Evangelist, (as appears from the first words of it,) for the most part an eye-witness to the things he records, being constantly a fellow-laborer with Paul. His purpose," they add, "in writing this narrative was, as he intimates in his first preface, that the church might have the *certain knowledge* of Christ, his gospel, and kingdom; that our faith might not be built on the uncertain reports of pretenders to truth." Hence, admitting the writer to be a faithful and pious historian, and writing purposely for the direction of the Church of Christ in all following ages; and, above all, under the influence of the Spirit of God, we may safely rely, not only on the accuracy of the accounts, but on the fulness and sufficiency of the information to answer the professed purpose.

We have here, on infallible record, NINE INSTANCES of the administration of baptism, which we will examine in their own order.

13. *The Baptism at the Feast of Pentecost.*

On this memorable occasion, which was but ten days from the ascension of Christ, when the Apostles and Disciples were together at Jerusalem, it pleased God to accomplish the promise of sending them the Holy Ghost. By his miraculous power they were enabled to speak in different languages to the multitude then assembled at Jerusalem from different nations: so that every one heard, in his *own tongue, the wonderful works of God.* Peter delivers to the multitude an impressive discourse, in which he charged the Jews with having crucified the Lord of glory; but added, that God had raised him from the dead, and exalted him to his right hand, as the only Lord and Christ. Upon this follow the verses relating to the ordinance, and descriptive of the subjects of it.

Acts ii. 37. Now when they heard *this*, they were pricked in their heart, and said unto Peter, and to the rest of the Apostles, Men *and* brethren, what shall we do? 38. Then Peter said unto them, Repent and be baptized, every one of you, in the name of Jesus Christ, for the remission of sins; and ye shall receive the gift of the Holy Ghost: 39. For the promise is unto you, and to your children, and to all that are afar off, *even* as many as the Lord our God shall call. 41. Then they that gladly received his word, were baptized; and the same day there were added *unto them* about three thousand souls. 42. And they continued steadfastly in the Apostles' doctrine and fellowship, and in breaking of bread, and in prayers. 47. Praising God, and having favor with all the people. And the Lord added to the church daily such as should be saved.

Here we must observe how the Apostle Peter obeys his Lord's direction in the Commission. He begins by *preaching*, and never mentions a word about baptism, till he evidently found some of his hearers answering the character, "he that believeth." Hence, the persons who were baptized are thus described,—1. Their hearts were deeply penetrated by the truth they heard, so that they cried, *What shall we do?* 2. They are exhorted to repent of their sins. 3. They, at length, "GLADLY RECEIVED THE WORD," and thereon were baptized, and added to the church. 4. They afterward *continued steadfast* in the doctrine of the gospel, and in the practice of its duties. Not a word of this will apply to *infants.*

There is, however, one clause in the 39th verse of the above scriptures, "The promise is to you, *and to your children,*" which is commonly urged in favor of infant baptism; as if the Apostle alluded to some promise, on the ground of which infant children were deemed proper subjects of Christian baptism. To answer which, let the *three* following things be considered:—

I. The promise to which the Apostle alludes, has no relation to *infant* children, it being the promise of the gift of the Holy Ghost, joined with its effects, of which infants are incapable. My reader will observe that the people, on this occasion, were astonished at the effects produced by the gift of the Spirit. The Apostle assures them, verses 16–18, that it was the fulfilment of the prophecy of Joel; which prophecy is thus expressed, chap. ii. 28: "*I will pour out my Spirit upon all flesh; and your sons and your daughters shall prophesy,*" &c. The Apostle having delivered an impressive discourse, observing his hearers deeply affected and amazed at the gifts of the Spirit, in order to turn their amazement into hope and joy, refers them a second time to this promise, and to their own interest in it, in the following words, ver. 38, 39, "Repent, &c., and you [yourselves] shall receive the gift of the Holy Ghost; FOR [by this I assure you of it] the *promise* is to you and to your children." Now, as the gift of the Spirit, with his miraculous powers, is the object of *the promise* and as *infant* children are *incapable* of that gift, children in infancy cannot be intended. Thus,

WHITBY. "These words will not prove a right of infants to receive baptism; the promise here being that only of the

Holy Ghost, mentioned in verses 16, 17, 18, and so relating only to the times of the miraculous effusion of the Holy Ghost, and to those persons who, by age, were capable of these extraordinary gifts." *Annot.* on the place.

DODDRIDGE. "*The promise is to you and to your children.* Considering that the gift of the Spirit had been mentioned just before, it seems most natural to interpret this as a reference to that passage in Joel, which had been so largely recited above, ver. 17, &c., where God promises the effusion of the Spirit *on their sons and their daughters.*" *Fam. Expos.* Note on the place.

II. The word, in the original, τεκνα, rendered *children*, signifies *posterity;* and does not necessarily imply *infancy.*

HAMMOND. "If any have made use of that very unconcludent argument, [referring to this passage, Acts ii. 39,] I have nothing to say in defence of them. The word *children* there, is really the posterity of the Jews, and not peculiarly their infant children." *Works,* Vol. I. p. 490.

LIMBORCH, a learned divine of Amsterdam. "By τεκνα the Apostle understands, not infants, but posterity; in which signification the word occurs in many places of the New Testament; see, among others, John viii. 39. [*If ye were Abraham's* CHILDREN, *ye would do the works of Abraham.*] Whence it appears, that the argument which is very commonly taken from this passage, for the baptism of infants, is of NO FORCE, and GOOD FOR NOTHING." *Comment. in loc.*

III. The words of the Apostle immediately following, explain his own meaning in the most decisive terms: "The promise is to you, and to your children, and to all that are afar off, even TO AS MANY AS THE LORD OUR GOD SHALL CALL,"— "to *as many* of you and your children, and the Gentiles afar off, as God should call by his word and Spirit to this great privilege."

MATTHEW HENRY. "To this general, the following limitation must refer *even as many of them,* as many particular persons in each nation, *as the Lord our God shall call* effectually into the fellowship of Jesus Christ." *Expos.* of the place.

Inference. From the whole, it appears most evident, that none were, in this case, encouraged to hope for Christian baptism, but such as gave evidence of being *called* effectually by grace; and NONE WERE, IN FACT, baptized, but such as "*gladly received the word.*" So far, the word of God is our plain guide.

14. *Philip baptizing at Samaria.*

Acts viii. 5. Then Philip went down to the city of Samaria, and preached Christ unto them. 6. And the people with one accord gave heed unto those things which Philip spake, hearing, and seeing the miracles which he did. 8. And there was great joy in the city.

12. But when they believed Philip preaching the things concerning the kingdom of God, and the name of Jesus Christ, they were baptized, both men and women. 13. Then Simon himself believed also; and when he was baptized, he continued with Philip, and wondered, beholding the miracles and signs which were done.

In this instance, as in the former, the commission of Christ is literally fulfilled. Philip began his work by *preaching Christ to them;* and when they had heard the doctrines and saw the miracles, they were filled with joy. Not a word about baptizing, till some of the people "*believed*" the things concerning Jesus Christ; then "*they were baptized, both men and women.*"

Now, if it were the will of Christ that infants should be baptized, and it were true that the Apostles, (like Pædobaptist Missionaries among the Heathen,*) were accustomed to

* In the accounts we are often receiving from Pædobaptist Missionaries among the Heathen, our brethren naturally inform us of the children, as well as the adults, they baptize. For example, in the "*Missionary Register*" for the year 1821, at page 19, a Report from South Africa states—"During the

baptize children together with the parents; then, if *any* of those "men and women" at Samaria had children, (which surely is highly probable,) Philip must have baptized them: but had he baptized *men, women, and children,* is it to be imagined that the inspired historian, writing, (as he says,) "of ALL that Jesus began to do and to teach," and "having had perfect understanding of *all things* from the very first;" and his avowed design being that his reader "might know the certainty of things;" is it to be imagined *that he would particularize the two,* out of the three descriptions of the baptized, *and omit the third?* This I conceive impossible, and therefore draw this

Inference. When the Evangelist states, "they were baptized, both men and women," had infants also been baptized, he must have added, to have completed the record of the circumstance, "and children;" but not making that natural and necessary addition, I infer, that men and women *only* were baptized; and that no infants *received the ordinance* with them; therefore, that the practice at that time did not exist.

15. *The Baptism of the Ethiopian Eunuch.*

The eunuch described in this chapter was a person of high authority in the kingdom of Ethiopia, but it would seem a proselyte to the Jewish religion. He is here returning from

year 1819, 20 adults and 21 children were baptized." At page 293, a Missionary in Western Africa states—"September 3d, Sunday—I preached, &c., and then baptized 23 adults and 3 infants." Page 294, Nov. 29th—"On the first Sunday of this month I baptized 34 adults and their children; 48 in all."

Rev. C. Mault writes from *Nagercoil,* East Indies, in March, 1826: "Last month I baptized 5 adults and 4 children." Rev. C. Barff writes from *Huahine,* South Sea Islands, June 5, 1825, "30 were added to the church during our visit, and a number baptized. Among those baptized were 16 infants." —*Missionary Chronicle,* for November, 1826.

Are not such accounts quite natural where infant baptism prevails? And why is there a perfect silence throughout the history of apostolical labors on this subject? Their practice surely was not the same.

Jerusalem. Philip is directed to meet him in his way. He found the eunuch reading, as he proceeded in his chariot, the prophet Isaiah, chap. liii. 7. "He was led as a sheep to the slaughter," &c. He is desirous that Philip should explain to him, Whether the prophet, in that place, spake of himself or of some other? and he took him up into his chariot for that purpose: upon which the Evangelist adds:

Acts viii. 35. Then Philip opened his mouth and began at the same scripture, and preached unto him Jesus. 36. And as they went on *their* way, they came unto a certain water: and the eunuch said, See, *here is* water; what doth hinder me to be baptized? 37. And Philip said, If thou believest with all thine heart, thou mayest. And he answered, and said, I believe that Jesus Christ is the Son of God. 38. And he commanded the chariot to stand still; and they went down both into the water, both Philip and the eunuch; and he baptized him. 39. And when they were come up out of the water, the Spirit of the Lord caught away Philip, and the eunuch saw him no more: and he went on his way rejoicing.

My reader will not need to be reminded of the *Commission* of his Redeemer, after perusing these verses. We have here a plain example of the practice of the Apostles, before they admitted a person to baptism. Philip might have deemed the eunuch, after having heard the gospel, a proper subject for baptism, by being directed from heaven to teach him—he might have inferred it, also, from his sincere request of it; yet he does not, he dares not, baptize him, until he openly profess to "*believe with all his heart;*" remembering, no doubt, that Christ had appointed the ordinance for such, and for such only. Nothing can demonstrate more clearly than this, that a DECLARATION OF FAITH WAS INDISPENSABLY REQUIRED PREVIOUS TO BAPTISM.*

* Those who contend that servants and children were all baptized in those days, with, and on account of, their masters and parents, would find it difficult to support their hypothesis in this case. It is the greatest absurdity to

16. *Of the Mode of the Eunuch's Baptism.*

We have, in this case, the *circumstances* attending the administration of baptism more minutely described than in any other instance recorded in the New Testament. The reader is requested to observe the following things:

1st. If *sprinkling* or *pouring* were the mode of baptism ordained by Christ, and practiced by the Apostles, we are assured, by the best authority, that travelers through those deserts "never omitted" to furnish themselves with vessels of water for their journeys; that this provision was "absolutely necessary;" and, if so, the eunuch had all that was required for the ordinance, *without waiting till they came to a place of water.* See Doddridge, as presently cited, and Shaw's Travels, as referred to by him.

2d. We are here, however, informed, verse 36, that they proceeded on their journey till "they came" (επι, *ad*) "UNTO a certain water." And it appears that it was the sight of this place of water that suggested to the eunuch his immediate submission to the ordinance. "See, here is water; what doth hinder me to be baptized?" How unmeaning would this be if he had the requisite water before!

3d. If we admit that the eunuch was not previously provided with water, *now*, when they were "come to a water," it would have been easy, and natural to be expected, for one of the attendants *to have conveyed* to him as much water as was required, without his, or Philip's, proceeding farther. But, though "he commanded the chariot to stand still," no command is given upon this point,—of *bringing water* to him. But,

suppose that Philip would admit the eunuch's servants to baptism, without any profession, or even instruction, when he would object to the pious master, after he requested it, unless he was able to give a frank and open profession of faith in Christ. But he baptized NONE but the eunuch; and, therefore, we may safely conclude, the apostles had "no such custom, neither the churches of God."

4th. Leaving the chariot, verse 38, "they went down INTO the water;" (εις το ὑδωρ, *in aquam.*) Here the reader will remark, It was not sufficient to come *to the water*, (which we are often told is all that the original means,) for this they had done before; but here is a *second* circumstance,—after they had come *to it*, they went down *into it.*

5th. The inspired historian also adds, that it was not the eunuch *alone* that went into the water, but "they went down BOTH;" and this is repeated again, as if to make quibbling or doubting on this subject impossible, "both Philip and the eunuch." Such was the mode of baptism, as now established by the Son of God, that it could not, in this case, be administered unless Philip *attended* the eunuch *into the water*. And

6th. While in this situation, both of them in the water and surrounded therewith, "he baptized him;" that is, if the word be translated, "he *immersed* him," in the name of the Tri-une Jehovah. For this solemn act, the circumstances before noticed were *necessary*, but for any other mode they would be absurd.

7th. The sacred rite being performed, it is lastly added, "when they were come up, (ἐκ του ὑδατος) OUT OF the water," they were parted asunder; probably to meet no more till they should enter the presence of Him to whom they now rendered this act of prompt and cheerful obedience.

It is not easy to imagine how the mode of this sacred ordinance could be more minutely described. That we have here an example of IMMERSION, is allowed by the learned and candid of all denominations.

MR. TOWERSON. "For what need would there have been of Philip and the eunuch going down INTO this [water], were it not that the baptism was to be performed by immersion, a very little water, as we know it doth with us, sufficing for an effusion or sprinkling?" *In Pæd. Exam.* Vol. I. p. 209.

CALVIN, in his Comment on this place, observes, "Here we

perceive how baptism was administered among the ancients, for they immersed the whole body in water." *Ibid.* p. 194.

DODDRIDGE. "*They both went down to the water.* Considering how frequently bathing was used in these hot countries, it is not to be wondered that baptism was generally administered by immersion, though I see no proof that it was essential to the institution. It would be very unnatural to suppose, that they went down to the water merely that Philip might take up a little water in his hand *to pour* on the eunuch. A person of his dignity had, no doubt, many vessels in his baggage, on such a journey through a desert country: a precaution absolutely necessary for travelers in those parts, and never omitted by them.—See Shaw's *Travels,* Preface, p. 4." *Fam. Expos.* Note in loc. See numerous other authors in Booth's *Pæd. Exam.* Vol. I. p. 191 to 224.

Inference. If I find one sufficient proof of the mode of baptism in the days of the Apostles, whatever that mode may be, I infer that I have ascertained what was their *invariable* practice. Because it cannot be imagined that the Apostles (having probably witnessed, and certainly knowing well, the mode by which the Lord Jesus was baptized, and having all received *the same instructions* from their Lord and Master,) could be *divided* either in sentiment or practice. And if immersion be proved in one case, and from thence it be granted that JESUS was THUS baptized, and that HE COMMANDED the ordinance THUS to be administered, would not the amiable and pious Doddridge, who grants above, "baptism was *generally* administered by immersion," allow me to infer, (from the authority of Christ's example and command,) that this mode is "essential to the institution?" Here I have an instance of immersion, and from this I am authorized to conclude, and I do it with the utmost confidence and satisfaction of mind, that IMMERSION WAS WHAT CHRIST ORDAINED, and his obedient Apostles and Disciples INVARIABLY PRACTICED; and, consequently, any departure from this practice is *a departure from the revealed will of Christ;* and such an act can be viewed in no other light than an act of rebellion against his Divine authority.

17. *The Baptism of the Apostle Paul.*

SAUL, while breathing out threatenings against the disciples of Christ, is met, in his career of persecution, by the Lord himself, at whose exceeding glory he falls prostrate on the ground. Ananias, a devout disciple, is directed of God to go to him, and teach him what he is to do; and for his encouragement in visiting the persecutor, he is informed that Saul was *praying*, and that God has made him *a chosen vessel* to himself.

Acts ix. 17. And Ananias went his way, and entered into the house; and putting his hands on him, said, Brother Saul, the Lord, *even* Jesus that appeared unto thee in the way as thou camest, hath sent me, that thou mightest receive thy sight, and be filled with the Holy Ghost. Chap. xxii. 14. And he said, The God of our fathers had chosen thee, that thou shouldst know his will, and see that Just One, and shouldst hear the voice of his mouth. 15. For thou shalt be his witness unto all men of what thou hast seen and heard. 16. And now why tarriest thou? arise, and be baptized, and wash away thy sins, calling on the name of the Lord. Chap. ix. 18. And immediately there fell from his eyes as it had been scales; and he received sight forthwith, and arose, and was baptized.

The promptitude of Ananias in baptizing Saul, "who also is called Paul," as soon as he had received the message from his Saviour, and the restoration of his sight, shows how strictly this ordinance was observed in the days of the Apostles; and, consequently, how it should be observed to the end of time. Paul is exhorted to *arise, and be baptized, and wash away his sins, &c.* He was to arise, and yield obedience to the command of Christ, in baptism, and, at the same time that his body received the washing of water, he was to *call on the name of the Lord,* that his soul might be washed and purified by being, through faith, bathed in the "fountain opened for sin." This spiritual purification, *immersion in water* would strikingly represent. Thus the pious poet,

> COWPER.—"There is a fountain filled with blood,
> Drawn from Immanuel's veins;
> And sinners *plung'd* beneath that flood,
> Lose all their guilty stains."

In this instance, we have the SPIRITUAL DESIGN of the ordinance very plainly referred to. "The meaning is not," says an excellent writer, "as if remission of sins were obtained by baptism; but that, by means of the ordinance, they might be led to the sufferings, death, and bloodshed of Christ *represented* in it."

All our three inquiries are answered in the baptism of this illustrious man. 1. Respecting the *Person* to be baptized,—Paul was *a believer* in Christ. 2. To the *Mode*,—he himself refers when speaking of his baptism, and that of others, comparing it to *a burial;* "Therefore WE are BURIED with him by baptism." Rom. vi. 4. And, 3. The *Spiritual Design* is to represent a *washing away of sin*, obtained in "calling on the name of the Lord."

18. *The Baptism of Cornelius and his Friends.*

The next instance records the baptism of the first Gentiles received into the Christian Church. Cornelius was "a devout man, and one that feared God, with all his house." He is directed from Heaven to send for Peter the Apostle; and against his comimg, he called together his kinsmen and near friends. The Apostle having taught them the leading doctrines of the gospel, concludes by repeating what Christ had commissioned his Apostles to do as their first and chief work, and the testimony of the prophets concerning him, in the two first verses below; after which we have the ordinance in question.

Acts x. 42. And he commanded us to preach unto the people, and to testify that it is he which was ordained of God *to be* the Judge of the quick and the dead. 43. To him gave all the prophets witness, that through his name, whosoever believeth in him, shall receive remission of sins. 44. While Peter yet spake these words, the Holy Ghost fell on all them which heard the word. 45. And they of the circumcision which believed, were astonished, as many as came with Peter, because that on the Gentiles also was poured out the gift of the Holy Ghost. 46. For they heard them speak with tongues, and magnify God. Then answered Peter, 47. Can any man forbid water, that these should not be baptized, which have received the Holy Ghost as well as we? 48. And he commanded them to be baptized in the name of the Lord. Then prayed they him to tarry certain days.

The order of the commission is here also observed. Peter began by *preaching;* and never a word of baptism is found, till the people had heard the gospel, and had given *certain evidences* of their conversion. Then, and not till then, Peter pleads for their baptism; and, what should be particularly observed, he pleads for it upon the ground of their being, most evidently, true BELIEVERS, and as *having received the Holy Ghost.* His language, in verse 47, implies that, if they did not appear to be regenerate persons, any one might object to their baptism; but as they had given evidences that could not be disputed, he infers, no one could deny the propriety of their being baptized. Hence, they were converts to the faith of Christ. Accordingly,

MR. HOLLAND had infallible authority for his observation. "In the first plantation of Christianity among the Gentiles, such only as were of full age, after they were instructed in the principles of the Christian religion, were admitted to baptism." *In Wall's Hist. Inf. Bap.* Vol. II. c. ii. § 14.

As to the *manner* by which these persons were baptized, nothing is said of it, by the sacred historian, beyond the simple fact. It has been suggested, however, that Peter, by the words, "Can any man forbid water," intimates that he required *a little water to be brought to him*, in a cup or basin, for the purpose of sprinkling; but the Apostle neither speaks of *little* nor *much* water, nor about *bringing* it, but simply of *water*, and, no doubt, he intended as much as the ordinance required. It is most improper to form conjectures upon inconclusive statements of Scripture, against that which, by other Scriptures, is evidently confirmed and established. When persons are said to be baptized, we are bound to infer that they were baptized *according to the Pattern and Authority of Christ.* This, I conclude, was the case in this, and in every other instance.

19. *The Baptism of Lydia and her Household.*

The three following instances, as they relate to "*households*," are commonly urged in favor of infant baptism; and, indeed, as being the principal support of that practice in the New Testament. The reader will, therefore, the more particularly examine the Scriptures below in reference to the persons that constituted these households, and if he find recorded the baptism of one infant, or any thing in the text which evidently indicates it, he will consider the point as settled forever in favor of infant baptism; but if the text does not contain such an indication of infants, but describes the baptized households as consisting of persons arrived at the years of understanding, and so capable of *hearing and believing the gospel*—and especially if what is recorded implies that they actually did *hear* and *believe*, then it must be granted that adult and believers' baptism receives all the support these instances afford. The *first* is of Lydia and her household.

Paul, whose baptism we have just considered, is now become an Apostle of Christ. He, with Silas, (and with them, probably, Luke, the writer of this history,) are commissioned from heaven to proceed to Macedonia, and to Philippi, a chief city of it, to preach the gospel. Having arrived, they began their work in the following way, and with the following success:

Acts xvi. 13. And on the Sabbath we went out of the city by a river side, where prayer was wont to be made; and we sat down, and spake unto the women which resorted *thither*. 14. And a certain woman named Lydia, a seller of purple, of the city of Thyatira, which worshiped God, heard *us*: whose heart the Lord opened, that she attended unto the things which were spoken of Paul. 15. And when she was baptized, and her household, she besought *us*, saying, If ye have judged me to be faithful to the Lord, come into my house and abide *there*. And she constrained us. 40. And they [that is, Paul and Silas, who afterward had been imprisoned at Philippi] went out of the prison, and entered into *the house of* Lydia; and when they had seen the brethren, they comforted them, and departed.

Lydia herself, it is evident, had a right to be baptized, according to the order of Jesus Christ, being a BELIEVER. But of what does it appear, from the text, did her household consist? of children, or grown persons? Before we answer this question, we observe, there are *four things* which a Pædobaptist must admit and take for granted, before he can urge this place in his favor; but if he can *prove* none of them, his argument (to use the learned Limborch's phrase) "is good for nothing."

1st. That Lydia had, at this time, or lately, a husband.

2d. That she had children, and children then in infancy.

3d. That these children were with her at Philippi.

4th. That such children were actually baptized.

The whole of these admissions I strongly question; for,

The 1st is *improbable;* for, had she a husband, she was not likely to be thus engaged in business: and especially as no mention is made of him, though the Apostles were repeatedly at her house.

The 2d is *uncertain;* because there are thousands of households where there are no infant children.

The 3d is *incredible;* for if, as the text indicates, Lydia was come from Thyatira (a journey, including both sea and land, of probably not less than 300 miles) ON BUSINESS, it is not to be believed she would bring young children with her, if she had any.

The 4th is *inconclusive;* because the word *household* or *house* is used in Scripture, when the whole of the family is not included, but the principal part only. See 1 Sam. i. 21, 22.

The argument, therefore, for infant baptism, grounded upon the baptism of Lydia's household, is extremely weak, as there is NO EVIDENCE SHE HAD EITHER HUSBAND *or* CHILDREN : and certainly, before any such custom can from this case be supported, as an ordinance of the New Testament, it ought to be UNDENIABLY PROVED, from the text, that she had infant children, and that they were actually baptized.

Should it be replied, in favor of infant baptism, that Lydia at this time was probably *a resident* at Philippi, although originally from Thyatira, and that consequently her infant children must be with her—this I would answer by asking, Must not then her husband be with her? But this evidently was not the case, for this reason—If Lydia had a husband with her, he surely must be ONE of the "household"—if he was one included in this household, he must have been *baptized*, because the household was—if he was baptized and joined in the same union with Paul and Silas, as Lydia, would she say, "Come into MY house?" or would Luke say, "they entered into the house *of Lydia*," supposing there was a believing husband at the head of the family? Impossible. The language employed by the inspired historian evidently implies, "A SINGLE FEMALE AT THE HEAD OF A FAMILY, AND AT THE HEAD OF A BUSINESS." And the fair conclusion is, that her household were her *servants;* or, if her *children*, that her husband was deceased, and her children so far advanced in life as to join in her journey, her business, and her worship; and thus they would be capable of instruction, faith, and baptism, as Christ commanded; and as in effect plainly stated of the household in the next section.

But, more satisfactory to the pious reader than ten thousand surmises, the question of the persons of Lydia's household, may be answered, with the greatest probability, from the last verse above cited. Paul and Silas being delivered from prison, and *quitting the jailer's house and family,* according to his own request, ver. 34, 36, they "entered into the house of Lydia," (for my reader will remember, this was the only other Christian house in the city, and in this family the only other persons baptized ;) and here, undoubtedly, they would meet with her "household" which they had baptized: having entered, we read, "when they had seen THE BRETHREN, they COMFORTED THEM, and departed." If then Lydia's household be denominated "brethren," and were capable of being "comforted" by the word, they must have been BELIEVERS IN CHRIST.

MR. WHITBY seems to consider this unquestionable. "And when she, and those of her household, *were instructed* in the Christian faith, in the nature of baptism required by it, she was baptized and her household." *Paraphrase* on the place.

LIMBORCH. "An undoubted argument, therefore, cannot be drawn from this instance, by which it may be demonstrated that infants were baptized by the Apostles. It might be, that all in her house were of a mature age; who, as in the exercise of a right understanding they believed, so they were able to make a public profession of that faith when they received baptism." *Comment. in loco. In Pœdobap. Ex.* Vol. II. p. 359.

MR. T. LAWSON, referring to this argument, says, "Families may be without children; they may be grown up, &c. So it is a wild inference to ground infant baptism upon." *Baptismalogia,* p. 92.

ASSEMBLY OF DIVINES. "*Of the city of Thyatira*—a city of Asia—here dwelt Lydia, that devout servant of God."—"*And entered into the house of Lydia:* doubtless to confirm them in the faith which they had preached to them—Lydia and HERS hearing of their miraculous deliverance, could not but be *comforted* and confirmed in the truth." *Annot.* on Acts xvi. 14, 40.

The place at which Lydia was taught and baptized must have been remarkably convenient for immersion. The people were "by a river side," ver. 13, and at a place frequented by the Jews for religious purification, by washing in the water. Thus

MR. DODDRIDGE. "On the Sabbath day we went out of the city to the side of the river Strymon, where, according to the custom of the Jews, there was an oratory, or a place of public prayer."—"It is certain that the Jews had a custom of building their oratories or proseuchas, or places of public prayer, by the sea side, or near rivers, for the sake of purification." *Fam. Expos.* on the place.

JOSEPH JOHN GURNEY. "Although the baptism practiced by John and by the Apostles, did not, in all its circumstances, resemble those Jewish washings to which I have now adverted; yet it was precisely similar to them in that main particular of IMMERSION in water." *Observ. on the Pecul. of Friends,* p. 61.

Inference. If the Divine word, which records the baptism of Lydia and her household, and subsequently refers to them, is to be my only guide upon the inquiries before us, I must infer, "that they were all believers in Jesus, and were baptized as their Saviour was."

20. *The Baptism of the Philippian Jailer and Household.*

Paul and Silas, having been cast into prison at Philippi, are delivered from their confinement at midnight, by the miraculous interposition of God. An earthquake shook the foundations of the prison, the doors of it were opened, and the prisoners' bands loosed. The jailer, suspecting the escape of the prisoners, drew his sword to destroy himself, but which Paul prevented, by assuring him the prisoners were all there. Then follow his conversion and baptism:—

Acts xvi. 29. Then he called for a light, and sprang in,

and came trembling, and fell down before Paul and Silas. 30.
And brought them out, and said, Sirs, what must I do to be
saved? 31. And they said, Believe on the Lord Jesus
Christ, and thou shalt be saved, and thy house. 32. And they
spake unto him the word of the Lord, and to all that were in
his house. 33. And he took them the same hour of the night,
and washed *their* stripes; and was baptized, he and all his,
straightway. 34. And when he had brought them into his
house, he set meat before them, and rejoiced, believing in God
with all his house.

Here observe, 1. The jailer, bringing Paul and Silas out of the prison, being persuaded that they were the servants of the true God, and were now delivered by his power from their unjust and cruel punishment; and deeply convinced, at the same time, of his own guilt and danger, urges them to tell him *what he should do to be saved!* To this greatest of questions, he received a direct answer. *Believe on the Lord Jesus Christ, and thou shalt be saved, and thy house.* It is probable, many, if not all the jailer's family, alarmed at this awful event, ran to his assistance, as his life they would consider imminently in danger, both by the prisoners in order to escape, and especially by the law, if any had fled. Hence Paul indirectly spake to the whole, *Believe, and thou shalt be saved,* yea, *and thy house too,* in the same way.

DODDRIDGE. "*Thou shalt be saved and thine house.* The meaning cannot be that the eternal salvation of his family could be secured by *his faith;* but that if they also themselves believed, they should be entitled to the same spiritual and everlasting blessings with himself; which Paul might the rather add, as it is probable that many of them, under this terrible alarm, might have attended the master of the family into the dungeon." *Fam. Expos.* Note on the place.

2. We may next learn, from the text, in the most satisfactory manner, of what the jailer's household consisted; that they were not infants, or persons so young as to be incapable

of being taught the gospel, and of believing it; for thus we read, ver. 32, "*They spake unto him the word of the Lord,* AND TO ALL THAT WERE IN HIS HOUSE." This household is *instructed,* instructed ALL, and then baptized. Infants, therefore, cannot here be included.

3. Luke further describes the jailer and his household, and shows thereby how the Lord's commission was still strictly obeyed. Paul and Silas first *preached the gospel* to the whole house, as observed above; and now we read, verse 34, the jailer *rejoiced,* BELIEVING IN GOD, WITH ALL HIS HOUSE." Then it follows, he had no infant children, or those words cannot include them; for of this faith they would be incapable.

MATTHEW HENRY. "The voice of rejoicing, with that of salvation, was heard in the jailer's house,—*he rejoiced, believing in God, with all his house:* there was NONE in his house that refused to be baptized, and so made a jar in the ceremony, but *they were unanimous* in embracing the gospel, which added much to the joy." *Expos.* on the place.

CALVIN is still more expressive. "Luke commends the pious zeal of the jailer, because he dedicated his whole house to the Lord; in which, also, the grace of God illustriously appeared, because it suddenly brought the WHOLE FAMILY to a pious consent." *Comment.* in loco.

Inference. As the same pre-requisites to baptism are here specified, in relation to the jailer's family, as to himself, viz.: 1st, that *the word of the Lord was spoken to them as to him;* and, 2d, that *he and they equally believed in God,* I must, on inspired authority, conclude, that we have here nothing more or less than a plain example of a BELIEVING HOUSEHOLD BAPTIZED, the whole being EQUALLY disciples of Christ; and as to the mode, that it was what the Lord sanctioned by his example and command, and nothing different therefrom.*

* Some, in opposing the practice of immersion, have imagined great difficulties in this case. They cannot conceive where the jailer could find a suitable place, and especially in the night, to receive the ordinance in this

21. *Paul and Household Baptisms at Corinth.*

The next instance is the baptism of several persons at Corinth, where we now find the same Apostle exerting himself to the utmost for the spread of the Messiah's kingdom. Here, though many *opposed themselves, and blasphemed,* yet he zealously persevered, and his labors were crowned with success; for thus we read :—

Acts xviii. 4. And he reasoned in the synagogue every Sabbath, and persuaded the Jews and the Greeks. 5. And when Silas and Timotheus were come from Macedonia, Paul was pressed in the spirit, and testified to the Jews *that* Jesus *was* Christ. 8. And Crispus, the chief ruler of the synagogue, believed on the Lord with all his house: and many of the Corinthians hearing, believed, and were baptized.

A church being formed in this place, Paul afterwards writes them two epistles. In the first of these, he laments the unhappy divisions that prevailed amongst them, in contending for different ministers, as if they had so many saviours, and

form. It is not for us, at this distance of time, *to state the place,* as the sacred historian has not done so. The Scriptures affirm that "he and his were baptized:" what do these words mean? We reply (from the sense of the word, and from the other Scriptures,) "they were immersed in the name of the Lord Jesus." Then it falls to the part of our opponents TO PROVE that they were not baptized in this way. These *imagined difficulties* have not a particle of weight upon that mind that admits that CHRIST'S AUTHORITY was Paul's only guide.

It may not be improper, however, to remind the reader how exceedingly common the practice of cold bathing was, and still is, in the East. That frequent bathing was usual among the Grecians, Romans, and now is in Turkey, in which country this city Philippi stood, is testified by

LORD BACON. "It is strange that the use of bathing, as a part of diet, is left. With the Romans and Grecians it was as usual as eating or sleeping; and so it is amongst the Turks at this day." *In Stennett's Answer to Addington,* p. 34.

GROTIUS, (the most learned and best informed man in Europe in his time,) held it as highly probable, from the practice of the country, that the jail at Philippi was provided with baths, which would admit of the ordinance in this form without delay.

had been baptized in their separate names. Upon which he reasons:—

1 Cor. i. 13. Is Christ divided? was Paul crucified for you? or were ye baptized in the name of Paul? 14. I thank God that I baptized none of you, but Crispus and Gaius. 15. Lest any should say that I had baptized in mine own name. 16. And I baptized also the household of Stephanas: besides, I know not whether I baptized any other. 17. For Christ sent me not to baptize, but to preach the gospel.

Chap. xvi. 15. Ye know the house of Stephanas, that it is the first fruits of Achaia, and *that* they have addicted themselves to the ministry of the saints.

Paul at Corinth, as at all other places, begins his work by "testifying" to the people "the things concerning Jesus Christ," and by teaching, not by baptizing, he makes disciples to Christ. He continued his labors at Corinth a year and six months, in which time, "many hearing" his preaching, "believed, and were baptized." He himself baptized but few, namely, Crispus, Gaius, and the household of Stephanas, and in this he afterwards rejoiced, as none of them, in their angry contentions, and excessive partiality, could say "they were for Paul; for, Paul baptized them, and that in his own name;" for, he adds, the first and chief work for which Christ sent him, was, "not to baptize, but to preach the gospel."

It is not said, the household of Crispus were baptized, though, had it been so, it is certain they were proper subjects of the ordinance, agreeably to the words of the institution; for, he "believed on the Lord, WITH ALL HIS HOUSE." Their baptism, if obedient to Christ, was a matter of course.

The persons who composed "the house of Stephanas," (the last household said to be baptized,) are not described where their baptism is recorded; and had nothing, in any other place, been said of them, this would have been the only house left in *such uncertainty;* but, as if it were the design of the Holy Spirit to leave no room for dispute, as to the proper persons to receive the ordinances of Christ, we find this family also described at the end of this epistle, as cited above: they were the "first fruits" of the word of God in Achaia, and "they addicted themselves to the ministry of the saints." They exerted themselves in acts of zeal and charity, in reference to their fellow, but poorer, or more afflicted disciples; and hence, (we scarcely need add) could not be infant children.

DODDRIDGE. "*They have set themselves, &c.* This seems to imply, that it was the generous care of the whole family to assist their fellow Christians; so that there was not a member of it which did not do its part." *Fam. Expos.* Note on the place.

GUISE. "It therefore seems that the family of Stephanas were all adult believers, and so were baptized on their own personal profession of faith in Christ." *On the place.*

HAMMOND. "I think it unreasonable that the Apostle's bare mention of baptizing his [Stephanas'] household, should be thought competent to conclude that infants were baptized by him; when it is uncertain whether there were *any such at all* in his house." *Works,* Vol. I. p. 492. *In Pæd. Exam.* Vol. II. p. 358.

MACKNIGHT. "The family of Stephanas seem all to have been adults when they were baptized, for they are said, chap. xvi. 15, *to have devoted themselves to the ministry of the saints.*" *Apos. Epis.* Note on 1 Cor. i. 16.

22. *Reflection on the Baptism of Households.*

We have now found the record of *Three Households* baptized by the Apostle Paul, or Silas, his companion: *Lydia's,* the *Jailer's* and *Stephanas'.* If it were the constant practice of the Apostles to baptize *children with their parents,* (as our Pædobaptist friends maintain,) we should reasonably have expected, and, no doubt, should have found, in various places of Scripture, after naming the baptism of believers, the words added, "and their children," or "and their little ones;" as families of young children are expressed in the Old Testament. And I infer that this must have been a fact in MANY instances, because we find in this book MANY THOUSANDS of adults believing, and being baptized, or added to the Lord. See Acts ii. 41, iv. 4, v. 14, &c. Would it, then, be probable that *three* families only would be specified AS FAMILIES, while *hundreds*, or, it may be, *thousands of other families*, are not referred to in the most distant way? This I conceive next to impossible, and, therefore, infer that the baptism of *families* was comparatively of rare occurrence.

But in these *three* cases we have not the words "and their little ones;" nor yet "and their children;" (and this expression might be used without necessarily implying infants,) but the term "house" or "household" is used, which conveys no idea as to THE AGE of the persons intended, nor whether they were the *children* or the *servants* of the heads of the families; and, therefore, had nothing been said descriptive of them, it would have been exceedingly inconclusive to have inferred A PRECEDENT FOR INFANT BAPTISM from the use of the word *household;* because *there are thousands*, yea, *millions* of families that have no infant children. The writer of this pamphlet has baptized households, and, among others, a "Lydia and her household," and yet never baptized a child. From the word "household," therefore, to infer the baptism of infants, is completely *begging the question.* But, as my reader has seen, there *is* something said of these three households, which describes the constituents of them: from this it is DEMONSTRABLY CERTAIN, that the jailer's and Stephanas' were professedly believers in Christ, and that which is said of them is of infants *impossible.* And as to Lydia's, if "the brethren" Paul and Silas "comforted" in her house were her household, (and there were no other Christians in the city but the family they had just quitted,) there is no more uncertainty respecting them. Thus, while households out of number are referred to in the Scriptures, and nothing is added by which we could learn of what they consisted, it has pleased God to give such information of the *baptized households*, as to lead the reader to infer, that they all were (as the same Apostle testifies of the church of which Stephanas and his household were members) "called of God to the fellowship of his Son Jesus Christ our Lord." 1 Cor. i. 9.

The celebrated Pædobaptist writers I have cited, candidly allow that the Scriptures, regarding these households, teach nothing further upon our inquiries than what I have endeavored to make plain to the reader. To his own judgment I cheerfully leave his decision.

23. *Certain Disciples at Ephesus Baptized.*

This is the NINTH and LAST PLACE, in the Acts of the Apostles, relative to our present inquiries. The question whether the persons here referred to were baptized *twice*, first with John's baptism, and now Christ's, does not affect the object of our examination.

Acts xix. 1. Paul, having past through the upper coasts, came to Ephesus; and finding certain disciples, 2. He said unto them, Have ye received the Holy Ghost since ye believed? And they said unto him, We have not so much as heard whether there be any Holy Ghost. 3. And he said unto them, Unto what then were ye baptized? And they said, Unto John's baptism. 4. Then said Paul, John verily baptized with the baptism of repentance, saying unto the people, That they should believe on him which should come after him, that is, on Christ Jesus. 5. When they heard *this*, they were baptized in the name of the Lord Jesus. 6. And when Paul had laid *his* hands upon them, the Holy Ghost came on them; and they spake with tongues, and prophesied. 7. And all the men were about twelve.

That in these persons we have an example of adult baptism is clear. For, 1. They are called "disciples."—2. They "believed."—3. They "received the Holy Ghost."—4. They "spake with tongues and prophesied;" and were in number twelve

MEN. We need not, therefore, add another word respecting them.

24. *Conclusion of the Acts.*

We have now, Christian reader, passed through all the Acts of the Apostles, and examined all the instances of the administration of this ordinance recorded in this sacred history, and to this place, we can confidently assert, *That we have nowhere found a single place or passage that describes, records, or implies the baptism of any infants.* The reader will not suppose this a hasty conclusion, when he hears the following Pædobaptists :—

GOODWIN. "Baptism supposes regeneration sure in itself first. Sacraments are never administered to *begin*, or *work* grace. Read ALL the Acts, still it is said, they *believed, and were baptized.*" *Works*, Vol. I. P. I. p. 200.

MR. T. BOSTON. "There is no example of baptism recorded in the Scriptures, where any were baptized but such as appeared to have a saving interest in Christ." *Works*, p. 384.

LIMBORCH. "There is no instance can be produced, from which it may indisputably be inferred that any child was baptized by the Apostles." *Complete Syst. Div.* B. V. Ch. xxii. § II.

MR. BAXTER. (The appeal he makes to *Mr. Blake*, in this place, might be made, with all confidence, to every Pædobaptist.) "I conclude, that all examples of baptism in Scripture do mention only the administration of it to the professors of saving faith; and the precepts give us no other direction. And I provoke *Mr. Blake*, as far as is seemly for me to do, to name ONE PRECEPT OR EXAMPLE for baptizing any other, and make it good if he can." *Disput. of Right to Sacram.* p. 156. *In Pæd. Exam.* Vol. II. p. 29.

THE EPISTLES.

We now proceed, lastly, to examine those passages in the Apostolical Epistles, which refer to this ordinance.

25. *Passages which contain an express allusion to Baptism.*

Rom. vi. 3. Know ye not, that so many of us as were baptized into Jesus Christ, were baptized into his death? 4. Therefore we are buried with him by baptism into death; that like as Christ was raised up from the dead by the glory of the Father, even so we also should walk in newness of life. 5. For if we have been planted together in the likeness of his death, we shall be also *in the likeness* of *his* resurrection.

Colos. ii. 12. Buried with him in baptism, wherein also ye are risen with *him* through the faith of the operation of God, who hath raised him from the dead.

The object of the Apostle Paul in these places, and their connection, is to show the churches to which he is writing, the necessity of a *holy walk and conversation.* To this end, he puts them in mind of their baptism, the profession they made in it, and the obligation they took upon themselves to live according to those truths symbolically taught by and in the ordinance. "*Know ye not,*" says he to the Romans, "*that so many of us as were baptized into Jesus Christ,*" into a profession of his religion, "*were baptized into his death,*" into a reliance upon, and conformity to his death, the great design of which was to take away sin; and, consequently, as our Lord died, and was *buried* on account of it, so should we die and be *buried* to the love and practice of it? Then follows this plain and striking allusion to the particular *act* by which the rite in question is administered, in verse 4, which, with the same allusion in the Epistle to the Colossians, reads to this effect:—

"THEREFORE (that is, *to express this very design*) WE ARE BURIED BY and IN BAPTISM, with Christ our Lord; and as He WAS RAISED UP from the dead by the glory of the Father, so are we at our baptism, WHEREIN we likewise are RAISED UP to walk thenceforth in newness of life; and this is not of ourselves, but THROUGH THE FAITH of the operation of God, who thus raised up his Son from the sepulchre to live and reign forever."

In these places the Apostle does *twice* describe baptism as effecting a *burial* and a *resurrection*, and as such to be a continued *representation* of the burial and resurrection of Christ, our Pattern and Lord; and this is realized only *in immersion.*

By these plain allusions to the *Mode* of the ordinance, the sense of the word "baptize" is most plainly exhibited and confirmed; and the necessity of "going down INTO, and coming up OUT OF the water"—of "baptizing IN THE JORDAN," and where "there was MUCH WATER;" (which phrases we found in connection with baptism,) is here evidently explained. Pædobaptist divines, of the greatest celebrity for learning and information, have frankly allowed what we have above asserted. We have no difficulty but in making such a selection as would be most highly esteemed by the reader. The following are, perhaps, the most unexceptionable that could be produced:—

MR. WALL, *Vicar of Shoreham, in Kent, and author of that famous work, " The History of Infant Baptism," for which he received the thanks of the whole clergy in convocation.* "As to the manner of baptism then generally used, the texts produced by every one that speaks of these matters, John iii. 23, Mark i. 5, Acts viii. 38, are undeniable proofs that the baptized person went ordinarily into the water, and sometimes the Baptist too. We should not know from these accounts whether the whole body of the baptized was put under water, head and all, were it not for two later proofs, which seem to me to PUT IT OUT OF QUESTION: *one,* that St. Paul does twice, in an allusive way of speaking, call baptism a BURIAL; *the other,* the custom of the Christians, in the near succeeding times, which, being more largely and particularly delivered in books, is KNOWN to have been generally, or ordinarily, a TOTAL IMMERSION." *Defence of the History of Infant Baptism*, p. 131.

ARCHBISHOP TILLOTSON. "Anciently, those who were baptized, were immersed and BURIED in the water, to represent their death to sin; and then did rise up out of the water, to signify their entrance upon a new life. And to these customs the Apostle alludes, Rom. vi. 2–6." *Works*, Vol. I. *Serm.* vii. p. 179.

ARCHBISHOP SECKER. "BURYING, as it were, the person baptized in the water, and raising him out again, WITHOUT QUESTION, was anciently the more usual method; on account of which Saint Paul speaks of baptism as representing both the death, burial, and resurrection of Christ, and what is grounded on them—our being dead and buried to sin, and our rising again to walk in newness of life." *Lect. on Catechism*, L. xxxv.

MR. SAM. CLARKE. "*We are buried with Christ by baptism*, &c. In the primitive times the manner of baptizing was by immersion, or dipping the whole body into the water. And this manner of doing it was a very significant emblem of the dying and rising again, referred to by St. Paul, in the above-mentioned similitude." *Expos. of the Church Catechism*, p. 294, ed. 6.

MR. WELLS. "St. Paul here alludes to immersion, or dipping the whole body under water in baptism; which, he intimates, did typify the death and burial (of the person baptized) to sin, and his rising up out of the water did typify his resurrection to newness of life." *Illust. Bib.* on Rom. vi. 4.

MR. NICHOLSON, Bishop of Gloucester. "In the grave with Christ we went not; for our bodies were not, could not be buried with his; but *in baptism*, by a kind of analogy or resemblance, while our bodies are under the water, we may be said to be BURIED with him. *Expos. of the Church Catechism*, p. 174.

MR. DODDRIDGE. "*Buried with him in baptism.* It seems the part of candor to confess, that here is an allusion to the manner of baptizing by immersion." *Fam. Expos.* Note on the place.

MR. GEORGE WHITEFIELD. "It is certain that in the words of our text, Rom. vi. 3, 4, there is an allusion to the manner of baptism, which was by immersion, which is what our own church allows," &c. *Eighteen Sermons*, p. 297.

MR. JOHN WESLEY. "*Buried with him*—alluding to the ancient manner of baptizing by immersion." *Note* on Rom. vi. 4.

MR. WHITBY, *author of a Commentary on the New Testament, and more than forty other learned works.* "It being so expressly declared here, Rom. vi. 4, and Col. ii. 12, that we are BURIED with Christ in baptism, by being buried under water; and the argument to oblige us to a conformity to his death, by dying to sin, being taken hence; and *this immersion being religiously observed by* ALL CHRISTIANS FOR THIRTEEN CENTURIES, and approved by our church, and the change of it into sprinkling, even without any allowance from the author of this institution, or any license from and council of the church, being that which the Romanist still urges to justify his refusal of the cup to the laity; it were to be wished that this custom might be again of general use, and aspersion only permitted, as of old, in case of the Clinici, or in present danger of death." *Note* on Rom. vi. 4.

The Apostle uses the figure of *Planting*, as well as of *Burying*, in allusion to baptism, verse 5. "If we have been planted together in the likeness of his death, we shall be also in the likeness of his resurrection." This also is in perfect agreement with the same *Mode* of administering it. The circumstance in nature, from which the figure is borrowed, is the same as that employed by our Lord, John xii. 24. "Except a corn of wheat fall into the ground and die, it abideth alone, but if it die, it bringeth forth much fruit." The seed to be *planted* must be *buried* in the soil; so the Christian in baptism is "planted in the LIKENESS of the death, that he may be also in the likeness of the resurrection of his Lord."

MR. MACKNIGHT. "*Planted together in the likeness of his death.* The burying of Christ and of believers, first in the water of baptism, and afterwards in the earth, is fitly enough compared to the planting of seeds in the earth, because the effect, in both cases, is a reviviscence to a state of greater perfection." *Note* on Rom. vi. 5.

ASSEMBLY OF DIVINES. "*If we have been planted together,* &c. By this elegant similitude, the Apostle represents to us, that as a plant that is set in the earth lieth as dead and immovable for a time, but after springs up and flourishes, so Christ's body lay dead for a while in the grave, but sprung up and flourished in his resurrection; and we also, when we are baptized, are *buried,* as it were, in the water for a time, but after are *raised up* to newness of life." *Annot. in loco.*

Inference. With certainty I may gather from the Scriptures at the head of this section, That the outward form of baptism in the apostolic age was a BURIAL IN WATER. It is made infinitely interesting to the heart of a Christian by that which it was intended to represent, viz., the death, burial, and resurrection of the Redeemer; and here too I may infer the infinite and irresistible obligation the baptized person is under to devote his life to that Lord to whose death and resurrection he is thus emblematically conformed in the baptismal rite: and I see also in these verses, by what principle and power this is all to be realized, "through faith, which is of the operation of God." In none destitute of that living principle can this intention of the ordinance be fulfilled. If sprinkling were the mode, and infants the subjects, these passages never could have been written. To the baptism of believers alone, and that administered by immersion, will these passages apply.

26. *Occasional Mention of Baptism.*

Eph. iv. 5. One Lord, one faith, one baptism.

1 Cor. xii. 13. For by one Spirit we are all baptized into one body, whether *we be* Jews or Gentiles, whether *we be* bond or free; and have been all made to drink into one Spirit.

Gal. iii. 27. For as many of you as have been baptized into Christ, have put on Christ.

1 Cor. xv. 29. Else what shall they do which are baptized for the dead, if the dead rise not at all? Why are they then baptized for the dead?

To the *Ephesians* and *Corinthians* the Apostle is recommending peace and unity; that they should be all of one heart and mind, so that there be no schism in the body, as all were one in Christ. To urge which, he puts them in mind of what they had been uniformly taught, that there was but "ONE LORD, ONE FAITH, ONE BAPTISM;" and that "all were baptized into ONE BODY, whether Jews or Gentiles." We should here observe, (what we have so frequently noticed before,) that the Apostle places *faith* BEFORE *baptism*, as Christ the great Lawgiver had done, *He that believeth and is baptized.* "*One faith, one baptism.*" If this passage were to be expressed according to the general practice of the *present* day, the order both of Christ and the Apostle must be "*reversed.*" See Simeon, at p. 28.

In the above verse to the *Galatians*, the Apostle is thought to be alluding to the change of garments which must necessarily take place after the administration of the ordinance; to which may allude the expressions "putting off the old man with his deeds," and "putting on the new man," Eph. iv. 22, 24; Col. iii. 9, 10; and especially, as here, "putting on Christ," as "the Lord our righteousness."

ADAM CLARKE. "When he [the person baptized] came up out of the water, he seemed to have a *resurrection* to life. He was therefore supposed to throw off his old Gentile state, as he threw off his clothes, and to assume a new character, as the baptized generally put on new or fresh garments." *Comment.* on Rom. vi. 4.

The last verse cited above, 1 Cor. xv. 29, has obtained many interpretations, as the meaning of the Apostle in the words, "for the dead," is not certain.

JOHN EDWARDS. "Some of the fathers hold that the Apostle's argument in the text is of this sort: If there should be no resurrection of the dead hereafter, why is baptism so significant a symbol of our dying and rising again, and also of the death and resurrection of Christ? The immersion into the water was thought to signify the death of Christ, and their coming out denotes his rising again, and did no less represent their own future resurrection." *In Stennett's Answer to Addington,* p. 105.

MACKNIGHT. "Christ's baptism was an emblem of his future death and resurrection. In like manner, the baptism of believers is emblematical of their own death, burial, and resurrection." *Apost. Epis.* Note on Rom. vi. 4.

Inference. If faith PRECEDED baptism in the Apostles' days, and the persons who received that ordinance had *imbibed the influence of that* ONE SPIRIT, and had *put on* CHRIST as the robe of righteousness, the spiritual adorning of their souls, hoping for their part in the first resurrection at His appearing and glory, it is most manifest, that none but a genuine convert to Christ could thus be baptized, or enjoy such high and delightful privileges.

27. *Baptism illustrated by Events recorded in the Old Testament.*

These are the LAST PASSAGES we find in the New Testament which relate to the subject of our examination.

1 Cor. x. 1. Moreover, brethren, I would not that ye should be ignorant, how that all our fathers were under the cloud, and all passed through the sea; 2. And were all baptized unto Moses in the cloud and in the sea.

1 Pet. iii. 20. The long-suffering of God waited in the days of Noah, while the ark was a preparing, wherein few, that is, eight souls, were saved by water. 31. The like figure whereunto *even* baptism doth also now save us (not the putting away of the filth of the flesh, but the answer of a good conscience towards God), by the resurrection of Jesus Christ.

The better to understand the Apostle Paul, in the first passage above, the reader would do well to peruse the account, in the Old Testament, in Exod. xiv., to which he refers. In verse 22, we are told, that the Israelites "*went into the midst of the Red Sea upon dry ground,*" that the water divided, opening a passage for them, and forming "*a wall unto them on the right hand and on the left.*" We also learn, that "the cloud" which had conducted them, now removed its situation; stood between the two armies, and overspread and concealed the Israelites from their enemies; that it was bright, and "*gave light*" to the former, while it was "*darkness*" toward the latter. It does not appear that any water *actually touched* the Israelites in *any sense whatever;* and hence, the word "baptized" must be used by the Apostle in a *figurative sense;* and if it has a reference to the *mode,* we have only to ask, Does the situation of the Jews, "IN *the cloud, and* IN *the sea,*" best agree to sprinkling *with water,* or a total burial *in it?* Pædobaptists of the highest celebrity will answer:—

"WITSIUS (says Mr. Booth) expounds the place to this effect, 'How were the Israelites baptized *in the cloud, and in the sea,* seeing they were neither immersed in the sea, nor wetted by the cloud? It is to be considered that the Apostle here uses the term 'baptism' in a figurative sense, yet there is some agreement to the external sign. The sea is water, and a cloud differs but little from water. The cloud hung over their heads, and the sea surrounded them on each side; and so the water in regard to those that are baptized.'" *In Pæd. Exam.* Vol. I. p. 185.

WHITBY. "They were *covered with the sea on both sides,*

Exod. xiv. 22; so that both the cloud and the sea had some resemblance to our being covered with water in baptism. Their going into the sea resembled the ancient rite of going into the water; and their coming out of it, their rising up out of the water." *Ibid.* p. 187.

By the Apostle Peter, in the passage cited, we are taught that as Noah and his family "*were saved by water,*" so baptism, the antitype of the water of the deluge, "now saves" the believer; not by a washing of his person, or a ceremonial purification, which cannot take away sin; but the water being a "like figure" in both cases, that is, EXHIBITING CHRIST AND HIS MERITS, the believer is saved by the SACRED REALITY *signified.* In this case baptism is "*The answer of a good conscience toward God:*" both the answer given to inquiry at baptism, and the subsequent testimony of the mind to God, are *conscientious,* being in accordance with a sincere and heartfelt faith in the merits of the dying and rising Saviour.

OWEN. "I deny not but that there is a great analogy between the salvation by the ark, and that by baptism, inasmuch as the one *did represent,* and the other *doth exhibit* Christ himself." *On Hebrews,* Vol. IV. p. 138, Williams's Abr.

MACKNIGHT. "This *answer of a good conscience* being made to God, is an *inward answer,* and means the baptized person's sincere persuasion of the things which, by submitting to baptism, he professes to believe; namely, that Jesus arose from the dead, and that at the last day he will raise all from the dead to eternal life, who sincerely obey him." *Apost. Epist.* Note in loc.

Inference. If the exercise of "a good conscience" is associated with the ordinance of baptism, in none but a believer in Christ can this union be realized.

28. *Conclusion of the New Testament.*

Having now, my reader, completed the chief design of this pamphlet, *in transcribing and laying before you every passage of this sacred volume that relates to the subject of our inquiry,* and contains any information, whether on the *subjects, mode,* or *spiritual design* of baptism, I have, I humbly hope, fulfilled the title I have assumed, in presenting you with "THE SCRIPTURE GUIDE TO BAPTISM." Our Divine Master commanded us to "search the Scriptures," and I have no doubt but that it would meet with His gracious approbation, if this plan were adopted, in reference to *any* subject pertaining to His cause or kingdom. "To the word and to the testimony," is an inspired maxim in theology, and one from which no Protestant will dissent. "Ye do err," said our Redeemer, "not knowing the Scriptures."

We ought, therefore, now to be able to answer the three inquiries proposed at the beginning:

I. Who are proper *subjects* of Christian baptism, according to the authority of Christ, and the practice of his Apostles?

Answer. We have met with the baptism of many thousands of persons, and the ordinance administered on many different occasions; but we have no where found, through all this sacred book, *any one person* baptized (Christ excepted) that we have the slightest reason to suppose was not FIRST INSTRUCTED *in the doctrines of the gospel, and had professed to* BELIEVE; but this is either expressly testified, or so implied of all, as to leave no just ground of dispute.

II. By what *mode* should the ordinance be administered?

Answer. We have no where met with a single verse, word, or circumstance, which indicates *the application of water,* by pouring or sprinkling; but wherever any thing is found descriptive of this ordinance, IMMERSION (as the word *baptism* undeniably signifies) is plainly implied in circumstances, and confirmed by allusions.

III. What is its *spiritual design,* and in whom is it realized?

Answer. The passages that have been before us plainly indicate that it was the Divine intention that this ordinance should exhibit and teach the important change produced by the efficacy of grace on a sinner, namely, *his* PURIFICATION *from sin,* and BURIAL as to the love and practice of it; his RESURRECTION to a new and religious life; the UNION and FELLOWSHIP into which *the Christian* enters with the Tri-une God; and *his* RISING *from the dead,* through his risen Lord, at his coming.

CHAPTER IV.

Infant Baptism.—Pengilly on the grounds of Infant Baptism, its rise and supposed benefits. 1. Strange that Infant Baptism still exists. 2. No Infant Baptism in the New Testament. 3. The Saviour blessing little children. 4. Pedobaptist grounds of Infant Baptism. 5. The children of believers, 1 Cor. vii. 14. 6. The children of believers no better by nature than those of others. 7. The promise of God to Abraham and his seed. 8. Circumcision and the Abrahamic Covenant. 9. Infant salvation. 10. The authority on which Infant Baptism is founded. 11. The time when Infant Baptism was introduced. 12. Tradition. 13. Other innovations introduced. 14. The Christian fathers and Infant Baptism. 15. Sponsors introduced, because infants could not believe. 16. Views of modern Pedobaptists. 17. The use of baptism. 18. The first Christian writer who defends Infant Baptism.

1. PERHAPS nothing is stranger in the history of religion, than that infant baptism should have been so long, and by so many pious persons, received and practiced as an ordinance of the Church of Christ. Baptists have from the commencement rejected it; and in no case have they shown it any favor; and nothing has been more fully and fairly proved, than the correctness of the Baptist position on this subject. Wide-spread, indeed, are the doubts among Pedobaptists; and extensive is the neglect of the so-called ordinance, as is evident from the long and loud complaints of the people, by their religious teachers. Still infant baptism is a law of the Pedobaptist denominations.

Though enough is said in the preceding remarks on the general subject, to convince the candid, we deem it important to give the Baptist arguments more fully, and know of nothing better adapted to our design, than Pengilly's article on Infant Baptism. Besides, it is constructed to follow the general article on Baptism, and I here insert it, almost entire, asking for it the serious consideration of our readers. We do not see how any one can resist such arguments.

PENGILLY ON THE GROUNDS OF INFANT BAPTISM, ITS RISE, AND SUPPOSED BENEFITS.

2. *No Infant Baptism in the New Testament.*

Question. Although in the passages of Scripture you have cited, I have not found an express authority, either by *command* or *example*, for the baptism of infants, yet will Pædobaptist divines allow that no such authority is to be found in the New Testament?

Answer. BISHOP BURNET. "There is no express precept or rule given in the New Testament for baptism of infants." *Expos. of the Articles*, Art. xxvii.

MR. S. PALMER. "There is nothing in the words of institution, nor in any after accounts of the administration of this rite, respecting the baptism of infants: there is not a single precept for, nor example of, this practice through the whole New Testament." *Answer to Priestley on the Lord's Supper*, p. 7.

LUTHER. "It cannot be proved by the sacred Scripture, that infant baptism was instituted by Christ, or begun by the first Christians AFTER the Apostles." (*In Pæd. Exam.* Vol. II. p. 4.) See also GOODWIN, BOSTON, LIMBORCH, and BAXTER, at page 44 of this pamphlet.

3. *On the Saviour's blessing little children.*

What, then, are we to make of those words of our Saviour, and his subsequent conduct? Mark x. 14, 16. "Suffer the little children to come unto me, and forbid them not; for of such is the kingdom of heaven. And he took them up in his arms, put his hands upon them, and blessed them."

Answer. If, when our condescending Saviour took these children in his arms, it had been added, "and he baptized them," instead of the words "and blessed them," then this passage with propriety might be adduced, and, indeed, would have decided the subject; but as the Holy Spirit has recorded the circumstance, it no more refers to infant baptism, than to infant communion, or infant circumcision. It is certain Christ did not baptize these children, for he never baptized at all, John iv. 2; and if his disciples, who baptized for him and by his authority, had been commanded by their Lord to baptize infants, it is certain they would not have "rebuked" the parents or friends of these children for bringing them.

But this passage, by fair inference, and implication, contains an argument *against* infant baptism. Here you observe parents bringing their children to Jesus to crave his blessing upon them; or, at least, that he would "pray," Matt. xix. 13, that the blessing of heaven might attend them.

Now let me ask, If baptism would have brought these children into the covenant of grace, or into Christ's church, or secured to them any spiritual benefit, would the Lord Jesus have concealed that circumstance from these parents, and from his disciples? Would he "take them in his arms and bless them," and give them back to the parents *without baptism*, and without a word upon that ordinance? Was it ever known that any spiritual benefit was sought from him, and he bestowed it not? Here the spiritual good of these children was sought at his hands, and if baptism was the key, the seal, the door to all the spiritual blessings of the covenant of grace, (as Pædobaptists often describe it,) would the Lord Jesus refuse it—or send them away without it? This is impossible; and therefore I infer that infant baptism is no part of the will of Christ, that it can communicate no good, and ought not to be observed. Some of the most learned Pædobaptists are aware that this passage serves not their cause.

POOLE'S CONTINUATORS. "We must take heed we do not found infant baptism upon the example of Christ in this text; for it is certain that he did not baptize these children. Mark only saith, He took them up in his arms, laid his hands on them, and blessed them." *Annot.* on the place, in Matt xix. 14.

BISHOP TAYLOR. "From the action of Christ's blessing infants, to infer they are to be baptized, proves nothing so much, as that there is a want of better arguments; for the conclusion would with more probability be derived thus: Christ blessed infants, and so dismissed them, but baptized them not; therefore, infants are not to be baptized." *Liberty of Prophecy*, p. 230.

4. *Pædobaptist grounds for Infant Baptism.*

If the New Testament does not afford an authority for infant baptism, upon what grounds do Pædobaptist divines practice and defend it?

Answer. MR. EDW. WILLIAMS, (one of its most zealous advocates,) affirms, "The champions [for it] are by no means agreed upon this question, On what is the right of infants to baptism founded?"*

Their grounds are various and contradictory. The early fathers who practiced it, urged *the virtue* of the ordinance in taking away sin, and securing eternal life; adding, the certain ruin of those that neglected it.†—The church of Rome holds, "If any one shall say that baptism is not necessary to salvation, let him be accursed."‡—The Greek church, by Cyril, patriarch of Constantinople, affirms, "We believe that baptism is a sacrament appointed by the Lord, which except a person

* Notes on Morrice's Social Religion, p. 68.

† See Origen, Cyprian, and Ambrose in Mr. Wall's Hist. of Infant Bap. Vol. I., chap. 6, 13, 14.

‡ Catechism of the Council of Trent, Part II. p. 164.

receive he has no communion with Christ."*—The Lutheran church, and the church of England, hold both the ordinances "as generally necessary to salvation." The former, agreeing with Calvin and Melancthon, "own a sort of faith in infants," affording them a right; while the English church hesitates not to baptize them, "Because they (the infants) promise by their sureties" repentance and faith, "which promise, when they come to age, themselves are bound to perform."†

Many learned writers, as well as churches, have expressed their views upon this inquiry. Mr. Wall, Mr. Hammond, and many others, hold that the practice of "Judish proselyte baptism" is the foundation of the Christian rite, and as infants received the former, so they should the latter: but Mr. Owen, Mr. Jennings, and others, have *proved* that no such practice existed among the Jews to afford such a pattern till generations after Christ.‡—Sir N. Knatchbull assumes *circumcision* as the proper foundation.—Beza, and after him Mr. Doddridge and others, considered the *holiness* of the children of believers, as making them proper subjects.§—Mr. Matt. Henry and Mr. Dwight contended that "the profession of faith made by the parents" to be their children's right.‖—Mr. H. F. Burder affirms, "The identical principle which pervades and unites the whole of the argument—is that infants are to be baptized SOLELY on the ground of *connection with their parents;*" and this he explains,—"It is a connection in the covenant of grace, the covenant of redemption, the everlasting covenant, embracing all that man can desire, or all that Jehovah can impart."¶—An anonymous writer affirms that "children by baptism are actually *brought into* the covenant of grace."

* Confess. Christ. Fidei, chap. xvi.

† See Church Catechism, and Pædobap. Exam. Vol. II. p. 491, et seq.

‡ Mr. Judson's Serm. on Christian Baptism, pp. 62, 63.

§ See Beza and Doddridge on 1 Cor. vii. 14.

‖ Treatise on Baptism, p. 76, and Dwight's Theology on the subject.

¶ Sermon of the Right of Infants to Baptism, pp. 7, 25; cited by Mr. I. Birt in Strictures on ditto, p. 18.

This is denied by another, who replies that the "children of believers are really and truly in the covenant of grace *before* their baptism."*

5. *The Children of Believers in* 1 *Cor.* vii. 14.

Some of the grounds assumed by those churches and eminent men, appear to have weight. Does not the "holiness" referred to, existing in the children of believers, and founded on 1 Cor. vii. 14, afford the ground required? "For the unbelieving husband is sanctified by the wife, and the unbelieving wife is sanctified by the husband; else were your children unclean, but now they are holy." If *holy*, they are surely proper subjects of baptism.

Answer. So many good men have thought: but *holiness* is no where required in God's word as a pre-requisite to baptism. And is there not an absurdity in the thought that baptism, which is the outward sign of *washing away sin*, Acts xxii. 16, should be administered to infants, because they are *holy?*

But what is the holiness intended in the above passage? The Apostle says, it results from an UNBELIEVER being *sanctified.* Now this sanctification cannot be *spiritual;* for that is the work of the Holy Ghost upon the mind and heart, and in which an unbeliever has no share or part, Acts viii. 21. If attention be paid to the subject upon which the Apostle is speaking, his meaning can readily be perceived. He is advising the Corinthians upon the question, "Whether, if a husband or wife who is converted to Christ, has an unbelieving partner, either Jew or idolator, the believer should *separate from the connection;*" as in Ezra x. 1–14. The Apostle advises, "If the unbelieving partner be pleased to dwell with the believer, the believer should not cause the separation." Then follows the passage before us, "For the unbelieving husband is sanctified by the wife;" or, as Doddridge renders it, "is sanctified to the wife," &c.

Now, in what sense can any thing, or person, be *sanctified,*

* In Pædobap. Exam. as before.

in which there is no moral or spiritual holiness communicated, and the sanctification is not the work of the Holy Spirit? The Scriptures afford the reply. The temple, the altar, the offerings, the official garments, &c., under the law, were expressly said to be *sanctified*, when they were appointed by God's law, and set apart to certain specified purposes. Apply this to the subject before us. Marriage is an appointment of God; and when a man or woman enters into that contract, he or she, by God's law, is set apart, or sanctified, to stand in the relation of husband or wife; and hence the union is lawful, becoming, and pleasing to God, and shall continue to be so, though one of the parties shall be converted and the other be an unbeliever.*

Taking this, which appears to me to be the sense of the passage, the inference which the Apostle draws from this sanctification, or legal appointment and constitution by Divine law, is natural, "else were your children unclean, but now are they holy;" i. e., If the marriage union was not according to the law of God, your children would be the fruit of uncleanness; but now, the union being in harmony with God's will, they are "holy;" they are free from illegitimate impurity. So some of the greatest and best Pædobaptist writers understand the Apostle. Thus, among a multitude of others:—

MR. T. WILLIAMS, of London. "The unbelieving husband is sanctified by the (believing) wife, &c., so that the connection is perfectly lawful, and the children are *legitimate*, or in a ceremonial sense, *holy*." *Cottage Bible*, on the place.

* MR. GILL, on the verse in question, cites a number of passages from Jewish writings, in which the word *sanctified*, in the phraseology of common use, is used for *legally espoused*. If this reading were adopted in this passage, it would not only convey good sense, but make the reasoning of the Apostle evident. If the word *holy* must be taken in a spiritual sense, and infant baptism inferred from it, the word *sanctified*, being evidently here of a kindred meaning, would unquestionably afford equal ground for the baptism of the unbelieving parent! Nor should it be forgotten that the word *children* in this place, as in Acts ii. 39, signifies *posterity* of any age.

MELANCTHON, the Reformer. "The connection of the argument is this, 'If the use of marriage should not please God, your children would be bastards, and so *unclean;* but your children are not bastards, therefore the use of marriage pleaseth God.' How bastards were unclean in a peculiar manner the law shows, Deut. xxiii." *In Pœdobap. Exam.* Vol. II. p. 375.

SUARES AND VASQUES. "The children are called *holy,* in a civil sense: that is, legitimate, and not spurious. As if Paul had said, 'If your marriage were unlawful, your children would be illegitimate. But the former is not a fact; therefore not the latter.'" *Ibid.* p. 373.

CAMERO. "The holiness of which the Apostle speaks is not opposed to that impurity which by nature properly agrees to all on account of Adam's offence, but to the impurity of which believing wives were apprehensive from their cohabiting with unbelieving husbands." *Ibid.* p. 372.

Inference. If the holiness which is merely *legitimacy of birth,* is no title to baptism, then the passage we have considered favors not the baptism of infants.

6. *The Scriptures do not authorize the plea that the children of believers are better by nature than those of unbelievers.*

From this interpretation, it would appear that the children of believers are no better, or more *holy* by nature, than the children of unbelievers. Is this in accordance with the Scriptures?

Answer. Most unquestionably so. Thus, Psalm li. 5, "Behold, (saith the son of pious Jesse,) I was shapen in iniquity, and in sin did my mother conceive me." Eph. ii. 3, "We (says the Apostle Paul, for himself and all the primitive Christians,) were BY NATURE the children of wrath, even as others." Romans v. 12, "Wherefore, as by one man sin entered into the world, and death by sin; so death passed upon all men, for that all have sinned." Chap. iii. 9, 10, "What then, are we better than they? No, in no wise: for we have before proved both Jews and Gentiles that they are ALL under sin; as it is written, there is none righteous, no, not one." And our Saviour adds, "That which is born of the flesh is flesh, and that which is of the Spirit is spirit. Ye must be born again." John iii. 6, 7.

CHURCH OF ENGLAND. "Original sin is the fault and corruption of the nature of every man; and therefore in every person born into this world it deserveth God's wrath." *Articles*, Art. ix.

MR. DORRINGTON. "Although the parents be admitted into the new covenant, the children born of them are not born within that covenant, but are, as all others, born in a state of rebellion and misery." *Vindicat. of the Church*, p. 44.

MR. ADAM CLARKE. "All are born with a sinful nature,—there has never been one instance of an immaculate human soul since the fall of Adam. Through his transgression all come into the world with the seeds of death and corruption in their own nature; all are sinful—all are mortal—and must die." On Rom. v. 12, 13.

MR. DODDRIDGE. "As we ALL proceed from a corrupt original, we do not more evidently bear the image of the earthly Adam in the infirmities of a mortal body, than in the degeneracy of a corrupted mind." *Fam. Expos.* Improv. on John iii. 1–10.

7. *The Promise of God to Abraham and his Seed.*

But God was pleased to promise to Abraham to be "a God to him and to his seed." Gen. xvii. 7. Now believers in Christ are Abraham's *spiritual seed;* must not *they*, therefore, and *their seed*, be included in that promise, and possess the same spiritual benefits?

Answer. The statement introducing this question is an important truth, that God promised to be "a God to Abraham and to his seed;" and so it is *true* that believers in Christ are Abraham's *spiritual seed*, and also that the God of Abraham is *equally* their God; but it would be not only *not true*, but an alarming and dangerous error, to assert that the children of believers are, on that account, also the spiritual seed of Abraham, and enjoy the same benefits. The children of believers must *themselves* become believers, must possess the same faith with their parents, and be Christ's genuine disciples, in order to be included in that promise and blessedness.

Hear the Apostle Paul, Gal. iii. 6, 7, "Abraham believed God," i. e., in reference to the coming Messiah, "and it was accounted to him for righteousness. Know ye, therefore, that they which are OF FAITH, the same are the children of Abraham;" ver. 29, "and if ye are CHRIST'S, then are ye Abraham's seed, and heirs according to the promise." And ver. 9, "So then they which be OF FAITH are blessed with faithful Abraham."

No doctrine can be more dangerous, (because calculated to be fatally delusive,) than this, "That because persons are *born of pious parents*, they are therefore under some peculiar spiritual and advantageous distinction, on account of which they are entitled to sacred privileges, and do not need equally with others the same converting grace and mercy, and the same atoning sacrifice." John the Baptist applied the axe to the root of this tree, at the dawn of this dispensation. "Think not to say within yourselves, We have Abraham to our Father." Ye are a "generation of vipers! Who hath warned you to flee from the wrath to come?" So our Redeemer, when the Jews uttered their usual vaunt, "We be Abraham's seed," replied, "I know that ye are Abraham's seed. If GOD were your Father, ye would love me. Ye are of your father the devil, and the lusts of your father ye will do." John viii. 33, 37, 42, 44. Such is CHRIST'S testimony of the carnal circumcision!

If, then, Abraham's *own descendants* were not his spiritual seed, while destitute of faith and love, surely none can contend that the unbelieving descendants of believing Gentiles can be that spiritual seed.

MR. EDW. WILLIAMS exposes this error in strong terms, in his Notes on Morrice's *Social Religion.* "Our author takes considerable pains to maintain a favorite point, which I shall pronounce a very precarious hypothesis. It is that of *hereditary grace,* if I may so express the notion,—that all the children of the godly are absolutely interested in all new covenant blessings. . . . But that interpretation of the Abrahamic promise, Gen. xvii. 7, which Mr. M. and some others have adopted, and which considers the words in their undistinguished application, is REPLETE WITH VERY ABSURD CONSEQUENCES. Jehovah, surely, was not the God of Abraham and of his UNBELIEVING descendants in the SAME respects. . . . The New Testament saints have nothing more to do with the Abrahamic covenant than the Old Testament believers who lived prior to Abraham." *Notes,* p. 312–317.

MATT. HENRY. "Grace doth not run in the blood, nor are saving benefits inseparably annexed to external church privileges; though it is common for people thus to stretch the meaning of God's promise to bolster themselves up in a vain hope. . . . The children of the flesh, as such, by virtue of their relationship to Abraham—are not *therefore* the children of God." *Expos.* on Rom. ix. 6–13.

8. *Circumcision and the Abrahamic Covenant no ground for Infant Baptism.*

But did not circumcision bring those that received it into the covenant of grace?

Answer. No: in no case whatever. The covenant of grace, (as Mr. Burder expresses it, cited at p. 54,) is "the covenant of redemption, the everlasting covenant." Nothing can bring into that covenant but the grace of God in Christ Jesus. It existed from the beginning of the world, and righteous Abel enjoyed its blessings. It has been an ever-flowing river, communicating its saving streams to the Church of God THROUGH ALL AGES, and ALL DISPENSATIONS. *Enoch, Noah,* and, no doubt, thousands of others, *though uncircumcised,* enjoyed the blessedness of this covenant before Abraham was born. Circumcision, therefore, is *no part* of the "covenant of grace;" and that it did not bring *Abraham* into it, is undeniably clear, for he enjoyed it and all its blessedness many years *before* circumcision was instituted; when he was, says the Apostle, "not in circumcision, but in uncircumcision." Rom. iv. 10. And that this rite did not bring *children* into the covenant of grace is equally evident, from the addresses of all the holy prophets and Apostles, and of Christ himself, to those who had thus received that rite, and who are addressed as *persons entirely destitute of the grace of God, and being by natare the children of wrath, even as others.* See, among innumerable passages, Isa. i. 2–15, John viii. 42–44, Eph. ii. 3, Acts vii. 51, 52.

In what sense, then, is circumcision "a seal of the covenant," if it had not this efficacy?

Answer. Common as it is to denominate circumcision *a seal of the covenant*, it is no where so denominated in the word of God. In one place, Rom. iv. 11, it is called *a seal of righteousness;* but except the whole verse be cited, the sense of the Apostle is entirely lost. The words are these: "And he (that is, Abraham) received the sign of circumcision, a seal of the righteousness of the faith which he had, yet being uncircumcised." In no other place is circumcision called *a seal;* and let my reader try, after carefully looking at the whole passage, to make this applicable to infants, or to infant circumcision or baptism, or to unbelievers in any case, if he can. He will remark,

1. Circumcision is here spoken of, not in reference to its general administration to the *Jewish nation*, but to Abraham in particular. 2. It is spoken of, not as it might be received by a person *destitute of vital piety*, for it is called "a seal of the righteousness OF FAITH," &c. 3. It is not spoken of as sealing what was *in future* to be bestowed or enjoyed, but of

a blessing long before possessed—"of the faith which he had, yet being uncircumcised."

I appeal to the serious judgment of the reader, what a perversion of the sense of God's word it must be, to call circumcision, from this passage, "a seal of the covenant," or "a seal of righteousness," thereby referring to the *national* administration of that rite to the Jews, and as *sealing to them the blessings of salvation*, when the Apostle so guardedly expresses himself as sealing only what a TRUE AND LIVING FAITH had previously obtained! This passage can apply to none but to Abraham, and those of his posterity, who, like their progenitor, possessed a converting and saving faith.

VENEMA. "Circumcision was a seal of the righteousness of faith, as the Apostle affirms; but this only in respect of such Israelites as were believers." *In Pædobap. Exam.* Vol. II. p. 268.

Why, then, was circumcision administered to infants at all?

Answer. It pleased God to enter into a *particular covenant* with Abraham, which he had not done with the other patriarchs, though they equally enjoyed the blessings of the covenant of grace, in which particular covenant, described in Gen. xvii. 1–14, the Almighty promised to Abraham, "I will multiply thee exceedingly—make thee exceeding fruitful; and I will make nations of thee, and kings shall come out of thee. And I will give unto thee, and to thy seed after thee, the land wherein thou art a stranger, all the land of Canaan for an everlasting possession; and I will be their God."

My reader need not be told, that an EARTHLY KINGDOM is here promised to Abraham and his seed. He was to multiply into a nation, or nations, and kings were to arise amongst them; the land of Canaan was to be their country, and their perpetual residence. In it they were to dwell from generation to generation, and to continue a separate people from all other nations, until the SPECIAL PROMISED SEED, that is, CHRIST, should appear, in whom, as afterwards declared, Gen. xxii. 17, 19, "all the nations of the earth shall be blessed."

To *this covenant* it pleased God to append the institution of circumcision. Thus it is given, Gen. xvii. 9–23: "Thou shalt keep my covenant, therefore; thou, and thy seed after thee, in their generations. This is my covenant which ye shall keep,—Every man-child amongst you shall be circumcised; he that is eight days old, he that is born in thy house, or bought with money of any stranger, must needs be circumcised; and my covenant shall be in your flesh for an everlasting covenant. And Abraham took Ishmael his son, and all that were born in his house, and all that were bought with money, every male among the men of Abraham's house, and circumcised the flesh of their foreskin in the self-same day, as God had said unto him."

My reader will here perceive how the right of circumcision pertained to Abraham's household. *Every male* from eight days old, and every *servant or purchased slave,* of any age, willing or unwilling, must submit to this rite; and if he refused, "that soul (it is added, v. 14,) shall be cut off from his people." Can this rite, thus indispensably administered to all the males of a house, because the master received it, be *to them* the seal of the covenant of grace? This, I think, no enlightened Christian can for a moment imagine.

The Divine intention in making this ordinance a national rite, and requiring it to be so strictly observed upon all the male offspring of Abraham, and to those who were incorporated among them, appears evidently to be, THEIR SEPARATION AS A PEOPLE FROM THE REST OF THE WORLD, *that in them, in after ages, God might accomplish his wise and gracious purposes;* FIRST, in the coming of the PROMISED SEED, the Saviour of sinners; and beyond that event, in what the prophets have foretold of Israel, to be fulfilled at a period yet to come. For these designs, God was pleased to separate the Jews, by this indelible sign upon their persons: and as it was to be a national distinction, it must necessarily be a national rite, and in effecting this SEPARATION the Divine wisdom appears in applying it in early infancy.

WITSIUS. "The descendants of Abraham were separated by circumcision from other nations, and renounced their friendship: as appears from the open declaration of the sons of Jacob, Gen. xxxiv. 14, 15. A circumcised person, say the Jews, 'has withdrawn himself from the whole body of the nations.' And, indeed, circumcision was a great part, and, as it were, THE FOUNDATION OF THE MIDDLE WALL OF PARTITION." *Econ. of the Cov.* Book iv. ch. 8. § 20.

MR. ERSKINE. "When God promised the land of Canaan to Abraham and his seed, circumcision was instituted for this, among other purposes, to show that descent from Abraham was the foundation of his posterity's right to those blessings." *Theolog. Dissert.* p. 9.

In what sense then are we to consider the Abrahamic covenant as continued into the gospel dispensation, and enjoyed by Christians?

Answer. My reader, by comparing Gen. xv. 5, 6, 18, and chap. xvii. 1–14, will observe that the covenant (or rather covenants) made with Abraham were TWO-FOLD. 1 *Spiritual and internal*, pertaining to Abraham's acceptance with God, and salvation, as a believer in the coming Messiah; and which was all realized in Abraham's *believing* posterity, as we have already shown. 2. *Worldly and external*, pertaining to the land of Canaan; with which were to be united the services of the temple, a worldly sanctuary, a material altar, carnal sacrifices, and a changing priesthood; and the whole of this was intended as "a shadow of good things to come." See Heb. vii. 23, ix. 1–10, and x. 1.

Now, all that is *spiritual* and *internal* in this covenant, and as enjoyed by Israel under it, is what is called "the covenant of grace," and is *continued* in the Christian church by the Holy Spirit: while what is *worldly*, *external*, and *typical*, is fulfilled and done away is the coming of CHRIST, and in the SPIRITUAL privileges of his church. We have now, *as Christians*, no worldly kingdom, nor have we a temple, altar, or sacrifices, as the Jews; nor are we required to be separated from the nations of the world, so as to be one distinct nation; and hence no *carnal* distinction is necessary.—"My kingdom (said Christ) is not of this world." John xviii. 36. It is not worldly in its nature, seat, form, government, or privileges; but *spiritual*, and, as such, denominated "the ministration of the Spirit;" and consists "in righteousness, peace, and joy in the Holy Ghost." Rom. xiv. 17; 2 Cor. iii. 7.

VENEMA. "Circumcision, according to a two-fold covenant, INTERNAL and EXTERNAL, which then existed, had likewise a two-fold aspect, SPIRITUAL and CARNAL. The *former* referred to the internal covenant of grace; the *latter* to a legal, typical, and external covenant. *That* was concerned in 'sealing the righteousness of faith,' as the Apostle asserts: *this* in the external prerogatives of Judaism, and in conférring external benefits. *That* was peculiar to the believing Israelites; *this* was common to the whole people." *In Pœd. Exam.* Vol. II. p. 243.

Is there, then, nothing *typical* in the rite of circumcision?

Answer. I replying to this question, it is my happiness to be able to refer my reader to an authority which, as a Christian, he will esteem decisive and infallible. Circumcision was a type, but not of baptism, (a figure, a type of a figure!) but of "*the circumcision of the heart*" and "*the putting off the sins of the flesh.*" And this blessed work is accomplished, not on babes in age, but "*babes in Christ;*" born from above, and children of God. Hear the infallible authority to which I refer, Rom. ii. 28, 29, "For he is not a Jew, (an Israelite indeed,) which is one outwardly, neither is that circumcision, (in God's ultimate design,) which is outward in the flesh. But he is a Jew which is one inwardly; and circumcision IS THAT OF THE HEART; in the spirit and not in the letter, whose praise is not of men, but of God." Phil. iii. 3, "For we are the circumcision which worship God in. the spirit, and rejoice in Christ Jesus, and have no confidence in the flesh." Col. ii. 11, "Circumcised with the circumcision made without hands in the putting off the body of the sins of the flesh by the circumcision of Christ."

According to this, baptism was not instituted IN THE ROOM OF CIRCUMCISION, and so became its end and fulfilment.

Answer. It is certain that this was not the case. 1st. Because when the Apostles and Elders were assembled at Jerusalem, to consider the question, *Whether those who were turned to God from among the Gentiles should be circumcised?* Acts xv., not a word was said about *the end and fulfilment* of the Jewish rite in the Christian: and had this been the known appointment of Christ, *this must have been the decision* of the subject. 2d. Because had this been the appointment of the Saviour, it would have been an affront to his authority to *continue circumcision* for another day after he had substituted baptism in its place: but circumcision was observed, even by the Apostle Paul, long after Christ had instituted the New Testament rite. See Acts xvi. 3. This would have been a similar impropriety to the offering of "a sacrifice for sin," according to the law, after Christ had "put away sin by the sacrifice of himself."*

* The absurdity of urging the baptism of infants from the institution of circumcision, will appear by observing, 1st. That *male children only* were to receive that rite; and 2d. That *men servants* and *slaves* were equally commanded to be circumcised when the master was, and that upon pain of being cut off, or put to death. If that Divine command, therefore, be applied as descriptive of the subjects of baptism, it will *equally require* the baptism of servants and purchased slaves, willing or unwilling, as well as of infants; and it wonld *restrict* the Christian ordinance to the male sex alone. This being so plainly contrary to the revealed will of Christ on baptism, proves the fallacy of the doctrine.

In the word of God I see no connection or resemblance between circumcision and baptism, except in this, that they were both *initiatory ordinances;* the one into the *body-politic* of Israel of old, the subjects of which rite are

As you allow that circumcision was a *seal* in reference to Arbaham as a believer, is not baptism equally a seal under the New Testament, in a believer's case?

Answer. If it be so, it must be understood in the same sense in which the Apostle expressed it in the case of the patriarch; and then it would be "a seal of the righteousness of the faith which the believer had, yet being unbaptized." But we cannot do better than allow the New Testament to answer our inquiries; and here I am *no where* taught that any external ordinance is a seal of the covenant of grace, but most plainly instructed, (in beautiful harmony with the *spiritual nature* of the Messiah's kingdom,) that *the work of the Spirit* on the heart is the only seal of that covenant.

2 Cor. i. 22. "Who hath also sealed us, and given the earnest of the Spirit in our hearts."

Eph. i. 13. "Ye were sealed with that Holy Spirit of promise."

Eph. iv. 30. "Grieve not that Holy Spirit, whereby ye are sealed unto the day of redemption."

CHARNOCK. "God seals no more than he promises. He promises only to faith, and therefore only seals to faith. Covenant graces, therefore, must be possessed and acted, before covenant blessings be ratified to us." *Works*, Vol. II. p. 781, ed. 1.

VITRINGA. "The sacraments of the New Covenant are of such a nature, as to seal nothing but what is *spiritual*, nor to be of any advantage, except in regard to those who really believe in Jesus Christ." *In Pæd. Exam.* Vol. II. p. 268.

How, then, is the doctrine of the Church of England to be understood, by which we are taught, that a child by baptism is "incorporated" and "grafted into the body of Christ's Church;"

all the male inhabitants—the other into the *body of Christ, which is his church*, and the subjects of which are *all believers in him*. To this the Apostle seems to refer in Col. ii. 11–13.

and in another place, "made a member of Christ, a child of God, and an inheritor of the kingdom of heaven?"

Answer. To support that doctrine by any thing said in the Scriptures of this ordinance, (as the reader of the preceding pages must be aware,) is impossible; to make it agree with the analogy of faith as taught by the concurring testimony of the whole of Divine revelation, is equally impossible. What is here attributed to baptism, the Scriptures ascribe to the omnipotent agency of the HOLY GHOST in regeneration, and to the infinite efficacy of the REDEEMER'S cross in securing eternal life!! See 2 Thes. ii. 13, 1 Pet. iii. 18. Baptism, then, is here said to do what nothing short of the power and grace of God is able to perform; and that children, as they advance in life, should be taught to *express and believe* such a doctrine, and to consider themselves in the possession of such spiritual advantages, merely by having received this external rite, destitute as it is of all saving efficacy, is inexpressibly lamentable and dangerous; because it might prove, as it is fitly calculated to be, fatal to their souls!

MR. JOHN HYATT, (the late excellent minister of the Tabernacle, London.) "If the Church of Christ is his body, and every real believer is a member of that body, how important the question, Are we members of the body of Christ? Millions have been taught to say, that in baptism they are made members of Christ, who have given indubitable proofs that they uttered falsehood!! The members of the body of Christ are united to him as a head; and there are no dead, no unsanctified members. All are useful, active, and obedient. Ah! my hearers, beware of deception—beware of substituting the name for the reality—the form of godliness for the power. Surely, licentious characters cannot presume that they are members of the mystical body of the Son of God. A holy head, and impure members; a pure fountain, and corrupt streams; a good tree, and bad fruit;—these are anomalies. If you are united to him, you are of one spirit with him." *Sermons on various Subjects*, p. 363.

9. *Infant Salvation.*

But if infants are not to be received into the Church by baptism, and they should die in infancy, is not their salvation endangered?

Answer. By no means. How can the want of *that* endanger salvation which God hath nowhere enjoined or required? Did not our Lord receive UNBAPTIZED children into his arms, when on earth, and bless them, and send them away unbaptized, and without uttering a word about baptism? See question 2. And who then will say that baptism is necessary, that He should receive them to himself in heaven, especially when they remember his gracious declaratian in reference to these *unbaptized children,* "Of such is the kingdom of heaven?" See Mark x. 14, and Matt. xviii. 10.

Persons dying incapable of faith in Christ, are without doubt saved, *not by water,* nor by *the work of man;* but by *the blood of Christ,* and by the power of the Spirit. In like manner persons dying in faith, but having no opportunity of being baptized, as the penitent on the cross, are saved by the same infinitely efficacious, and the ONLY sufficient means.

If we do for our children what God hath required, we shall find this quite sufficient, without attempting to do what God hath *not* required. And should it please God to remove them from us in infancy, it is better to commit their souls to the merits of Christ, than to the unauthorized application of water to their bodies. The former we are sure saves. 1 John i. 7. And we are equally sure baptism cannot save; Acts viii. 13, 23; and is not necessary to salvation, Luke xxiii. 43. To apply baptism *for salvation,* therefore, is making a false saviour of the ordinance, and implies a criminal unbelief in the all-sufficiency of Christ.

10. *On what Authority is Infant Baptism founded?*

Admitting the want of Scripture authority for infant baptism, on what other authority is it supposed to be originally founded?

Answer. Some have urged in its behalf *apostolical tradition.* Others, a *council of bishops,* held at Carthage, A. D. 253. Higher authority it has not; and neither of these can Protestants admit.

MR. FIELD. "The baptism of infants is therefore named a *tradition,* because it is not expressly delivered in Scripture that the Apostles did baptize infants; nor any express precept there found that they should do so." *On the Church,* 375.

BISHOP PRIDEAUX. "Pædobaptism rests on no other Divine right than *Episcopacy.*"* *Fascicul. Contro.* Loc. iv. § iii. p. 210.

11. *The time when Infant Baptism was introduced.*

If this be granted, when was infant baptism supposed to be introduced?

Answer. There is no certain evidence of it earlier than the beginning of the third century after Christ. At that period it was practiced in Africa, and is mentioned, for the first time, by Tertullian, about the year 204, in his work entitled "De Baptismo," which I shall cite presently.

CURCELLÆUS, (a learned divine of Geneva, and professor of Divinity.) "The baptism of infants, in the two first centuries after Christ, was altogether unknown; but in the third and fourth was allowed by some few. In the fifth and following ages, it was generally received. The custom of baptizing

* In the Edict drawn up in the year 1547, by command of Charles V. Emperor of Germany, to allay disputes between the Romanists and the Reformers, *Tradition* is expressly stated as the ground of infant baptism: "Habet præterea Ecclesia traditiones, &c., quas qui convellit, is negat eandem columnam esse et firmamentum veritatis. Hujus generis sunt Baptismus parvulorum et alia;" i. e., "The Church moreover has traditions handed down to these times from Christ and the Apostles, through the hands of the bishops: which, whoever would overturn, he must deny the same (viz., the Church) to be the pillar and ground of truth. Of this sort are the baptism of little ones, and other things." *In Dr. Ryland's Candid Statement,* Notes, p. 28.

infants did not begin before the third age after Christ was born. In the former ages, no trace of it appears—and it was introduced without the command of Christ." *In Pœd. Exam.* Vol. II. p. 76.

SALMASIUS AND SUICERUS. "In the two first centuries no one was baptized, except being instructed in the faith, and acquainted with the doctrine of Christ, he was able to profess himself a believer; because of those words, *He that believeth, and is baptized.*" Ut supra.

VENEMA. "*Tertullian* has no where mentioned pædobaptism among the traditions or customs of the church, that were publicly received, and usually observed.—For in his book, *De Baptismo,* he dissuades from baptizing infants, and proves the delay of it to a more mature age is to be preferred. Nothing can be affirmed, with certainty, concerning the custom of the church before *Tertullian,* seeing there is not any where, in more ancient writers, that I know of, undoubted mention of infant baptism." Ut supra, p. 74.

The passage alluded to, containing the FIRST MENTION of infant baptism, is the following:

TERTULLIAN. "The delay of baptism may be more advantageous, either on account of the condition, disposition, or age of any person, especially in reference to little children. For what necessity is there that the sponsors should be brought into danger? because either they themselves may fail of the promises by death, or be deceived by the growth of evil dispositions. The Lord, indeed, says, *Do not forbid them to come to me.* Let them, therefore, come when they are grown up; when they can understand; when they are taught whither they are to come. Let them become Christians when they can know Christ. Why should this innocent age hasten to the remission of sins? Men act more cautiously in worldly things; so that Divine things are here intrusted with whom earthly things are not. Let them know how to seek salvation, that you may appear to give to one that asketh. . . . If persons understand the importance of baptism, they will rather fear the consequent obligation than the delay: true faith alone is secure of salvation."

Now I request my reader to observe—1. That there is confessedly no mention of infant baptism in the writings of any of the Fathers, before Tertullian, in the beginning of the third century; though the baptism of believers is repeatedly found, in various authors; some of which I shall cite in the next part of this appendix. 2. That when infant baptism is *first* mentioned, in the Christian Father above quoted, it is in a passage where the rite is referred to, not as of something of universal practice and approbation; but where it is OPPOSED AND REASONED AGAINST as something unknown in the age of Christ and the Apostles, and destitute of their authority, for with him their authority would not have been questioned for a moment; and as something implying *danger* in reference to sponsors, and *absurdity* relative to children. Thus,

REGALTIUS, the learned annotator upon Cyprian. "In the Acts of the Apostles, we read that *both men and women were baptized* when they believed the gospel preached by Philip, but not a word of infants. From the age of the Apostles, therefore, up to the time of Tertullian, the matter remained in obscurity, [or doubtful, in ambiguo;] and there were some who from that saying of our Lord, *Suffer little children to come unto me,* to whom the Lord nevertheless did not command water to be administered, took occasion to baptize even newborn infants. And as if, (seculare aliquod negotium cum Deo transigeretur,) they transacted some secular business with God, they offered sponsors or sureties to Christ, who engaged that they should not revolt from the Christian faith when grown up; which indeed displeased Tertullian." *In Stennett's Answer to Russen,* pp. 69, 73, and in *Mr. Wall's Hist.* Vol. II. chap. 2.

12. *Tradition no Authority for Infant Baptism.*

Tradition from the Apostles is declared by the Church of

Rome to be the authority for infant baptism; is this said to be its authority where the practice is *first* mentioned?

Answer. No such authority is ever once hinted at.

VENEMA. "Tertullian dissuades from baptizing infants—which he certainly would not have done, if it had been a tradition, and a public custom of the church, seeing he was VERY TENACIOUS of traditions; nor, had it been a tradition, would he have failed to mention it?" *See after next question.*

13. *Other innovations introduced.*

Do we find any other innovation introduced into the Church of Christ, about the same period?

Answer. Several. We never read of—1. The consecration of the baptismal water; 2. The use of sponsors; 3. The imposition of hands at baptism; 4. The use of material unction at confirmation; 5. Offering prayers and oblations for the dead, &c.; we never read of any of these in any Christian writer before Tertullian; and hence, learned Pædobaptists infer that they were *introduced about that time.* Thus, Mr. Pierce, speaking of the third of these, says, that Tertullian is "the most ancient author that mentions this rite;" and adds, "We make no doubt it began about the time of Tertullian." *Vindication of Dissenters,* Pt. III. ch. vii. pp. 172, 175. We come to the same conclusion, for the very same reason, respecting the baptism of infants. The celebrated and learned divine I cited in the former question seems willing to admit this:—

VENEMA. "I conclude therefore, that pædobaptism CANNOT be plainly proved to have been practiced before the time of Tertullian; and that there were persons in his age who desired their infants might be baptized, especially when they were afraid of their dying without baptism; which opinion Tertullian opposed, and, BY SO DOING, INTIMATES THAT PÆDOBAPTISM BEGAN TO PREVAIL." *In Pœd. Exam.* Vol. II. pp. 79, 80.

14. *The Christian Fathers and Infant Baptism.*

Did the first Christian Fathers, who supported the baptism of infants, suppose that some spiritual benefit was communicated to them by that ordinance?

Answer. They did. They held that baptism was necessary to salvation; that forgiveness accompanied it; that infants by it were purged from the pollution of original sin; and that all prsons dying without baptism were lost. Thus,

CYPRIAN, A. D. 253. "As far as lies in us, no soul, if possible, is to be lost. It is not for us to hinder any person from baptism and the grace of God; which rule, as it holds to all, so we think it more especially to be observed in reference to infants, to whom our help and the Divine mercy is rather to be granted; because by their weeping and wailing at their first entrance into the world, they do intimate nothing so much as that they implore compassion."

AMBROSE, A. D. 390. "For no person comes to the kingdom of heaven, but by the sacrament of baptism.—Infants that are baptized are reformed back again from wickedness to the primitive state of their nature."

CHRYSOSTOM, A. D. 398. "The grace of baptism gives cure without pain, and fills us with the grace of the Spirit. Some think that the heavenly grace consists only in *the forgiveness of sins:* but I have reckoned up TEN advantages of it." "If sudden death seize us before we are baptized, though we have a thousand good qualities, there is nothing to be expected but hell." See the original of these passages in *Mr. Wall's Hist. of Inf. Bap.* Vol. I. ch. 6, 13, 14; and II. ch. 6.

These extracts, which I might have increased a hundredfold, are sufficient to prove that some of the Fathers, from about the middle of the third century, considered baptism as *essentially necessary to salvation;* and in this false view of the ordinance, the baptism of infants originated. To this agree the following learned writers:—

SUICERUS, Professor of Greek and Hebrew at Zurich. "This opinion of the absolute necessity of baptism arose from a wrong understanding of our Lord's words, *Except a man be born of water and of the Spirit, he cannot enter the kingdom of heaven.*" *In Pæd. Exam.* Vol. II. p. 129.

SALMASIUS, the very learned historian and critic. "An opinion prevailed that no one could be saved without being baptized; and for that reason the custom arose of baptizing infants." *Ibid.* p. 128.

15. *Sponsors introduced as infants could not believe.*

But if a profession of repentance and faith was always required before baptism in the apostolic age, how could Christian ministers, or churches, so early as the days of Tertullian, admit of the baptism of infants, by whom no such profession could be made?

Answer. The deficiency, in reference to infants, was ingeniously supplied by introducing "sponsors." They would not *dispense with the profession*, but they would admit it *by proxy.* Two or three persons, and, in the case of an infant of high rank, from twenty to an hundred, were admitted as "sureties," who professed, *in behalf of an infant*, to repent, renounce the devil and his works, and to believe the doctrines of the gospel. These sureties are first mentioned by Tertullian, A. D. 204, in the passage I have copied, pp. 65, 66, where they are called "sponsors," i. e., persons who answer, and make themselves answerable for another.

Here is *religion by proxy;* real, personal, experimental religion! a thing unheard of before since the world began. But when so many strange absurdities were introduced into the church, as those before mentioned, p. 67, we need not be much surprised at this. To a reader, however, who knows by his own experience, and by the concurrent testimony of every part of the Bible, that there is no religion but that which is between God and the soul, and is God's gift, and in which another can have no share or part, it is grievous to reflect seriously on this alarming innovation.

16. *Views of modern Pœdobaptists.*

But do modern Pædobaptists entertain the same view as the ancients, as to the necessity of baptism to salvation?

Answer. The MAJORITY of professed Christians have ever avowed, and do still avow, the same doctrine! The Church of Rome has honored those who dare deny it with an "anathema;" and the Greek church, though not so ready to anathematize, entertains the same opinion. The reformed churches, and the different denominations of Protestant Pædobaptists, whether bearing the name of Episcopalians, Presbyterians, Independents, Congregationlists, or Wesleyans, while they generally disavow that doctrine, yet they hold opinions which, when fairly carried out to their consequences, come little short of the same amount. They have seen in the doctrine of the ancients, and of Rome, "that no one can be saved without their baptism," too plain a demonstration of the "little horn" of antichrist,*—the mystery of iniquity which began to work in the Apostles' days,†—to avow that doctrine *in the same terms.* But let me ask my respected brethren in these communities, If baptism makes its subjects, as some of them say,‡ "children of God and inheritors of the kingdom of heaven;" or, as all of them, by their leading writers, have said, that it brings its subjects "into the Church of Christ" or "into the covenant of grace," or "seals to them the benefits of that covenant," and which is "the covenant of redemption, embracing all that Jehovah can impart;" whether this is not tantamount to the doctrine guarded by Rome's anathema? If baptism brings into, or seals the benefits of, the covenant of grace, it will bring to heaven; for God hath joined these two together. And if there be not *another way* of bringing into this "covenant of grace and redemption," what must become of those who are *not* brought in, and who die in that situation? Thus

* Daniel vii. 8–21. † 2 Thes. ii. 3–10. ‡ See Authorities at pp. 54, 55.

pressed to consequences, I see no other conclusion to be come at from these premises, but that of Chrysostom, just cited, horrible as it sounds! Let my brethren who would recoil at the thought of that conclusion, examine rigidly and honestly whether the virtues they join to the rite of baptism afford not the just and fair ground of it. And if the conclusion be denied, let them deny the premises from which it is drawn; but while they avow the premises, I must be allowed to insist upon the conclusion.

17. *What is the use of Baptism in the Church?*

If no spiritual or saving benefit necessarily attends the ordinance of baptism, (which evidently is, and ever has been, conceived as the basis and reason of infant baptism, by the MAJORITY of those that have practiced it,) why is the ordinance administered at all? and of what use is it in the Church of Christ?

Answer. "God is his own interpreter." The ritual ordinances appointed of God in his church were never, under any dispensation, intended by him to carry salvation with them. For that purpose "neither circumcision availeth anything, nor uncircumcision," as the Apostle affirms; and the same may be said of baptism and the Lord's Supper. Salvation proceeds from a source entirely distinct and separate from these ordinances. It may be fully enjoyed without them; and they may be administered, and repeated a thousand times over, without it. The penitent malefactor was saved without baptism; Simon Magus was baptized without part or lot in salvation.

What, then, you inquire, is the use of baptism? I reply, It is a solemn, sacred institution of Jesus, intended by him, as I have before observed, TO EXHIBIT AND TO TEACH the way of salvation. It saves in no way of itself; but it presents a figurative and an impressive representation of saving—of that real saving, which is through the purifying merits of a crucified and risen Saviour. As such Christ instituted it; and as such it is the duty and privilege of his followers to observe it, till he come. Thus the Apostle Peter, cited p. 49, when he says, *Baptism saves;* he immediately guards against error upon this subject,—*it is not the putting away the filth of the flesh,* or impurity, or sin of any kind, which can only be cleansed by the blood of Christ. But it saves as a "figure;" it symbolically presents "the fountain opened for sin and uncleanness," and to *that* fountain it directs the penitent to flee, and therein by faith "to wash away sin, calling on the name of the Lord." Acts xxii. 16. When this is realized, then baptism affords *the answer of a good conscience,* satisfied that Christ is obeyed, guilt purged away, and the soul saved through the blood of the Lamb. Pædobaptist divines affirm the same. Thus,

MR. DAVID DAVIDSON, on 1 Peter iii. 21. "Lest any should imagine spiritual deliverance secure by the external rite, in any other sense than figuratively, the Apostle adds, that the baptism he chiefly meant was the cleansing of the conscience, which is by faith in Christ. The same figure and reality are repeatedly thus stated. See Eph. v. 26; Tit. iii. 5; Heb. ix. 14." *Commentary on the New Test.* p. 459.

18. *The first Christian writer who defends Infant Baptism.*

Who is the *first* Christian writer that defended the baptism of infants?

Answer. The first that mentioned the practice *at all* was Tertullian, A. D. 204. It was named next by Origen, A. D. 230. But the first writer that *defended* the practice was CYPRIAN, A. D. 253. At this period the plan of admitting a profession by sponsors became so general, at least in Africa, where it commenced, and the security the rite afforded of eternal life was deemed so important, that the practice of it became general. Hence Synods and Councils were held to sanction the practice, and to consider the time after birth when the ordinance may be properly administered. Thus, the very learned writer cited before—

REGALTIUS. "Most men thinking this opinion of Tertullian unsafe, were of Cyprian's mind, that even new-born children *ought to be* made partakers of the laver of salvation; which was pitched upon in the decree of this Synod, AND SO THE DOUBT WAS TAKEN AWAY." *In Stennett's Answer to Russen*, pp. 69–73, and in *Mr. Wall's Hist.* Vol. II. ch. 2.

CHAPTER V.

Dr. Fuller on Infant Salvation, Dedication, and Baptism. 1. Are infants, dying such, saved? 2. Ought parents to dedicate their children to God? 3. Where is the difference in baptism? 4. What harm can baptism of infants do? 1st. It perverts the Gospel; 2d. It makes void the command of God by human tradition; 3d. It attacks and insults the mercy of God; 4th. It dishonors the Saviour; 5th. It does a serious injury to children.

THE following tract, published by the American Baptist Publication Society, is by Rev. Richard Fuller, D. D. It is eminently worthy of the perusal of parents, stating in the most satisfactory manner the Scriptural view of the subject.

1. *Are not infants, dying in infancy, saved?* Certainly. Of a child which was the fruit of sin, David says, "I shall go to him, but he shall not return to me" (2 Sam. xii. 23.) It would be horrid blasphemy, to suppose that God can consign to hell infants who have never known good from evil. There is no controversy between Baptists and evangelical Pedobaptists on this point.

2. *Ought not parents to dedicate their children to God?* Assuredly. A Christian consecrates himself and all he has to Christ. And this is to be done by parents themselves, not by priests or ministers. In Mark x. 13, it was the parents, not the Apostles, who brought infants to Jesus. Yes, fathers and mothers, take your little ones to Him who is the same Jesus

now; supplicate his blessing on your offspring. Do more. Show, by your conduct, that you are sincere. When they are old enough, pray with them, send them to the Sunday School, and, above all, let your example point to heaven, and lead the way. To neglect this duty to our children, is to be ungrateful to God, who has given them to us; it is to be most perfidious and unnatural to our offspring, who inherit from us depraved natures; in a word, it is to prepare for ourselves sorrow while our children live, and the bitterest reproaches of our consciences if they are cut off in sin. There is no difference between Baptist and Pedobaptist brethren on this article.

3. Where, then, is the difference? It is as to *baptizing infants*. Jesus Christ commands all to repent—to believe—to be baptized. These are *personal* duties. The command is not to parents to do something for their children, but to each individual, requiring him to obey for himself. Can a parent obey, for a child, the command to repent? All answer, No—the child, when it grows up, must repent for itself. Can a parent obey, for his child, the command to believe? All reply, Certainly not—the child, when of sufficient age, must believe for itself.

Now the command to be baptized is just like these commands, and yet our Pedobaptist brethren maintain that parents can obey for their children. They teach that a parent and minister can do something for an unconscious babe, by which it may be said that the babe has obeyed the command to be baptized, so that the child is absolved, when it grows up, from the duty of personal obedience. As your friend, as the friend of Christ, as the friend of your children—for I am myself a parent—I wish affectionately to warn you against this error.

My friend, your common sense must convince you of the fallacy of such a doctrine. Your reason teaches you that we cannot obey God by proxy; that obedience to God is a personal duty, and that no one can obey for another. It is sometimes said that Christian parents must baptize their children, because Jewish parents circumcised theirs. But you see the sophistry of such reasoning. The command to circumcise was to *parents and masters as such.* "He that is eight days old shall be circumcised among you, every man-child in your generations; he that is born in the house, or bought with money of any stranger that is not of thy seed." (Gen. xvii. 12.) This is a command *to parents*, to perform a certain act on an infant eight days old; and *to masters*, to perform a certain act on a servant as soon as they purchased him. But baptism is not a command of this sort. It is a command to each individual, to be obeyed by himself. "Go preach the gospel to every creature: he that believeth and is baptized shall be saved." (Mark xvi. 15, 16.) Here the *being saved* is personal salvation; the *believing* is personal faith; and the *baptism* is an act of personal obedience.

When a general sends an order to his officers, the officers have no authority to go beyond that order. They must read it and obey it. If the commission is, "*First instruct and train men, and then enlist them into the army*," the officers cannot enlist men not instructed nor trained; it would be absurd to say that they can enlist infants. When these infants grow up they may be trained and enlisted, if they choose. And this is just the fact as to baptism. Jesus has given his written order as to baptism. The order requires ministers first to "*preach the gospel*," to "*teach*" people, then to "*baptize*" those that believe. This, of course, forbids the baptism of any who are not taught, or do not believe. Infants cannot listen to preaching, cannot be taught, cannot believe, and, therefore, cannot be subjects for baptism.

Let no one throw dust in your eyes by saying, "If infants cannot be baptized because they cannot believe, then infants cannot be saved." We have already said that infants are saved, saved through the blood of Him who "died for all." But the command to believe and be baptized is addressed to those who can believe and be baptized. It is absurd to suppose that God requires faith, or baptism, or any duty from babes.

Open your Bible. You find there not a trace of infant baptism. If infants are to be baptized, Jesus would have baptized the children brought to Him. But this was plainly never thought of, either by the parents, or by the Saviour and his Apostles. "He took them up in his arms, and put his hands upon them, and blessed them." (Mark x. 16.) In all the cases of baptism recorded in the Scriptures, the parties were intelligent beings, who heard and acted for themselves. It is sometimes said that households were baptized. What then? This clearly proves nothing, unless it be shown that there were infants in those households. "Mr. Smith and his family were at church;" does this prove that there are infants in Mr. Smith's family, and that infants were at church? The Baptists often baptize families. But we are not left to conjecture here. In the case of the jailer's household, it is expressly said that they "believed" and "rejoiced." (Acts xvi.) Of the household of Stephanas it is declared, that they "addicted themselves to the ministry of the saints." (1st Cor. xvi. 15.) The only other household is that of Lydia. From the history (Acts xvi.) all we know is, that she was a woman keeping her own dyeing establishment. Dr. Whitby, (a learned Pedobaptist,) in his commentary on this passage, says, "When she and those of her household were instructed in the Christian faith, in the nature of baptism required by it, she was baptized and her household." She and those employed in her establishment were baptized. There is not a word about her being married, or having children. The whole account, and her reception of the Apostles afterwards, (v. 15,) shows that she was a woman having her "own house," and doing business on her own account.

The advocates of this error sometimes quote Acts ii. 39. "For the promise is to you and to your children." Read the whole passage. It will expose this plea, drawn from a garbled quotation. "Repent, and be baptized, every one of you, and ye shall receive the gift of the Holy Ghost. For the promise is to you and to your children, and to all that are afar off, even as many as the Lord our God shall call. Then they that gladly received his word were baptized." What is the promise here mentioned? At verse 16th we are expressly informed that it included the miraculous gifts of the Holy Spirit, which babes do not, of course, receive. "This is that which is spoken of by the prophet Joel. And it shall come to pass in the last days, I will pour out my Spirit upon all flesh, and your sons and your daughters shall prophesy." To whom is the promise made? "To you" (Jews) "and your children;" that is, the Jews and their posterity, (as Joel says, "your sons and your daughters shall prophesy;" not babes, but children who can prophesy;) "and to all that are afar off;" that is, the Gentiles; (as Joel says, "all flesh;") "even as many as the Lord our God shall call." How absurd to talk about infants being called! The remaining words settle the matter. "Then *they that gladly received the word* were baptized."

Baptism is a New Testament institution, and the New Testament teaches us who are to be baptized. They are believers only. Those who go to the Old Testament and the Jewish circumcision for arguments, plainly confess that the New Testament is against them. Baptism is a Christian command, to be obeyed by each individual for himself or herself. Circumcision was a command to the Jewish nation, requiring them to put a certain national mark on all male infants and slaves. The two things are as distinct as any two commands in the whole Bible. I will, therefore, not dwell on this fallacy, except to remark, that when circumcision is spoken of in the New Testament with reference to Christians, it is never used as typical of baptism, but as emblematical of conversion and holiness. The very passage often cited by Pedobaptists proves this. It is Coloss. ii. 11, 12. Read the passage, and you will see that the Apostle is describing a "*complete*" Christian,

(v. 10.) And he notices two things: his conversion, or the inward change; and baptism, or the outward confession. First, (v. 11,) because in circumcision a part of the flesh was cut off, conversion is called "putting off the body of the sins of the flesh by the circumcision made without hands, the circumcision of Christ;" that is, the change which Christ by his Spirit performs on the heart. Then, afterwards, (v. 12,) comes baptism, which is compared, not to circumcision, but to a burial and resurrection. "And ye are complete in him, which is the head of all principality and power. In whom also ye are circumcised with the circumcision made without hands, in putting off the body of the sins of the flesh by the circumcision of Christ: Buried with him in baptism, wherein also ye are risen with him through the faith of the operation of God, who has raised him from the dead."

Parents, dedicate your children to God; but do not, in the very act, commit that which God has not commanded, and which cannot, therefore, be pleasing to him.

4. Perhaps, however, you may say: After all, what harm can this ceremony do? To which I answer, it plainly does no good, and it does much harm.

1st. *It perverts the Gospel.* Jesus says, "My kingdom is not of this world." His kingdom is a spiritual kingdom. But read the writings of those who practice infant baptism, and you find they are forced to maintain that Jesus has a kingdom which is of this world, into which water can introduce an unconscious babe. Jesus says, "That which is born of the flesh is flesh, and that which is born of the Spirit is spirit." "Except a man be born again, he cannot see the kingdom of God." The advocates of infant baptism teach that a child born of the flesh can enter the kingdom of God, by having a little water sprinkled on it. This perversion of the gospel is the foundation of the Popish system, and of the union of Church and State in Protestant countries.

2d. *It makes void the command of God by a human tradi-*

tion. There is plainly no authority for baptizing infants in the Bible. It is equally plain that the practice began long after the Apostles. Curcellæus (a learned Pedobaptist) says, "Pedobaptism was not known in the world the two first ages after Christ. In the third and fourth centuries it was approved by few. At length, in the fifth and following ages, it began to obtain in divers places. Therefore we observe this rite indeed as an ancient custom, but not as an apostolical tradition. The custom of baptizing infants did not begin before the third age after Christ, and there appears not the least footstep of it in the first two centuries." (Crosby's Hist. Pref. 66.) This human custom, but for the Baptists, would entirely abolish from the earth the baptism of the New Testament, which is the immersion of believers.

3d. *Infant baptism attacks and insults the mercy of God.* For it originated in the horrid impiety, that infants will be damned without baptism. Thus Augustine, (A. D. 410,) says: "The Catholic Church has ever held that unbaptized infants will miss, not only the kingdom of heaven, but also eternal life." (Wall on Infant Baptism, vol. i. pp. 411, 412.) And it is still really perpetuated by the same shocking doctrine, though its advocates are now afraid openly to avow it. Their insinuations about "covenant mercies," about infants being "admitted into the kingdom," &c., and their haste to sprinkle water on a dying child, all mean this, and nothing else.

4th. *Infant baptism dishonors the Saviour.* It cherishes the injurious idea that his blood is not enough; that our children, dying in infancy, cannot be saved through his atonement, but that the parent and minister must perform some act on them and for them, besides what Christ has done.

5th. I will only add, that this unscriptural practice *does a serious injury to our children.* It nourishes in them a vague idea that something has been performed towards their salvation. It prevents their searching the Scriptures for themselves, when they grow up. It fosters deeply-rooted prejudices, and causes them to repel the thought that their parents could have been in error. And thus, the very love which your children bear you closes their minds against all investigation, and perpetuates in them, and in their children's children, error and disobedience, which would at once cease, if they were left to read the Bible, and judge for themselves as to this command.

In proof of what has just been said, my dear friend, I appeal to yourself. I ask you candidly, have you examined the Bible for yourself as to the question of baptism? You will confess that you have not. And why have you not? Because you have grown up with the idea that your parents attended to the matter for you. God commands "all men every where to repent;" none can so blind you, as to make you believe that your parents yielded to this command for you. God says to all, "Believe in the Lord Jesus Christ;" you are incapable of a delusion which would lull you into the folly of trusting that your parents had believed for you. You love the Saviour, and feel the absurdity of supposing that you need not love him because your parents loved him for you. How is it, then, that you can live and die under an illusion equally glaring? When God commands all believers to be baptized, how can you think that your parents obeyed this command for you? When Jesus says, "If you love me, keep my commandments," will you mock him, and do the grossest violence to your own reason, by saying, "I love Jesus, but this or that command I need not keep; my parents kept it for me?" Are you willing to die, and meet your Saviour with such a plea on your lips?

Do not suffer any one to perplex a plain thing by talking about "covenant mercies," and "circumcision," and the like. Search the Scriptures, and you will see that infant baptism is not a command of God, but an invention of man. It was introduced on account of the unscriptural, popish idea, that water washes away original sin, and that none can be saved unless baptized, no matter how impossible baptism may be. Do not lend your countenance to an error so insulting to God and so pernicious to your children. Believe and be baptized yourself. Train up your children in the way they should go. By prayer and counsel and example seek to win them to Jesus. And admonish them to search for themselves those Scriptures, "which are able to make them wise unto salvation." So shall the blessing of God be upon you, and "it shall be well with you and your children forever."

CHAPTER VI.

Communion.—1. Baptist terms of Communion the same with other denominations. 2. Robert Hall on Close Communion. 3. Baptists should not be called Close Communionists, to distinguish them from others. 4. Familiar Dialogue between Peter and Benjamin, on Close Communion.

1. Baptists are called close communionists; and it is generally supposed their terms of communion differ from those of other denominations. Such, however, is not the fact. All denominations unite in requiring baptism prior to the Lord's Supper, on the ground that this is the order of the two ordinances in the New Testament. Consequently, it is neither intelligent nor fair to call Baptists close communionists in distinction from other denominations. The difference between us is that of baptism, and not communion. Baptists believing that immersion alone is baptism, cannot invite to the Lord's table those who have only been sprinkled, because they in common with other denominations believe baptism precedes communion. Other denominations would not invite Baptists, if they supposed them unbaptized.

2. It is common for even well-educated Pedobaptists to quote Robert Hall, an open communion Baptist, who is the author of a work on the subject, against Baptists, as though his work was particularly against them, when it is against all

denominations, on the ground that baptism is not pre-requisite to communion. With Mr. Hall, close communion consists in making baptism precede communion, and consequently with him all denominations are close communionists. His language is, "The class of Christians whose sentiments I am relating, are usually known by the appellation of Baptists; in contradistinction from whom all other Christians may be denominated Pedobaptists. It is not my intention to enter into a defence of their peculiar tenets, though they have my unqualified approbation; but merely to state them for the information of my readers. It must be obvious, that in the judgment of the Baptists, such as have only received the baptismal rite in their infancy, must be deemed in reality unbaptized; for this is only a different mode of expressing their conviction of the invalidity of infant sprinkling. On this ground they have, for the most part, confined their communion to persons of their own persuasion, in which, as illiberal as it may appear, they are supported by the general practice of the Christian world, which, whatever diversities of opinion may have prevailed, has generally concurred in insisting upon baptism as an indispensable pre-requisite to the Lord's table. The effect which has resulted in this particular case, has indeed been singular, but it has arisen from a rigid adherence to a principle almost universally adopted, that baptism is under all circumstances a necessary pre-requisite to the Lord's Supper. The practice we are now specifying has usually been termed *strict communion;* while the opposite practice, of admitting sincere Christians to the Eucharist, though in our judgment not baptized, is styled *free communion.*"

3. With this explanation, no candid person will call Baptists close communionists, to distinguish them from other denominations. Our terms of *communion* are the same. Baptists are only entitled to a share with other denominations of the opprobrium of insisting upon the necessity of adhering to the order of the New Testament, in placing baptism before com-

munion. While Pedobaptists insist upon this order, and Baptists believe immersion alone baptism, the former can cast no blame upon the latter, except for being strict *Baptists*, not *Communionists*. How much occasion Baptists have for their strict adherence to immersion, we have seen.

4. I cannot deny myself the pleasure of quoting here a Tract, which I deem one of the best practical works on baptism and communion, which has been published. It is by Rev. Gustavus F. Davis, D. D., late pastor of the First Baptist Church, Hartford, Ct. It is entitled "A Familiar Dialogue between Peter and Benjamin, on the subject of Close Communion." We quote it, because it answers our purpose better than any thing we can write; and is well deserving circulation and the perpetuity which is implied in placing it in a bound volume, beyond what it could have in the tract form.

A FAMILIAR DIALOGUE BETWEEN PETER AND BENJAMIN, ON CLOSE COMMUNION.

Peter. Good morning, Benjamin; whither are you going so early?

Benjamin. I am going to the Baptist prayer meeting.

P. Then you attend the *Baptist* meeting, do you?

B. I do. I am a member of the Baptist Church—I go to the Baptist meeting from a conviction of duty, and I esteem it a great privilege.

P. I will go with you this morning, because I wish to have a little conversation with you on the peculiarities of your denomination.

B. You shall be welcome to a seat with me, and on the way I will explain to you as well as I can, the reasons for what you call our peculiarities.

P. Well, I must tell you that I have read and thought much of late on the ground of our differences; and with respect to the mode and subjects of baptism, I have come to the settled conclusion, that you have the best of the argument. I have satisfied myself that the original word *Baptizo*, signifies to immerse.

B. Can you read Greek?

P. No. But I find by all history that the Greeks, who certainly understand their own language, have from the beginning, until this day, practiced immersion. Their practice is a very satisfactory comment on the meaning of the word. Besides, I have read the ample concessions of more than eighty Pedobaptist writers, that this is the meaning of the original word, and that immersion was practiced by the Apostles and by succeeding Christians for thirteen hundred years from the commencement of the Christian era. As late as 1643, in the Assembly of Divines at Westminster, sprinkling was substituted for immersion by a majority of *one*—25 voted for sprinkling, 24 for immersion. This small majority was obtained by the earnest request of Dr. Lightfoot, who had acquired great influence in that Assembly. Among the concessions of *Presbyterians*, I find the Rev. Professor Campbell, D. D., of Scotland, confessedly the most learned Greek scholar and biblical critic of modern times, says—"The word, both in sacred authors and in classical, signifies *to dip, to plunge, to immerse,* and was rendered by Tertullian, the oldest of the Latin fathers, *tingere,* the term used for dying cloth, which was by *immersion.* It is *always* construed suitably to this meaning." Notes on Matt. iii. 11.

B. Have you found any thing in the *Bible* which seems to support the statement that immersion was the practice of the primitive disciples?

P. Yes. I perceive that they "*baptized in Jordan,*" and other places where there was "much water"—and the phraseology employed in describing the act of baptism, such as "Jesus when he was baptized came *up straightway out of the water;*" Philip and the Eunuch "*went down both into the water,*" &c., affords strong evidence that immersion was the act performed in the water. Then, again, the early believers in Christ are said to have been "*buried* with him by baptism." The figurative use of the word baptism, in the expression of Christ, also, relating to his sufferings, seems very conclusive, "I have a *baptism* to be *baptized* with." I was so struck with this expression, that I turned to the commentary of Dr. Doddridge, a pious and learned Pedobaptist minister, to see what he would say, and to ascertain whether the expression could be applied to a small degree, a mere *sprinkling* of sufferings. But I found he gave the meaning which seemed to me to appear on the very face of the passage.

B. Will you repeat his paraphrase?

P. With pleasure. "I have a baptism to be baptized with, i. e., I shall shortly be *bathed*, as it were, in blood, and *plunged* in the most *overwhelming* distress." And when I hear my brethren pray, as they often do, "May we be *baptized* with the Holy Ghost," I cannot but think that they attach a similar meaning to the use of the word, and intend by the petition to pray, May we be *deeply* and *thoroughly* imbued with divine influences.

B. Some of the passages which you have quoted relate to John's baptism. Have you never heard the objection that John's baptism was not Christian baptism?

P. Yes. But if the baptism to which *Christ* himself submitted, was not *Christian;* especially when he said in reference to it, "Thus it becometh us to fulfil all righteousness," or, as Campbell renders it, "to *ratify* every institution," I know not what can deserve the name. Have you any additional reasons for considering John's baptism not *Christian?*

B. Yes. Mark (i. 1) calls his ministry the "*beginning* of the gospel," &c. Dr. Scott, in his notes on this passage, gives my views of its import. "This was in fact *the beginning* of the gospel, the *Introduction of the New Testament Dispensation.*"

Luke (xvi. 16) says, "The law and the prophets were *until* John," &c. Those who object to John's baptism being under the New Dispensation, say that this dispensation did not com mence until *after the resurrection of Christ;* but this, you perceive, would throw back the Lord's Supper into the Old Dispensation, for it was instituted *before his death.*

P. I do; but I have been a little puzzled with the account given in Acts xix. 1–6, respecting the disciples whom Paul found at Ephesus. Do you think they were re-baptized?

B. By no means, and I think I can relieve your mind in a few words. I remark, in the first place, that these disciples were believers, and must have experienced the ordinary influences of the Holy Ghost. The inquiry of Paul related to the *special miraculous gifts* of the Holy Ghost; these gifts, after suitable inquiries and explanations, were conferred. Luke is considered the writer of the Acts. I will now read the verses, first naming the speakers.

Paul. Have ye received the Holy Ghost since ye believed?

Disciples. We have not so much as heard whether there be any Holy Ghost.

Paul. Unto what then were ye baptized?

Disciples. Unto John's baptism.

Paul. John verily baptized with the baptism of repentance, saying unto the *people* that they should believe on him which should come after him, that is, on Christ Jesus. When they (i. e., the *people* to whom John preached) heard this, they were baptized in the name of the Lord Jesus.

Luke. And when Paul had laid his hands upon them, the Holy Ghost came on them, and they spake *with tongues and prophesied.*

P. I am satisfied, and I fear, after all, that the reason for objecting to John's baptism, is to be found in the overpowering evidence that it was immersion.

B. Have you not heard some startling objections to the *possibility* of immersion, in certain cases mentioned in the Bible?

P. Yes. My minister said the other day, "that it seemed

to him improbable, if not quite impossible, that 3,000 were immersed on the day of Pentecost," and that it was not likely that the jailer and his household "the same hour of the night" went out to some river to be baptized, especially as the Apostles refused the next day to go out until they were honorably released.

B. And how did you dispose of these objections?

P. With regard to the first, I remarked to him, that Peter was preaching at the third hour, (9 o'clock in the A. M.,) and his sermon, one would judge from reading the 2d of Acts, must have been ended before 11 o'clock; and as there were twelve Apostles and "other seventy" administrators, I proved to him by *simple division* of 3,000 by 82, that there were less than 37 candidates a-piece. I also referred him to the fact, that a Baptist minister in Jamaica, not long since, immersed 129 in one day; another in Troy, 20 in nine minutes.

With regard to the second objection, I replied, that though the Apostles would not be released from the care of the jailer without an honorable legal discharge, yet under the care of that jailer they might go out to administer baptism. But there is no necessity for supposing that they did go out, as the jailer, before his conversion, "brought them out of the inner prison" into the outer court, and every one acquainted with the structure of an oriental prison, knows that in that court there were bathing fonts, in which prisoners were every day required to bathe. He and his family, I believe, were baptized in a font resembling a baptistery.

B. Really on baptism you reason like a Baptist. And are you equally convinced that believers are the only proper subjects of baptism?

P. Yes. I have been so for nearly two years. I have told my minister and some of the private members of our church, that it seems to me strange that they can doubt that penitents or believers are the only subjects of baptism, when they read such passages as the following:

Mark xvi. 16. "He that *believeth*, and is baptized, shall be saved."

Acts ii. 38. "*Repent* and be baptized every one of you." Acts viii. 12. "When they *believed* Philip preaching the things concerning the kingdom of God, and the name of Jesus Christ, they were *baptized, both men and women.*" Acts viii. 36, 37. "The eunuch said, See, here is water; what doth *hinder* me to be baptized? And Philip said, *If thou believest* with all thine heart, thou mayest."

Acts xviii. 8. "Many of the Corinthians hearing, *believed*, and were baptized."

B. But you know that they endeavor to find evidence in favor of infant baptism from an expression of Christ, in reference to children—from household baptism—and from circumcision.

P. Yes, I know they do. But though Jesus said, "Suffer little children to come unto me," &c., yet John (iv. 2) says, "Jesus himself *baptized not.*" Of the household of Stephanas, Paul says, (1 Cor. xvi. 15,) "It is the first *fruits* of Achaia, and they have *addicted themselves to the ministry of the saints.*" Paul preached the word of the Lord *to all that were in the house* of the jailer, and it is said (Acts 16) that he believed in God, and rejoiced in God with *all his house.*" There is no evidence that there were any children in the household of Lydia, and from the last clause of the chapter that gives us an account of her conversion and baptism, it appears that her household consisted of *brethren*—probably the servants that attended her on her trading journey. And have you never found any whole households that "believed and were baptized," in your denomination?

B. Yes, several. I called on a family of this kind not long since, in the town of Willington, Con. The father and mother and seven children and an apprentice, had all become members of the Baptist Church in that town. Such instances are not unfrequent among us. I believe you did not express your views of the argument drawn from circumcision.

P. I can see no analogy between the circumcision of a *male* Hebrew child, and the baptism of a *female* child of a believing Gentile. And if baptism came in the room of circumcision, I wonder the change was not thought of by the apostolical council to whom the dissension about circumcision was referred. It would have been easy for them to remove the difficulty by simply saying, "Baptism came in the room of circumcision, and is to be observed by believers in its stead;" but they "gave no such commandment." See Acts xv. 1–31.

B. You said you wished to converse with me on the *peculiarities* of the Baptist denomination. But thus far your sentiments and mine are the same. I can see no difference between us.

P. You will find there is one point at least on which we shall widely differ.

B. I would now ask you what that is, but the time for meeting has come; we will now close our conversation, and if you please, resume it again this evening at my house.

P. Very well. I will call at 8 o'clock.

B. Good evening, brother Peter. I am glad to see you. Be seated. Ever since our conversation this morning, I have been trying to imagine what you could mean by that "one point on which we shall widely differ."

P. There is one thing, and one only, which prevents me from being a Baptist; but that one thing seems to be an insuperable barrier.

B. Do tell me what it is.

P. O, your close communion!

B. Do we not commune just as you do? The only difference I can see is, we celebrate the Lord's Supper at the close of the day instead of the morning, because we think this season better adapted to the idea of a *Supper*. What do you mean by close communion?

P. You do not receive Christians of other denominations, and this is a great stumbling block to me.

B. Let me ask you one question, and the answer, I have reason to anticipate, will show that our difference of opinion on this point is not so wide as you imagine. Do you believe that baptism is a pre-requisite to communion?

P. Certainly; though I confess I should like to hear some of your reasons for considering it so.

B. I will give them with pleasure.

Christ commissioned his disciples to "Go teach (disciple) all nations"—admitting them immediately to the Lord's Supper? No; "*baptizing* them," &c. They were then to teach them all things which he had commanded. One of the commands afterwards to be taught the baptized disciples was, "Do this in remembrance of me." According to this commission, when Ananias became satisfied that Saul had become a disciple, he said to him, "Arise,"—and what next? Come to the table of the Lord? No. "Arise, and be *baptized*." He afterwards "assayed to join himself to the disciples." We have another example in the manner of building the Church at Jerusalem on the day of Pentecost. By consulting the second chapter of Acts, you will find that the joyful converts were first *baptized*, and then continued steadfastly in the Apostles' doctrine, in fellowship, in "*breaking of bread*," &c. Baptism seems to have been considered by all denominations (that have held to external ordinances at all) as a rite which should precede the reception of the Lord's Supper.

Justin Martyr says, "This food is called by us the Eucharist; of which it is *not lawful* for any to partake, but such as believe the things taught by us to be true, and have been *baptized*." Dr. Wall informs us, that "*No church* ever gave the communion to *any* persons before they were baptized. Among all the absurdities that ever were held, none ever maintained *that*, that any person should partake of the communion *before* he was baptized." Dr. Doddridge tells us, "It is certain that, as far as our knowledge of primitive antiquity reaches, *no unbaptized person* received the Lord's Supper." Again: "*How excellent soever* any man's character is, he must be *baptized before* he can be looked upon as completely a member of the Church of Christ." Mr. Baxter remarks—"What man dare to go in a way which hath neither precept nor example to warrant it, from a way that hath a full current of both? Yet they that will admit members into the visible church *without baptism*, do so." Equally to the point is the assertion of Dr. Dwight, late President of Yale College. He says: "It is an *indispensable qualification* for this ordinance, that the candidate for communion be a member of the visible Church of Christ, in full standing. By this I intend—that he should be a person of piety; that he should have made a public profession of religion; *and that he should have been baptized.*" And how is it in your church? Does your minister require candidates for admission first to be baptized?

P. I never knew him to receive any who had not been baptized according to his views of baptism. Indeed, I do not know of a Presbyterian or Congregational church in the country, that would admit persons to the communion *whom they considered unbaptized.* I never supposed that this ever could consistently be dispensed with in the churches; but I confess I never saw before so strong reasons in favor of first requiring baptism of candidates for admission to church privileges.

B. Well. You see that the principle on which we and all other denominations act in this instance, is precisely the same. Your minister believes that sprinkling, pouring, and plunging, are all equally valid baptism; and therefore invites such as are sprinkled, poured, and plunged, to the communion. My minister believes with Paul, that there is but "*one* baptism," and that is immersion; he therefore can invite only the immersed. There is no close *communion* here; if there is any closeness, it is close *baptism*. The Baptists and all other Christians refuse to commune with the unbaptized. The question then his, What is baptism? If we agree in settling this question, then there is no difference between us. And as they all believe that immersion is valid baptism, I have often wondered that they do not practice immersion instead of sprinkling, and end the strife. They have no doubt that we are baptized; if they had, they would not receive us. We do conscientiously doubt the validity of sprinkling for baptism. The sacrifice on their part to produce conformity would be nothing; on ours it would be the sacrifice of honest, conscientious principle.

P. I now see that your churches and ours act on the same principle respecting the admission of persons to the sacrament, but still I wish to name a few objections to your practice, which have existed in my mind, and which, I freely acknowledge, still have some influence upon me.

B. Go on, my brother; let me know all your difficulties on this subject.

P. You know the communion table is called the Lord's table; how then can you refuse to admit the Lord's people?

B. The very fact that it is the *Lord's* table, furnishes the answer. If it were *our* table, we would invite whom we pleased; but as it is the Lord's table, we must consult his word, and extend the invitation to those only who, by the Saviour's commission, and the apostolic examples, we find allowed to partake—viz., baptized believers.

And I think I can convince you that your minister does not invite all the Lord's people to come to the Lord's table.

P. O, he says he "can freely receive all that Christ has received."

B. But does not Mr. Goodman belong to his congregation,

and does not your minister believe that he has a name descriptive of his character?

P. Yes. I have often heard him regret that a man so eminently pious and exemplary should remain year after year, out of the church, where his influence is so much needed.

B. Mr. Goodman attends meeting on communion days, I suppose.

P. Yes; no man is more constant in his attendance on public worship.

B. And is he invited to come to the Lord's table?

P. O no. He was never baptized. He never joined the church.

B. And I have been told that within two months, many in your congregation have experienced religion.

P. Yes. A large number indeed have become pious.

B. Any of them before the last communion?

P. Yes; more than forty.

B. Is your minister satisfied with their piety?

P. I heard him say that he was never better satisfied with young converts.

B. Did he invite them to the Lord's table?

P. O no.

B. What! debar Mr. Goodman and more than forty others of the Lord's people from the Lord's table? Surely he is on the Baptist ground. And I have been told, too, that his mother and one sister are among the converts. How could he refuse to commune with his own mother and sister?

P. None of these had been admitted to membership, and I am now convinced that piety alone, even when found in our dearest earthly connections, does not give them a right to the Lord's table. The Lord's people must, if they come at all, come in the Lord's way. But what do you say to them, provided they seem to be *sincere?*

B. We tell them that sincerity is no proof of correctness. Saul of Tarsus was sincere before his conversion. He thought

18

he was doing God service when he was persecuting the church; and John Newton was sincere after his conversion, in continuing in the slave trade, until his eyes were opened to see the evil of this abominable traffic. But the sincerity of these men did not prove their conduct to be justifiable. But if sincerity be admitted as an evidence of correctness, then we claim to be correct ourselves; for we are as sincere in refusing to commune with those whom we consider unbaptized, as they are in refusing to commune with those whom *they* consider unbaptized.

P. I have another question which I presume you have often heard, and which has been a source of some perplexity to me —"If we cannot commune together on earth, how can we in heaven?"

B. "We plead for a communion on earth, with Christians of every sect, which shall bear a resemblance to that of heaven. We do not suppose that the communion of the 'just made perfect' consists in partaking of the symbols of Christ's death, but in high and spiritual intercourse; in mutual expressions of admiration and gratitude, while reviewing the dispensations of providence and grace towards them in this world; in mingled songs of praise to Him who hath washed them from their sins in his own blood; and in exalted converse concerning the glorious scenes which the revolutions of eternity will be continually unfolding to their delighted gaze. In such communion as this, although of a more humble character, we would be glad to participate with *all good men.*"

P. Really, my brother Benjamin, you have answered my questions in a clear and satisfactory manner. I am convinced of the correctness of your principles, and the consistency of your conduct. I see that the Baptist churches act in accordance with apostolic usage, and with the universal practice of Presbyterian and other churches, in requiring baptism as a pre-requisite to communion. I have for some time past been convinced that immersion is the only baptism, and believers the only subjects of the ordinance; and I am now more fully confirmed in the opinion that baptism should *in every instance precede communion.* But what shall I do? My parents and many other relatives belong to the Presbyterian Church. I receive much patronage in my business from the wealthy and respectable part of that church; I shall give offence by dissolving my connection, and you will admit that baptism is not really essential to salvation.

B. I will admit that baptism is not essential to salvation. The Baptists are so far from believing this, that they consider no one entitled to baptism, who is not in a state of salvation. Faith is essential to salvation; immersion is as essential to baptism, as roundness to a ball; and baptism is an essential pre-requisite to communion. Is not baptism as essential as communion? Are not both *external* ordinances? The Jews were required on one occasion to offer a *red* heifer. Had they a right to say, the color is *non-essential?* A white one will answer as well? Was not *redness* essential to obedience? But, my dear brother, will you do nothing for the honor of Christ, which is not absolutely essential to your salvation? "Is this thy kindness to thy friend?" Are you not to obey all his commands, and to imitate his examples, even though he might possibly save you if you were to neglect some of them? You must forsake father and mother, and brother and sister, and wife, and houses, and lands, if you would follow Christ, and be a consistent disciple.

Your mind is confessedly enlightened with regard to the institutions established in beautiful order and simplicity by Him who evinced his love to you, by freely giving his blood as a ransom for your soul.

"If ye *know* these things, happy are ye if ye *do* them."

P. The love of Christ constraineth me: and fearless of consequences, I will make haste, and delay not to keep his commandments.

PART III.

BAPTIST CHURCH POLITY, GOVERNMENT AND PRACTICE.

CHAPTER I.

1. The Bible the Law of the Church. 2. The Church a Spiritual Body. 3. The Independence and Unity of the Church.

1. THAT the Bible is the only law of the Church, appears in the first article of the Confession of Faith we have published, to which the reader is referred. We wish only to say, in addition, that this is the fundamental law of the Church. The Church is not a legislative, but an executive body. Her office is to execute the laws of God, and not to re-enact, increase or diminish them. This simplifies her work beyond measure, and imparts confidence to her decisions. As she tries every thing by the law and the testimony, the Bible, so she is to be thus tried. The only question she has to settle is, what saith the infallible rule, the Bible? And when she departs from it, she is of no authority. It is on this ground that the Baptist Church has from the commencement resisted, unto death, all innovations upon Bible laws in church affairs. On this foundation she has ever stood out in the world alone. Imperfect in spirit, as she humbly confesses, she claims to be perfect in laws, because she knows none but those of God. It is on this

ground that she rejects sprinkling for baptism, infant baptism, union of Church and State, persecution for belief, and superior and inferior orders of ministers.

To the Bible, then, we turn for the true and only church polity. What were the primitive churches? What their government, their practice, their officers, their discipline, their duties and privileges, and the like? The church which will not stand this test, is no church of Christ. It is because we believe the Baptist churches will stand it, that we commend them to all.

2. The Church is a spiritual, and not a secular institution. "My kingdom," said the Saviour, "is not of this world." In what sense is this passage to be understood? It is *for* the world, and is *in* the world; still it is not *of* the world. It is not for any secular purpose, civil or political, but is spiritual in its nature, promoting piety, and pointing to heaven. The union of Church and State is impossible; as the State is a secular institution, existing for such purposes, and securing its ends often by physical force. The Church is another kingdom, existing for another purpose, and promoted by other means. "If my kingdom," said the Saviour, "were of this world, then would my servants fight, that I should not be delivered to the Jews; but now is my kingdom not from hence." The conscience is not to be intimidated by the secular power, but is to be free to choose or reject the good and evil set before it. All secular dignity and ostentation are out of place in the church, where all are "brethren," acknowledging no "Master" but Jesus.

As the Baptist Church has always claimed these principles for herself, so she has freely and fully accorded them to others. As she has never admitted the right of the secular power to control her, and has given up her members to death by millions, in vindication of her rights and duty, so she has never resorted to persecution to make converts, and has yet her first death to cause, or act of oppression, for conscience sake, to perform. Pointing triumphantly to her history, in confirmation of her position, and to her cruel wrongs from Catholics and Protestants, Reformers and Pilgrim Fathers, as evidence of her patience and humility under suffering, her language is:

"It's not with flashing steel;
It's not with cannon's peal,
Or stir of drum;
But in the bonds of love,—
Our white flag floats above,—
Its emblem is the dove,—
It's thus we come."

3. The independence and yet unity of the Church. Churches are independent of each other, and of all ecclesiastical bodies, and solely accountable to God. They acknowledge no head or control, but Jehovah; and no law but the Bible. "Be ye not called Rabbi," said the Saviour, "for *one* is your Master, even Christ, and all ye are brethren." It is an assumption for any individual or combination to attempt to control or intimidate any church of Christ. The smallest, poorest church on earth is independent of all but Jehovah. It by no means follows that the largest, richest church in the city or country, has the most piety or wisdom, or is in any sense in a condition to dictate to others. The churches of the Bible, large and small, rich and poor, in the city and country, are addressed as equally distinct accountable bodies, required to act for themselves nobly, in the fear of God. We read of "the churches throughout all Judea," of "Galatia," "Asia," "Macedonia," "Corinth," "Cencrea," &c. There is not the least intimation of any combination of churches, for the control of others, in the word of God. Much less is there any intimation of any other ecclesiastical combination, as council, association, or synod, for the control of the churches. Jehovah approaches the churches directly, and all of them equally. The true place of other ecclesiastical combinations is in subordination to the Church, and deriving their authority from her.

And yet the churches are one, in that they have the same Lord, the same work, the same motives, and the same heaven. But they are one, as the particles of the earth, or the drops of the ocean. In this manner they exist in harmony as fellow-laborers, but not as dictators; and in proportion as they are founded upon Christ, and governed by his laws, will they be at the same time one, and yet distinct.

CHAPTER II.

The Church. 1. Origin and meaning of the term. 2. Formation of a Church. 3. The power, rights and duties of a Church—her power executive; she should extend the reign of Christ; select, educate, license, ordain, and support ministers of the Gospel; and choose her own officers.

1. *Origin and Meaning of the term Church.*—The English word church is supposed to be derived from a Greek word, meaning "pertaining to the Lord." The Greek word is Κυϱιακõν; the Saxon circe; the German kirche; Scottish kirk. The word in the New Testament, hence, generally translated church, is εκκλησια, (ecclesia,) meaning literally "called out or summoned." It does not therefore necessarily mean a religious assembly, but is so commonly used to designate such, that for all practical purposes, it is a sufficiently definite use of the term. See 1 Cor. i. 2; Rev. ii. 7, &c. Rev. William Crowell, in his excellent "Church Members' Manual," says—"A church, in the language of the inspired writers, is a society of believers, who meet in one place for the worship of God, and for the united observance of the ordinances of the gospel. In this sense the word occurs in the singular number upwards of fifty times, and the word churches upwards of thirty times,

in the New Testament. It is used with other significations in about sixteen or eighteen instances." Chancellor King, an Episcopalian, in his distinguished "Inquiry into the Constitution, Discipline, Unity and Worship of the Primitive Church," says: "The usual and common acceptation of the word (church) is that of a particular church, that is, a society of Christians meeting together in one place, under their proper pastors, for the performance of religious worship, and the exercising of Christian discipline."

It follows, that while in a sense any assembly may be called a church, the term is most properly applied to Christian assemblies; and that the Church of Christ is an assembly according to his directions.

2. *Formation of a Church.*—Nothing is more natural than that the disciples of Christ living near each other should become acquainted, and find they have views in common; and that it is for their interest, and is their duty, to combine for their mutual edification and happiness, and for the propagation and defence of "the faith once delivered to the saints." A Christian moves into a new place. One of the first things occurring to him is, is there a church here of which I can approve? If there is, he joins it by a letter from the church of which he was previously a member. If not, the next question is, are there any fellow-disciples, and in sufficient numbers to justify a combination for Christian purposes? The number justifying such a step, depends on circumstances, of which those particularly concerned must judge. A very small number answers the purpose, as we have no rule, human or divine, settling the question of numbers. It is better for a small number to associate, than for them to live separately, unknown to each other. At the same time, common sense dictates that a small, weak body should be prudent in their attempts to construct a house of worship, or to support a minister of the gospel, lest they should bring reproach upon the cause by failure. No such considerations, however, should prevent the combination

of any number of disciples of Christ in a given place, for the advancement of piety. Such a combination is a church; and, if constructed after the plan of the New Testament, is a church of Christ.

Brethren and sisters meeting together thus, and desiring further association with those of other places, can without difficulty ascertain to which of the denominations around them they belong; and apply to some of the neighboring churches of the same for recognition. When delegates are appointed, ordinarily consisting of the pastor and two or three brethren from some half-dozen or dozen neighboring churches, who assemble on a given day, and examine the views of the applying church, and if satisfied with their views, recognize them as a church of the same faith and order as themselves, by public divine service, generally by a sermon, charge, hand of fellowship, and devotional exercises. Thus any company of disciples become a church, by their own association, in conformity with the New Testament, and thus they become a church of the Baptist denomination.

This is a simple but natural state of things, not adverse to the New Testament, but in harmony with it, as far as can be gathered from its pages, so silent upon the method in which the primitive churches came into being, and entirely without laws for the constitution of future churches.

We know that brethren and sisters in Jerusalem, Antioch, Corinth, &c., became the churches of these places, for so the New Testament teaches; but as to just how the combination was accomplished, we are not informed, nor is it of any consequence. We presume it was as we have described. At the baptism on the day of Pentecost, we read, "the same day there were added unto them about three thousand souls." When Saul of Tarsus was converted, and baptized, he "assayed to join himself to the church," and though rejected at first, on account of his previous character, the brethren doubting his being a true disciple, yet, when introduced by Barnabas, he was received as a brother beloved. We have only such fragmentary intimations of the formation of the primitive churches, and their method of growth. As far as possible, we follow the primitive mode, and adopt such other rules as, in the silence of the Scriptures, seem desirable, and which do not contravene the laws of God.

3. *The Power, Rights, and Duties of the Church.*—By the power of the Church, we mean (to adopt one of Webster's definitions of the complicated term) "her command, right of governing, dominion, rule, sway, authority." Her power is executive, and not legislative. The Saviour's language is, (see Matt. xxviii. 18,) "All power is given unto me in heaven and in earth." All the power the church has, is derived from Him, and in her intercourse with the world, other churches, and individuals, she must govern herself accordingly. She has only to inquire, what doth the Head of the Church direct in any given case? So far, and no farther, may she go. To make rules governing her in this respect, in her ever-changing relations, is not necessary, if it were possible. To the word of God she must resort in every case; and so simple are its laws, that she need be in no doubt on this subject. She is no church of Christ, and has no power of any kind, as such, if she is not sufficiently imbued with the spiritual element, to conform entirely to His laws for her government.

The right and duty of the church is implied in what follows in the general command of the Saviour, in which he asserts his exclusive authority in heaven and in earth, quoted above. (See Matt. xxviii. 18–20.) "Go ye, therefore, and teach all nations, baptizing them in the name of the Father, and of the Son, and of the Holy Ghost: teaching them to observe all things whatsoever I have commanded you, and lo, I am with you always, even unto the end of the world. Amen."

It follows that she *may* and *should* do what she can for the extension of the reign of Christ. Her "field is the world," and her work is not done until "the kingdoms of this world are become the kingdoms of our Lord, and of his Christ." She has a spiritual kingdom to extend, however, and must accomplish it by spiritual means. All nations are to be "taught," and gathered into the kingdom of Christ as they are taught, convinced, persuaded. Is she to "compel them to come in, that his house may be filled," it is the compulsion of teaching, moral suasion.

Missionary societies, under the control of the church, have been resorted to, not because the Bible provides directly for them, but because they are supposed to be no infringement upon the Saviour's laws and successful church methods of accomplishing her work. Too much caution, however, cannot be used to prevent such societies from being above the church, and to confine them strictly to the Divine plan of promoting the growth of his kingdom. It is the right and duty of the church alone to extend the reign of Christ. It is indeed the right and duty of individual disciples to promote the cause of Christ, but it is also their right and duty to be members of the church, and as such, with such sanction, they can be most useful.

The church by her members can and should go into adjoining regions, as well as into distant ones, and teach and baptize and gather the converts into churches. They in turn should do likewise, and thus the cause is to be promoted until the end, until all churches militant are merged in the Church triumphant.

Each church has the right and is in duty bound to govern itself after the Divine method. While any individual may "assay" to join any church of Christ, as Paul did the "disciples at Jerusalem," the disciples must judge whether "he *is* a disciple," and can on the Saviour's authority be received as one of them.

It is the Saviour's requirement that the members of the Church should love each other, and walk together in the ordinances and duties and privileges of his house blameless. The church is to judge of the conduct of members, and discipline them according to the laws made and provided in the case in the Bible. See article in this work on the subject of Discipline.

It is the right and the duty of the church to sympathize with her members in all suitable matters. Most fully is this treated in Rom. 12th chapter, which should be engraven on the heart of every member of the body of Christ. "Lo, we being many (5th verse), are one body in Christ, and every one members one of another." Ordinary intelligence and piety will regulate the use of this passage, and indeed the chapter, and save church members, on the one hand, from an unsuitable intrusion, and on the other, from cold and selfish indifference and neglect. Ample provisions are made in the laws of Christ for the pecuniary aid of poor members of the church. John iii. 16–18. "Hereby perceive we the love of God, because he laid down his life for us; and we ought to lay down our lives for the brethren. But whoso hath this world's good, and seeth his brother have need, and shutteth up his bowels of compassion for him, how dwelleth the love of God in him? My little children, let us not love in word, neither in tongue, but in deed and in truth." See also 2 Cor. chap's 8th and 9th; and kindred passages.

It is the right and duty of the church to look to God for ministers; and, receiving such as he may give them, to provide for their preparation, their induction into the sacred office, their support; and for their discipline, if it becomes necessary. Matt. ix. 37, 38. "Then said he unto his disciples, the harvest truly is plenteous, but the laborers are few; pray ye, therefore, the Lord of the harvest, that he will send forth laborers into his harvest." God is pleased to give the church in answer to prayer such ministers as she needs. Eph. iv. 11, 12. "And he gave some apostles; and some prophets; and some evangelists; and some pastors and teachers; for the perfecting of the saints—for the work of the ministry—for the edifying of the body of Christ."

It follows that those to whom God has committed this important work are responsible for it. They cannot transfer it to one or many of their number of the clergy or laity. It is sufficient, also, to task the energies of the entire church. God has provided that his ministers shall be intelligent, able men, and it follows that the church should provide whatever may be necessary for the accomplishment of his plan. Induction into the sacred office by license and ordination, also belongs to the church, as God has committed to her the control of the ministry, and has not given these particulars of it to others.

"A license to preach the gospel" is the appointment of a member by the church to the office. She is prudently, in the fear of God, and in the light of the scriptures, to decide the probabilities of his being called of God to the work of the ministry, and on conviction of the fact, she gives him a certificate, called a license. This seems necessary in acknowledgment of her right and duty; for his commendation to others; and to prevent imposition on the part of those who may wrongfully assume the sacred office.

The "ordination" of ministers of the gospel is amply provided for in the scriptures. Acts xiv. 23. And when they had ordained them elders in every church, and had prayed with fasting, they commended them to the Lord on whom they believed. Titus i. 5. "For this cause I left thee in Crete, that thou shouldst set in order the things that are wanting, and ordain elders in every city, as I had appointed thee."

Rev. William Crowell, in his "Church Member's Manual," a work having the sanction of several worthy names, particularly of Rev. Henry G. Ripley, D. D., Professor of Sacred Rhetoric and Pastoral Duties in the Newton Theological Institution, says of ordination: "It consists of two things; first, the election by the church of one to be their pastor, or to perform some ministerial service in their behalf, either to them, or as an evangelist to the destitute. Second, his solemn induction or inauguration, in which the ministry publicly recognize him as one of their number, welcome him to their brotherhood, and by the consent and acting in behalf of their respective churches, pledge to him the fellowship, confidence, and affection of the ministry and churches. *The first is the essential act, without which no one could be properly invested with the office and functions of a Christian minister.* The New Testament sustains no other ordination. What else has become custom in the case, should be distinguished from this, and used with great caution, on the ground that the laws of Christ are sufficient for his church.

"As it is desirable that the ministers of a given church may become the ministers of other churches, the rule generally in use of consulting other churches in the ordination of ministers is suitable, and is no infringement of the independence of the church, as she convenes the council, which of necessity derives its power to act from her. Besides, she may proceed contrary to its decisions, if she deems it her duty. Other churches, on this account, may reject her ministers or herself, but cannot interfere with her rights and duties."

We subjoin the following, upon licensing and ordaining members to preach the gospel, from Rules of Church Order, by Rev. J. Newton Brown, D. D.:

"Any member who, in the judgment of the church, gives evidence, by his piety, zeal, and 'aptness to teach,' that he is called of God to the work of the ministry, after having preached in the hearing of the church, may be licensed to preach the gospel of Jesus Christ, provided three-fourths of the members present at any regular meeting shall agree thereto.

"If the church unanimously decide that one of its licensed preachers possesses the scriptural qualifications for full ordination, they shall call a council of ministers and brethren to examine the qualifications of the candidate, to which council the propriety of ordaining shall be wholly referred."

We quote also, on this topic, from Notes on Baptist Principles, attributed to Rev. Dr. Wayland:

I intended, at an earlier period, to have offered some suggestions on the subject of the licensure and ordination of ministers. What I should, perhaps, have done before, I will endeavor to do now.

I have often heard our mode of licensing ministers spoken of with marked disrespect. It has been said, How can we have any improvement in the ministry, while the authority of licensing ministers is held by the church? What do common, uneducated brethren know about the fitness of a man to preach the gospel? I do not say that other men have heard such remarks—I only say that I have heard them myself.

Now, with this whole course of remark, I have not the remotest sympathy. I believe that our mode is not only as good as any other, but farther than this, that it is, more nearly than any other, conformed to the principles of the New Testament. Let our churches, then, never surrender this authority to ministers, or to councils, or to any other organization whatever. I believe that Christ has placed it in their hands, and they have no right to delegate it. Let them use it in the manner required by the Master, and it can be placed in no safer hands.

In the Episcopal Church, the candidate is admitted to the ministry by the Bishop. In the Lutheran Church, I believe, substantially in the same manner. In the Presbyterian Church, it is done by Presbyteries. Have these means been successful in keeping the ministry pure in doctrine, and holy in practice? How is it in the established Church of England? How is it in the Lutheran churches in Germany, of whose tender mercies our own brother Oncken has had so large an experience? How is it with the old Presbyterian Church of Scotland? Of the former condition of this last, we may inform ourselves, by reading "Witherspoon's Characteristics." How much they have improved of late years, the secession of the Free Church might possibly inform us. But to bring this matter to a test, would we exchange our ministry, just as it is, for the ministry of either of these churches at the present day? Or, take our own country, where freedom of opinion, and the watchfulness of other denominations has had a powerful influence over these churches, in matters of admission to the ministry, and look at the result. The object of a church of Christ is to subdue the world to God. Which mode of admitting men to the ministry has here been most successful in this respect? For a long time after the settlement of the colonies, Baptist sentiments were confined almost exclusively to Rhode Island. Some of our Rhode Island ministers were whipped and imprisoned for holding a private religious meeting in Lynn, Massachusetts. The Revolution, however, abolished, for the most part, the power of the established orders, and our sentiments began to extend. At this period we were few and feeble. The men have but recently died, who remembered when our whole denomination embraced but two or three associations. The land was filled with Congregational, Presbyterian and Episcopalian churches. We now, I presume, outnumber them all, and we should have outnumbered them to a vastly greater extent, had we not swerved from our original practices and principles, for the sake of imitating our neighbors. We need not certainly speak lightly of a ministry, or of a mode of introducing men to the ministry, which has led to such remarkable results.

We want no change in our mode of licensing candidates. We do, however, need that the subject should receive more attention, and that in this, as in everything connected with the Church of Christ, we should specially act in the fear of God. If a church will act in this matter, with conscientious desire to please the Master, we know of no better hands into which we could entrust the power of admission to the ministry. Some twenty-five years since, I knew a church refuse a license to two young men, to whom, I presume, it would have been readily granted by almost any Bishop or Presbytery. Both were graduates of college; one was among the first scholars in his class, but his delivery was so exceedingly dull, that he could by no possibility interest an audience. He was refused a license, because the brethren could obtain no evidence that he was called to the work, inasmuch as he had *no aptness to teach.* He, however, persevered, obtained a license from some church less scrupulous, and, if I mistake not, went through a Theological Seminary, and received what is called a thorough training; but I think he was never called to be the pastor of any church, and, so far as I know, never entered upon the work of the ministry. The other was the case of a young man of brilliant powers of elocution, and very respectable scholarship, but of erratic and eccentric character. The same church refused to license him, because they deemed him wanting in the sobriety of character and consistency of example, which are required in a minister of Jesus Christ. Subsequent events proved that they did not act without good reason. If all our churches would act in this manner, we should want to go no further to find a safe depository of the power of admitting men to the ministry. If, on the other hand, we are false to ourselves, and treat this subject as a matter of form, to be acted upon without thought, or much consideration, it is not our principles, but ourselves that are in fault. Any system that man could devise, would make mischief, if it were treated with the thoughtlessness which I fear is fast overspreading many of our churches.

Let us, then, look for a moment upon this subject, as our churches profess to understand it. We believe that there is such a thing as a call to the ministry; that is, that a man is moved to enter upon this work by the Holy Spirit. This call is manifested in two ways; first, in his own heart; and secondly, in the hearts of his brethren. So far as he himself is concerned, it appears in the form of a solemn conviction of duty resting upon him, with such weight that he believes it impossible for him to please Christ in any other way than in preaching the gospel. He dares not enter upon any other pursuit, until he has made every effort in his power to be admitted to this work. I beg these remarks to be remembered. They may be considered by many as obsolete and behind the age. It may be so, and yet the age may be wrong. There is a word of prophecy surer than this age, or than any age. I know it is common to hear men, even among Baptists, talk of the choice of a profession, and of balancing in their minds whether they should be lawyers, ministers, or physicians. They will say, perhaps, they dislike the turmoil of politics, the hard and irregular labor of a physician, the monotony of teaching; they are fond of study, of writing, and of quiet mental improvement; and besides, they can enter the ministry, be married and settled so much more easily than would be possible in any other profession, that they, on the whole, prefer it. Now I would always dissuade such a man from entering the ministry at all. If he could, with just as clear a conscience, be a lawyer as a minister, let him be a lawyer by all means. The Church of Christ can do without him. He proposes to enter the ministry of reconciliation from mere selfish motives, and the Saviour has no occasion of his services. He makes a convenience of the ministry of the word, he uses it to promote his own objects, he is a hireling whose own the sheep are not. If he begins in this way, in this way he will, unless the grace of God prevent, continue. He will soon tire of the work, and leave it for something else, or he will continue in it, to shed around him on every side the example of well-educated, cold, worldly-minded selfishness.

And here, at the risk of being considered a Puritan of the deepest dye, I must hazard another remark. This notion of considering the ministry in the same light as any other profession, to be preferred merely on the ground of personal advantage, is working very grave evils in the Church of Christ. I rejoice, however, to declare that I believe these views to be much less prevalent among Baptists than among other denominations. A young man preparing for the ministry with these views, feels himself much in the condition of any other professional student. He takes frequently a pride in sinking every thing that smacks of the cloth. He is anxious to appear a man of the world. He will talk over fashionable insipidity and personal gossip, with the most amusing volubility. He converses about his sermons, as a young lawyer would about his pleas or political harangues. He is more at home at the evening party, than at the bed-side of the dying, and is oftener seen at the concert than the prayer-meeting. If any one should suggest that such a life was not quite consistent with the character of a young evangelist, he would probably ask, with most amusing innocence, What is the harm of all this? He means to discharge his professional duties, and this being done, why should he not indulge his tastes and love of society, just as well as any other professional man? The Apostle James seemed to think his question unanswerable, when he asked, "Doth a fountain send forth at the same place sweet water and bitter? Can a fig tree, my brethren, bear olive berries, either a vine, figs? so can no fountain both yield salt water and fresh." Many of our young evangelists, however, have found out the way in which this can be done. The same lips can discuss the insipidities of fashion during the week, and the solemn truths of repentance towards God, and the eternal judgment, on the Sabbath. Brethren, these things ought not so to be.

Suppose such a man enters the ministry and assumes the care of souls. He is continually comparing himself with men of other professions. *They* strive to advance themselves, why should *he* not do the same? His object is not to convert souls, but to distinguish himself as a writer, or speaker, and thus to secure some more eligible professional situation, a church in a city, a splendid edifice, a congregation of the rich, the fashionable and well-conditioned. Or, he may desire the fame of a lecturer, or may seek for any other form of distinction and notoriety, to which success in the pulpit may conduct him. If the ministry of the gospel is like other professions, why should he not? But if the Holy Ghost has called him to follow in the footsteps of Christ, and has committed immortal souls to his charge, and if he will be called to account for the proof which he has given of the ministry; in a word, if religion be a reality and no sham, if the crown of glory be bestowed only on those who fight the good fight, if only those who turn sinners to righteousness shall shine as the stars forever—why, then, it is a very different matter.

It is the right and duty of the church to support her ministry. It is God's plan that the ministry should be "wholly" devoted to its appropriate work. See Acts vi. 4 and 1 Tim. iv. 15. With an exclusive confinement to their appropriate work, they may well exclaim, "who is sufficient for these things?"

As a necessary concomitant of this principle, the church is bound to support her ministers. The passages are very numerous in the scriptures on this topic. We give only a specimen of them: Luke x. 1–8; 1 Cor. ix. 7–14. The expressions, in the former, "For the laborer is worthy of his hire;" and in the latter, "Even so hath the Lord ordained, that they which preach the gospel shall live of the gospel," sufficiently indicate the obligation of the church.

While the church is not to support her ministers in indolence or extravagance, it is perfectly obvious she should give them a living which is ample and fair; removed at once from ostentation on the one hand, and contempt and inadequacy on the other. Ministers may find it their duty to toil for little or no pecuniary aid, when blessed with an abundance from other sources; or when toiling for the good of the cause with a very poor church. But these are exceptions to the Divine rule, found indeed in the scriptures, but not in any way to infringe upon the rule. Paul labored with his hands for his support, but in some manner as we suggest, claiming at the same time his right to a support.

Churches should insist on their right and duty to sustain their ministers amply, according to their circumstances, that he may have an entire heart and mind to labor exclusively for the cause.

For the right and duty of churches to discipline their ministers, and to sustain public worship, we refer to articles "Discipline," and "Meetings."

It hardly need be added that it is the right and duty of the church to choose her own officers. Who else should choose them, or can in consistency with the obligation of the church?

If we had no direct Divine command or precedent on this subject, we should be thrown upon our natural rights to choose our own officers and servants. But we have Divine direction in that as we have seen it is the church to whom Christ commits the responsibility of obtaining ministers from him. The remark is equally true of deacons. Pastors and deacons are the only officers of the church, as we shall see. But what is more direct and perhaps more desirable evidence of the right and duty of the church to choose her own officers, is the practice of the primitive church. See Acts i. 15–26; Acts vi. 1–6; 2 Cor. viii. 19–23. The first of these passages is an account of the first assemblage of the disciples after the Saviour's ascension—in other words, the first meeting of the church at Jerusalem. Its object was to fill a vacancy in the Apostleship. "Peter stood up in the midst of the disciples" and proposed the filling of the vacancy, when "they (the disciples) appointed two" candidates, and in prayer asked God to direct their choice. "And they gave forth their lots; and the lot fell upon Matthias; and he was numbered with the eleven Apostles."

The next passage relates to the choice of deacons. The Apostles propose the appointment of deacons. "And the saying pleased the whole multitude, and they chose Stephen," &c., "whom they set before the Apostles."

The remaining passage concerns ministers appointed to go on an errand of charity for the church. The language of the passage is "chosen of the churches," and "messengers of the churches."

Precisely in this manner do the Baptist churches, as they ever have, perform this duty, not by a pope, or bishop, or synod, or presbytery, or council, but by their own vote.

CHAPTER III.

Members of the Church. 1. Spiritual persons. 2. How they become members. 3. Restoration of excluded members. 4. How persons of other denominations become members. 5. Rights and duties of church members.

1. CONVERSION and baptism are essential to membership in the church; and those who have experienced the one, and have submitted to the other, and they only, are entitled to the privilege. The kingdom of Christ is a spiritual kingdom, and its members of necessity must be spiritual persons. They only, and they ever, of whatever nation, "are fellow-citizens with the saints, and of the household of God." The commission is to teach and baptize and gather such into the kingdom; and it follows, only such.

That the primitive churches were composed of spiritual members, is also evident from the manner in which they were addressed, and all the circumstances attending primitive disciples. "Paul unto the church of God, which is at Corinth, to them who are sanctified in Christ Jesus, called to be saints." "To all the saints in Christ Jesus which are at Philippi." "They that gladly received the word were baptized; and the same day there were added unto them about three thousand souls." Saul of Tarsus was first converted, then baptized, and then received into the church. There is no greater perversion of the church, and no more certain method of death to her, than to admit unconverted, unbaptized persons to membership. Besides, it is inflicting great injury upon them, putting them in a false position, where they can neither be useful nor happy.

2. Individuals become members of the church, on application, and on giving evidence of the above-named qualifications, by election. Different churches have different rules of admission, but the only principles involved relate to the free offer of the candidate on his own part, and his free election on the part of the members of the church. The following is a common method in Baptist churches of reaching the above result; and most of its particulars are deemed essential, though in some minor points different usages prevail, and are admissible.

A person believes he is converted, and, as is common with those truly converted, he desires to join the church. He expresses his wish to a member of the church, who proposes him. Or some member believes him converted, and suggests that it is his duty to join, and, with his consent, proposes him. He then appears before the church, and relates his Christian experience. Any member proposes such questions as seem suitable to obtain an understanding of his views. He then retires, and if no member objects to him, he is elected to come into full membership, after baptism and the hand of fellowship. Previously to his examination, he is furnished with the articles of faith and rules of order in use in the church. While the intelligence and maturity of advanced experience is not expected or required of applicants, they must give evidence of conversion, and concur, in the main, in the belief and practice of the church, being fully settled on all plain fundamental principles. Any member is free to make suitable objections to him, and his conscientious scruples are regarded; but he is not permitted to insist on unreasonable, personal, and selfish objections. The examination is generally in private church-meeting, though not always, or necessarily; and the baptism and hand of fellowship, public. He is now a member in good and full standing, and can only be censured for his future conduct.

3. Excluded members of the church may be restored by suitable reformation and confession. Excluded members wishing to join other churches, should be restored to their original church, and come in regularly by letter. Cases may exist, however, in which it may be the duty of a church to receive excluded members of other churches on their experience, they being independent, and all churches being liable to errors in discipline. This is a vexed question, however, and great Christian prudence should characterize such action. On these several topics, see article "Discipline."

4. Persons of other denominations become members of Baptist churches by a relation of their Christian experience, as in the case of those who have not been members of any church.

5. The rights of church members are to the sympathy, and love, and watchful care of each other. They all have an equal voice and vote in all church matters. Each member has the right of private judgment, and is not liable to discipline therefor, provided his opinions are not fundamentally heretical, and he is evidently sincere in believing them in conformity with the word of God. All members, however, should be modest in their private judgment, while they maintain their rights in this direction. All are accountable to God for their opinions and usefulness, and are under obligations to him, to be insisted upon with humility against the world, if it becomes necessary.

We quote the following from Notes on the Principles and Practice of the Baptist churches, in the Examiner, attributed to Rev. Dr. Wayland:

"The private brethren of the church have *rights.* Jesus

Christ has called them to be his servants, and he has conferred on every one the privilege of working in his vineyard, and has promised to each laborer a rich reward. He has given to each servant some particular gift, and permitted him to use that gift for him. Of this right no man, or body of men, or ecclesiastical authority, may deprive him. Every Christian is Christ's freeman, and he has a right to labor for Christ in any place where his Master opens a door: and he is to seek diligently to ascertain where the door is opened for him."

On the general duties of church members, we quote from Rev. Dr. Brown's Rules of Church Order:

"The duties of members to *themselves* are, the acquisition of religious knowledge; constant progression in grace and spirituality; consistency of external conduct; and the control and eradication of every unholy temper.

It is the duty of members to honor, esteem, and love their *Pastor;* to pray for him, fervently and daily; to submit to him in the scriptural exercise of his official authority; to attend constantly upon his ministrations; to manifest a tender regard for his reputation; and to contribute towards his support, in proportion to their ability.

It is the duty of each member to cultivate and cherish brotherly love for all other members of the church; to visit and sympathize with them in affliction; to pray with and for them; to administer pecuniary relief to those who are necessitous; tenderly to regard their reputation; affectionately and privately to admonish them for faults and improprieties; and to strive by all proper measures to promote their spiritual benefit and prosperity.

Toward those who are not connected with the church, it is the duty of members to bear a prudent testimony against evil practices; to be exact in fulfilling obligations and performing promises; to live in a peaceable and neighborly manner; to perform offices of kindness and charity; to set an example of industry, honesty, and generosity; and, as opportunity and

20

ability may enable, to commend the religion of the gospel unto them.

It is the duty of all members removing from the vicinity of the church, to take letters of dismission to other churches of the same denomination; but should this not be practicable, to furnish their names and places of residence within three months after leaving the church."

CHAPTER IV.

Officers of the Church. 1. A Church may exist without them. 2. Bishops or Pastors and Deacons the only Officers. 3. Terms applied to Officers of the Church. 4. The authority, rights and duties of Pastors. 5. The origin, ordination, and duties of Deacons. 6. Other servants of the Church.

1. A CHURCH may exist without officers, but it is in the most limited sense of the term, as a mere "assembly" or "congregation." God has provided officers for his Church. The primitive churches had them, as have had all efficient ones since; and it may well be doubted if any combination can claim to be a church of Christ without them.

2. The only legitimate officers of the church are Bishops, or Pastors and Deacons. The Church at Philippi is thus addressed, (see Phil. i. 1,) "Paul and Timothy, the servants of Jesus Christ, to all the saints in Christ Jesus which are at Philippi, with the Bishops and Deacons." Here we have the true Church of Christ complete, consisting of members, bishops and deacons. In Paul's directions to Timothy, he particularly describes these two classes of officers, and no others. 1 Tim. iii. 1–10. "A bishop, then, must be blameless," &c. "Likewise must the deacons be grave," &c. The character and duties of these officers in the church, are named and

described in the above passage, in a manner to show their importance and permanence. Rev. Mr. Crowell has well remarked—"The wants of a church are all provided for in these two offices. They have no more occasion for the services of prelates, or diocesan bishops, to govern churches, and ordain ministers, and administer discipline, than a civil State has for those of an autocrat, or a dictator." It is singular, indeed, particularly in a republican country, that men will tolerate in the Church what they will not in the State, especially when Jehovah has forbidden it in the Church, by making *her* the responsible power.

Bishops, Pastors and other Preachers of the Gospel—Their Equality.

That other names of ministers do occur in the Scriptures, is obvious, but it is also obvious that some of them are limited to particular periods and duties, and some of them are synonymous with pastor. It is, in part, because this fact has been overlooked, that we have in some churches (never in Baptist churches) more officers than we have named, and they of different grades in the ministry. For instance, the words bishop and pastor are synonymous in the Scriptures, but some churches have assumed that they are not only different offices, but of different grades, and hence have their bishop over the churches, including their pastors; and, in addition, their pastors over the churches.

Another innovation upon the Scriptures, of more recent origin, and no more culpable, is that of one officer in the church superior to all, called the Pope, from the Greek, παπα, a term which does not occur in the Scriptures. The Episcopalians, the Methodists, and the Presbyterians, for their superior clergy, have adopted scripture terms, all describing, however, one and the same office; while the Papists have brought in a word not before known in church affairs. They all in common make offices in the church to suit themselves. The latter introduce a new term with the new office.

3. In evidence of the correctness of these positions, a brief notice of the different terms applied to preachers of the gospel, is desirable.

Apostle. This term was applied to the early ministers, and they were endowed with the power to work miracles, in evidence of their Divine commission. They were inspired, and in their office were infallible. This was necessary in the commencement of the kingdom of Christ. The office passed away with the original Apostles, inasmuch as no provisions were made for its continuance. Ample provisions were made for ministers, unlike the Apostles in these respects, as we have seen. The claim of popes or prelates to be the successors of the Apostles is unfounded, as God has authorized no succession. No claimant of this office since the original Apostles has been able to substantiate his claim by miracles. Claimants of this office have acknowledged the necessity of miraculous power in their profession of it; and in their attempts to prove its residence in themselves. But all such attempts have been failures, as all intelligent persons know. In regard to this office, see Matt. x. 1–4; Mark iii. 13–19; Luke vi. 12–19; Acts xx. 25–29; 2 Thess. ii. 1–17; 1 Cor. xii. 28; 2 Cor. viii. 23, &c., &c.

The Seventy Disciples. Their mission related to the Jews. They had also miraculous power, and have not since reappeared. Luke x. 1–6.

Prophets. This term was applied to the Apostles and others of their day. Prophetic power ceased with the original prophets, and of course the office was extinguished. See Acts xiii. 1, xv. 32, xi. 27, xxi. 10; 1 Cor. xii. 28, xiv. 32; Eph. iv. 11, &c., &c.

Teachers. This term is applicable to all who teach, independently of the subject; and is so used in the New Testament. It is thus applied to the Saviour, and his ministers generally. See John iii. 2; Eph. iv. 11; 1 Tim. ii. 7, &c., &c.

Elders. The word translated elders, in the New Testament, is πρεσβυτέρους (Presbyters), meaning ancient, and hence elder. It is applied in the New Testament to others than ministers; and to them indiscriminately, probably because they were ordinarily somewhat advanced in life. It is a scriptural and appropriate title for mature ministers of the gospel and other disciples. See 1 Tim. v. 1–17; Titus i. 5; 1 Pet. i. 5; 2 John i. 3; John i., &c., &c.

Ministers. This term is in very common use at the present day, as applicable to preachers of the gospel. The original word is διακονους (diakovous), and means servants. It is in use in the New Testament in application to all members of the church; and thus to preachers also. It is perhaps more suitable for general use as applicable to preachers of the gospel than the term elders, as it is equally applicable to young and old. See Luke i. 2; Rom. xiii. 6; 1 Cor. iii. 5, iv. 1; 2 Cor. iii. 6, vi. 4, xi. 15, 23.

Evangelists. The original word in this case is ευαγγελιστας (euaggelistas), and means messengers of good tidings. It occurs in three passages in the New Testament, and is evidently distinct from pastors or bishops, and relates to those who preach to different congregations; in modern phraseology, to missionaries. See Eph. iv. 11; Acts xxi. 8; 2 Tim. iv. 5.

Bishops. The original is επισκοπους (episcopous), and means overseers. It is applied in the New Testament to permanent preachers or teachers of the gospel, and means the same as pastors. It is once only applied to the Saviour in 1 Pet. ii. 25, in the same sense as it is applied to pastors. See 1 Tim. iii. 1, 2; Acts xx. 28; Phil. i. 1; Titus i. 7.

Pastors. The original word is ποιμένας (poimenas), and means shepherds. Shepherds are overseers, and the term is the same as bishops. See Eph. iv. 11; 1 Pet. v. 1–4; John x. 1–18.

Angels. This term is used in application to preachers of

the gospel in Rev. 2d and 3d chapters, and is evidently used in the sense of pastors or bishops.

Reverend, and doctor of divinity, are terms, I hardly need add, not found in the Bible, as applicable to preachers of the gospel, or at all, except as the former is once (Psalms cxi. 9) found in a description of Jehovah.

The conclusion of the whole matter then is, that (as already stated) the only ministerial office in the church is that of bishop or pastor, who are sometimes called also elders and teachers, all of equal dignity and authority. Evangelists, or missionaries, in the nature of their occupation, confined to no particular church in their labors, are not officers. If in the process of their work they raise up churches, and take the charge of one or more of them permanently, then they cease to be evangelists or missionaries, and become bishops or pastors. In either capacity, however, they may be elders and teachers.

The silence of the scriptures as to other ministerial officers in the church, and as to any grades indicating superiority or inferiority in office, is a sufficient rebuke of all pretensions in that direction. Besides, the merest tyro in church history, can turn to the pages showing when and how the abomination to which we refer, was fastened upon the church. Gieseler says: "After the death of the Apostles, to whom the general direction of the churches had always been conceded, some one among the presbyters of each church was suffered gradually to take the lead in its affairs. In the same irregular way, the title of episcopos (bishop) was appropriated to this first presbyter. Hence, the different accounts of the order of the first bishops in the Church of Rome."

Rev. Dr. Baird remarks on this subject:

"In regard to the 'supremacy of the popes,' allow me to say a few words. If I have read the history of the church and of the world aright, the state of the case is this:—Taking advantage of the words of our Saviour addressed to Peter, but intended, as the Protestants believe, for *all* the Apostles, the

Bishops of Rome, who claimed to be the successors of Peter in the Episcopate of that city (which was the capital of the Roman Empire, till Constantine the Great transferred that honor to Byzantium, in the fourth century), began at an early day to claim pre-eminence in the church, and to a certain extent gained it, notwithstanding the opposition of the Bishops (or Patriarchs) of Alexandria, Antioch, and Constantinople. After the transfer of the government to Constantinople, the pretensions of the Bishops of Rome rapidly augmented, as did the changes which they introduced into the doctrines, discipline, ceremonies, etc., of the church. Nor was it very long until, as Thierry justly affirms, (in his *History of the Conquest of England by the Normans,*) they began to conceive it to be possible for them to become virtually the 'successors of the Cæsars' at Rome, and govern the world by means of Christianity. What was a *conception* soon became a *deliberate purpose*, and the enterprise was for ages prosecuted with vigor, consummate wisdom and skill, and with astounding success. To be sure, the 'Great Schism' in the ninth century sadly interfered with their schemes, so far as the eastern part of Christendom was concerned. Still the western portion of it remained almost entirely submissive to the Bishops of Rome, until the 'Great Reformation of the sixteenth century' caused another immense 'defection.' In consequence of these two great 'disruptions,' there are more than seventy millions of people in the East, and eighty-five millions in the West, (including a portion of our own hemisphere,) who do not in any sense acknowledge the supremacy of the Bishops of Rome.

"In the eighth century the Bishops of Rome became kings or temporal rulers, in a direct and positive sense, by the grant of Pepin, which was confirmed by his son, Charlemagne. And for a thousand years and more they have ruled the 'Patrimony of St. Peter,' or 'States of the Church,' as their petty kingdom is called. That little country of less than three millions of inhabitants, is the only part of the world over which their *direct* and *material* sway has extended. Over this kingdom they have swayed their sceptres and reigned as *kings*. But they have sought to govern the rest of the world by another sort of dominion—a dominion which is emphatically founded in the souls of men, and by controlling them, has often controlled ther social and political, as well as their moral, relations and conduct. It is exactly this *politico-ecclesiastical, subtle,* and almost *indefinable* dominion that long made 'Rome under the popes,' almost as much the 'Mistress of the world' as was 'Rome under the Cæsars.' The foundation of all the claims of the popes to *temporal supremacy* was, after all, the 'keys,' or 'power of binding and loosing,' which, it is maintained, the Saviour 'gave' to Peter. It is from this grant that they claimed to be the 'Vicars' and 'Vicegerents of Christ,' and consequently the disposers of crowns and sceptres at their will. Indeed it would seem that some of them, or rather all of them, for a thousand years and more, believed that Christ, to whom the Father had given 'the heathen for an inheritance, and the uttermost parts of the earth for a possession,' had abdicated his throne in behalf of the 'successors of St. Peter,' and taken the position of a quiet spectator! If this be blasphemous, what shall we say of the language of those impious doctors of Rome, who have maintained that the pope can even do some things which God himself cannot?"

It was natural, when they abandoned the Scriptures, and permitted human innovations, that the pastors of the larger churches, being perhaps more talented, and eloquent, and learned, than those of the smaller ones, should assume to be superior in all respects; and that in process of time, this assumption should become the law of the church. Here we have episcopacy. This matter disposed of, and the process forgotten, it was equally natural that the Bishop of Rome, the prince of cities, should aspire to be the prince of the bishops and the churches. Here we have papacy, a papa or pope.

4. *The Authority, Rights, and Duties of Pastors.*

This is an important topic. While practically the intelligent and pious will have little difficulty in deciding what to demand on the one hand, and to grant on the other, unhappily all concerned are not in this condition, and untenable positions may be taken by both parties.

The passages relating to it are chiefly the following: 1 Thess. v. 12, 13. "And we beseech you, brethren, to know them which labor among you, and are over you in the Lord, and admonish you; and to esteem them very highly in love for their work's sake." Heb. xiii. 7, 17. "Remember them which have the rule over you, who have spoken unto you the word of God, whose faith follow, considering the end of their conversation. Obey them that have the rule over you, and submit yourselves, for they watch for souls, as they that must give account, that they may do it with joy and not with grief, for that were unprofitable for you." 1 Pet. v. 3. "Neither as being lords over God's heritage, but being examples to the flock." That something is implied in the terms "over you," "the rule over you," and "obey them," is obvious. The pastor's authority, on the other hand, is "in the Lord," and relates to "watching for souls," and is to be exercised not as "lords over God's heritage," and with reference to his "account." Nothing tyrannical, and destroying the free moral agency and accountability of the people, is admissible in the pastor. His authority is derived from God, and is to be exercised in his fear, and in the spirit and temper which he requires. It is evident that it relates to spiritual affairs: he "watches for souls." It follows that the people should cultivate a teachable, respectful, candid spirit toward him, as the servant of God, charged with affairs of the most momentous consequence. They are to "know him" as the servant of God, and to "esteem him very highly in love for his work's sake," "submitting" themselves to the claims of God.

There is no necessity for a pastor's authority in other than strictly spiritual matters, and no scriptural authorization of it, except in such matters. In church meetings he has but one vote, and is entitled only to such influence as his talents and abilities may command.

The rights and duties of pastors relate to but a small number of subjects, and are implied in the duty of the church to support him, and in his authority. See articles on these topics.

It is his right and duty to devote himself exclusively to his spiritual work; and of necessity he must be supported in it. His first duty is to preach the gospel, in the fear of God, and not of man, in the pulpit, and from house to house. He is subject to removal by the church, but not to dictation and neglect. He should have particular regard, as he goes from house to house, to the sick and suffering. He is none the less a citizen for being a pastor, except so far as the one office is necessarily modified by the other. In the nature of things, he cannot be extensively engaged in worldly matters of a business or political nature; but is nevertheless a citizen, having his responsibilities to such matters like others.

The rights and duties of other preachers of the gospel, as evangelists or missionaries, are very similar to those of pastors, being different only as they have charge of no particular church.

5. *Deacons.*

The origin and nature of this office is seen in Acts vi. 1–6. It related to providing for the temporal wants of "widows." The number originally chosen was "seven." They were set apart to the office by "prayer and laying on of hands." The office originated when the disciples had "all things common," and made one family.

This state of things passed away immediately, and with it some of the duties of deacons. But the office is made a permanent one, as we have seen. 1 Tim. iii. 8–13. In the absence of instructions as to the duties of deacons in their permanent capacity, we are led to infer that in its nature it is the same as originally, relating to the poor, and to temporal matters, to conform in particulars to the necessities of the churches choosing them. They should on these principles be chosen, more or less of them, by the church, to hold their office during adaptedness to it. They should be consecrated by "prayer and laying on of hands." They should attend to such secular matters as are necessary in the church, that the pastor may not be burdened with temporalities. It is not an exclusive office, and requires but a small amount of time, and is not therefore entitled to the pecuniary support of the church. In all other matters than those committed to deacons, they are the same as other members.

The term deacon, (διάκονος, diakonos,) means literally servant, and in this general sense was sometimes applied to pastors and missionaries, as in 1 Cor. iii. 5, where Paul and Apollas are called deacons, translated ministers. In this manner also it was applied to females useful in the church, as in Rom. xvi. 1, where Phebe is called our sister and deacon of the church, rendered servant. But all this is only a general application of the term, in which all members are servants, deacons. It has besides a specific application, as we have seen, to a permanent office in the church.

6. *Other Servants of the Church.*

Each church needs, and generally has, besides these divinely appointed officers, a clerk, treasurer, and committees, one of the committees, partly composed of reliable members of the congregation, being a body corporate for holding and managing church property. In Massachusetts, the deacons are the body corporate. See Revised Statutes, Part I., Tit. 8, chap. 20, sec. 39.

CHAPTER V.

Church Meetings. 1. For Worship. 2. For Business. 3. Of Committees. 4. Of Councils. 5. Of Associations. 6. Of State Conventions and Missionary Societies. 7. Of Ministers. 8. Church Letters.

1. *Meetings for the Worship of God.*

THESE should occur upon the Sabbath ; and upon such other occasions as the church, in the fear of God, may deem desirable, and for the promotion of piety. They should be for preaching and prayer and exhortation and singing. Baptism and the Lord's Supper should be administered upon the Sabbath.

2. *Meetings for Business.*

These are important meetings, and should be managed with eminent piety and wisdom. Each church will find peculiarities in itself, requiring its specific arrangements. With slight alteration, we insert here Rev. Dr. Brown's articles on "Meetings of the Church," and "Manner of Conducting Business :"

"The regular meeting for business shall be held as the church may direct.

Special meetings may be called by the Pastor or Moderator of the church. In case of his resignation, absence, impeachment, or refusal to act, the Clerk shall call such a meeting on a written request signed by not less than seven male members; and the notice shall be publicly given from the pulpit on the Lord's day preceding.

Nine male members shall constitute a quorum, for the transaction of business.

The Pastor of the church, or in his absence, any brother whom the church may appoint, shall act as Moderator in all meetings for the transaction of business.

It shall be the duty of the Moderator to keep order; state

and explain propositions; and, by his vote, decide questions upon which there is no majority.

He shall cause every meeting to be opened and closed by prayer.

He shall call for the business of the church in the following order:

Read the Minutes of the previous meeting.

Hear the experience of candidates for membership.

Receive letters of dismission from sister churches.

Grant letters of dismission to those requesting them.

Hear reports of committees, and other unfinished business.

New business.

He shall suffer no second motion to be entertained, until the one under consideration has been disposed of, except motions to amend, postpone, adjourn, or put the main question.

He shall call to order any member who, while speaking, introduces any subject foreign to the one under discussion.

He shall call to order any member who uses uncourteous language, or whose remarks are adapted to injure the reputation or feelings of any brother.

He may speak upon any subject under discussion, by inviting a brother to preside in his place.

Every member who wishes to speak shall rise, and respectfully address the Moderator.

Every proposition presented for the action of the church, must be introduced by the motion of one member—in writing, if requested—and seconded by another.

No member shall speak more than twice upon the same subject, without the expressed consent of the church.

Upon any point of order, a member may appeal from the Moderator to the church, whose decision shall be final.

All questions shall be decided by the vote of a majority, except the cases mentioned in other sections of these rules."

3. *Meetings of Committees.*

The church may appoint such committees as she deems

desirable. Much time and difficulty may be saved, by referring questions to judicious committees, either for decision, or for preparation for the meeting of the church. Committees have no authority, except what is delegated to them by the church. Members of the church are under obligations to act upon committees with sobriety, candor and wisdom. Committees should hold such meetings as may be necessary for the intelligent and faithful discharge of the trust committed to them. Care should be observed on the part of the church, not to compromise her own authority or dignity, by referring to committees questions which she herself should settle.

4. *Meetings of Councils.*

When churches are unable to agree upon questions of importance, they may request sister churches to send members to sit in council, and aid them in coming to a decision. Councils, like committees, have no authority except that which is delegated to them by the parties calling them. Members of a council are but referees, and they may meet for advice upon a given question, or for the decision of it, as they may be requested. Ordinarily, councils are comparatively useless, unless in the outset the parties agree to abide by their decision. When they thus decide questions, it implies no control over the churches, as they have only such authority as is delegated to them by the church. In this manner their action is hers. Councils are ordinarily called in Baptist churches to aid in ordaining or installing ministers, and in settling difficulties about which the church cannot agree. They should hold such meetings as may be necessary to a judicious performance of the duties committed to them. The meeting is called by letter from the church needing aid, and when thus convened, should be governed by the ordinary usage of other assemblages for business.

Baptist churches have always objected to councils of ministers or laymen having any control over the churches, except such as is delegated to them at the time, on the ground that the church is the highest authority and ultimate appeal.

Dr. Brown remarks on Convening a Council:

"In cases of difficulty, for the decision of which the church desire the advice and wisdom of disinterested brethren, letters may be sent to the neighboring churches, requesting them to appoint delegates to meet a delegation from the church on a specified day; to which council, when organized, the case shall be referred, and their advice shall be laid before the church for further action."

5. *Meetings of Associations* occur annually, and are made up of delegates from churches, consisting of the pastor and two or more laymen chosen for the purpose. Pastors, however, are not essential to associations, but are always sent as a part of the delegation, if the church has one at the time. The object of this meeting is to promote fraternity and piety among the churches. For this purpose, each church is represented by a letter, as well as by delegates, and the time of the meeting is devoted to the reading of the letters, preaching, devotional exercises, and action adapted to promote the missionary spirit and efficiency of the churches. Associations, like committees and councils, have no authority over the churches.

Dr. Brown remarks on Representation in Association:

"Once in each year delegates shall be appointed to represent the church in the Association, whose duty it shall be to furnish to the Association a statement of the condition of the church, including its changes; to faithfully represent the desires of the church; and to co-operate with the messengers of other churches in promoting the interests of the kingdom of Christ."

6. *Meetings of State Conventions, Missionary, Bible, Publication Societies*, &c., are of a similar character, originating in the church, and deriving all their consequence from her. Any

society or convention for church purposes, not dependent upon the church, is a departure from the divine plan for promoting Christianity upon earth.

Dr. Brown remarks on Benevolent Action in the Church :

" The church holds it to be an imperative duty to labor for the propagation of pure Christianity throughout the world, and will maintain some system by which all the leading objects of benevolence may receive their share of support, and all the members contribute, as the Lord prospers them.

All collections granted to churches, societies, or individuals, shall be counted by the deacons before paying over the same ; and the amount so collected shall be reported at the next church meeting."

7. *Ministers' Meetings.*

These occur with greater or less frequency, for the mutual improvement of ministers, and do not relate at all to the churches, acknowledging no control from them, and claiming none over them.

Societies for religious purposes, or any methods of promoting religion, not definitely recognized in the New Testament, are justifiable, when they harmonize with that which is revealed. Jehovah has given us the principles, and more or less of the detail of their execution. Of necessity, much of the detail is left to the church. It belongs to her to provide such detail, and to see that nothing is adopted which is unharmonious with the divine plan.

8. *Forms of Church Letters.*

We introduce here, as illustrative of Baptist usage, and as suitable specimens of letters for the use of churches, Dr. Brown's :

I. LETTER OF DISMISSION.

Philadelphia, ——, 18—.

To the —— *Baptist Church in* —— *:*

This certifies that —— —— is a member, in good standing, of the First Baptist Church, and in compliance with —— own request, is affectionately recommended and dismissed to your fellowship.

If notified within six months of —— union with you, we shall consider —— as dismissed from us; otherwise this letter shall be null and void.

In behalf of the Church,

—— ——, *Clerk.*

II. LETTER OF NOTIFICATION.

To the First Baptist Church, Philadelphia.

This certifies that —— ——, recommended and dismissed by you, by a letter dated ———, was on the ——— received as a member of the ——— Baptist Church in ———.

Attest: —— ——, *Clerk.*

III. LETTER OF OCCASIONAL COMMUNION.

——, ——, 18—.

This may certify that the bearer, —— ——, is a member of the ——— Baptist Church in ———, in good and regular standing; and as such is affectionately commended to the sympathy, watchcare, and communion of any sister church where Providence may lead ——.

This letter continues valid only one year.

—— ——, *Pastor.*

IV. A LICENSE TO PREACH.

This may certify that the bearer, —— ——, is a member of the ——— Baptist Church in ———, without reproach; and that he has the full and cordial approbation of his brethren, by a vote passed ———, to exercise his gifts in preaching the Gospel of Christ.

Attest: —— ——, *Pastor.*

—— ——, *Clerk.*

V. LETTER OF DISMISSION TO FORM A NEW CHURCH.

The ——— Baptist Church, in regular church meeting, ——, 18—.

On request of the following brethren and sisters, now in regular standing with us, viz., (Here follow the names,) to be dismissed from us for the purpose of uniting in the formation of a new church at ———, it was *voted*, that we cordially grant them letters of dismission for that purpose, and when regularly constituted as a church, shall cease to regard them as under our watchcare.

—— ——, *Clerk.*

VI. LETTERS FOR CALLING A COUNCIL.

1. To Recognize a New Church.

P———, ——, 18—.

To the Baptist Church of Christ in ——.

In behalf of a number of brethren and sisters belonging to different Baptist churches, who desire to be recognized as an independent and distinct church in this place, we invite you to send your pastor and two other delegates to sit in council with us, on the ———, in the house of ———, to assist us by your prayers and counsels; and if it shall be judged agreeable to the will of God, to recognize us as a regular Baptist Church in fellowship with you.

The number of brethren who unite in this request is ——; and of sisters ——; all of us with the knowledge and approval of the churches to which we belong, who have granted us letters of dismission for this purpose. The churches invited, are the following, viz., ———.

—— ——, } *Committee*
—— ——, } *of*
—— ——, } *Arrangements.*

2. For the Ordination of a Minister. 3. For the Dismission of a Minister 4. For the Trial of a Minister. The forms only vary with the subject and the occasion.

VII. MINUTES OF A COUNCIL.

——, ——, 18—.

An Ecclesiastical Council was convened at ———, on ——, by letters missive from the church in ———.

The Council was organized by the choice of —— ——, as Moderator, and —— ——, as Clerk. Prayer was offered by —— ——. The vote of the church inviting the Council was then read as follows: (Copy the vote.)

The credentials of delegates were called for, from which it appeared that the following brethren were entitled to vote in the Council, viz.:

Churches. *Pastors and Delegates.*

The Council then heard a statement of the business, &c.

—— ——, *Clerk.* —— ——, *Moderator.*

CHAPTER VI.

Church Discipline. 1. Its Origin. 2. Its Nature and Design. 3. Offences requiring it. 4. Discipline of Ministers. 5. Treatment of Excluded Members. 6. Their Reception by other Churches.

1. *The Origin of Church Discipline.*

IT has its origin in first principles. All combinations must be subject to discipline, for the good of the whole, or disorders will arise, injurious to all. It is necessary in families, in schools, and, indeed, wherever persons are associated, as well as in the church.

The New Testament makes ample provisions for discipline

in the church. Early in her history, the Saviour gives us the principle here involved. Matt. xviii. 15–18. Here members disagreeing are to seek reconciliation—first, privately; then by the aid of one or two brethren; if these fail, the next resort is to the church, whose decision is ultimate. She may call to her aid, in cases of difficulty, the advice of a council of brethren, but the responsibility of decision is hers. Evidence of the divine origin of church discipline is seen all through the New Testament.

2. *The Nature and Design of Church Discipline.*

It is reformatory in its nature and design, first to individuals, and second to the church. Erring members are to be "gained" over to the truth; and when this becomes impossible, for the purity of the church, they are to be expelled, to be to the church "as heathen and publicans." Matt. xviii. 15–17. This passage, as all others on the subject, provides for great tenderness on the one hand, and for decision on the other. Whilst every thing vindictive, and selfish, and personal, is prohibited, so is undue forbearance, "suffering wrong" in members.

The church is a band of brethren, who are to "love one another," under all circumstances. It is at the same time a band of Christians, persons who are like Christ; and none are to be tolerated within her pale who are not, or who cannot be induced, by a suitable discipline, to become fellow-laborers for the truth. The church is an organization for the furtherance of the cause of Christ, and, as such, is charged with the most holy and momentous work; and its discipline should be at once illustrative and promotive of its great enterprise. Its members, by its discipline, are to become better in all respects, and more efficient laborers for God. Discipline not having these effects is wrong. See, on this topic, Cor. xii. 24, 26. 1 Pet. iii. 8. Matt. v. 14. Col. ii. 5. Rom. i. 8. Rom. xii. 4–8. Gal. vi. 1. James v. 19, 20. Rev. ii. 14. 1 Cor. v. 6, 7. 1 Tim. v. 20. 1 Thess. iv. 14.

3. *Offences Requiring Church Action, and Method of Procedure.*

Dr. Brown's article on "Mode of Proceeding Against Disorderly Members," traverses the ground of these topics, and is scriptural and judicious.

"When offence is given to one member of the church, by the language or conduct of another, if the offence relate only to himself, and is known to none other, the offended shall, without consulting or informing any person, seek opportunity to converse privately with the offender, with an honest view to reconcile the difficulty, if possible. If satisfaction be given, he shall complain of the offender to none.

If satisfaction be not given, it shall be the duty of the offended to select one or two, or at most three others, choosing such as he may deem best adapted to effect a reconciliation, with whom he shall again privately converse with the offending brother; if satisfaction be given, he shall make no further complaint.

If these efforts fail to secure a reconciliation, it shall be the duty of the offended to lay the matter before the church, for further action.

If any member of the church shall be publicly guilty of any crime or gross impropriety, it shall be the duty of the member knowing the transgression, to see or write to the offender, and inform him of his intention to lay the matter before the church, that he may appear in his own defence.

When common rumor charges a crime or gross impropriety against a member, it shall be the duty of the member hearing it to visit or write to the accused, and inform him of the reports; and if he has reason to believe that they are true, to take the most judicious steps to ascertain their correctness, and lay the charge and its evidence before the church.

When peculiar circumstances render it impracticable to visit or write to a member, who is known, or currently reported to have been guilty of crime or gross impropriety, it shall be the duty of the member knowing or hearing of such conduct, to take the most judicious measures to ascertain the truth, and lay the matter before the church.

If a member, having erred, shall voluntarily confess it to the church, and manifest repentance, no further proceedings, in ordinary cases, shall be entertained against him.

If a charge be preferred against an absent member, he shall, if practicable, be cited to appear at the next meeting of the church; and no member, if absent, shall be censured or excluded, at the same meeting during which a charge is preferred against him.

Every member against whom a charge of misconduct is preferred, shall have the privilege of speaking in his own defence.

Written testimouy of any individual who is not a member of the church, may be admitted in cases of discipline; but not oral testimony, except the individual testifying be connected with some church of the same faith and order.

If a member fail to give satisfaction to the church, in relation to charges preferred against him, or perversely refuse to appear before the church when cited, he shall be excluded."

4. *Discipline of Ministers.*

Ministers are members of the church, and, of necessity, in general, subject to the same laws as other members. The only scriptural exception to this rule is that made in 1 Tim. v. 19. "Against an elder receive not an accusation, but before two or three witnesses." That by "an elder" here is meant a minister, and not merely an aged person, is evident from the context. They are those "who labor in word and doctrine," and who are "worthy of their reward." Ministers, more than ordinary members, are exposed to injury from evil-minded persons. It is their office to "reprove and rebuke," which is by no means acceptable to the wicked; and they often become their "enemy, because they tell them the truth." In the nature of their office, they occupy a prominent place—a place of exposure to the shafts of envy and enmity, which demands caution in proportion, in receiving accusations against them. One witness is not enough, though it may be in the case of those whose position is more private, and consequently less exposed. "Two or three witnesses" are positively necessary in the case of ministers. In all other respects, on the principle of equality which has ever characterized the Church of Christ, and in the silence of the Scriptures as to different rules for the discipline of ministers, they are subject to the same rules.

In point is the case of the Apostle Peter, as described in Acts xi. "And when Peter was come up to Jerusalem, they that were of the circumcision contended with him." Peter claims no special privilege on the ground of his ministerial character, but makes his defence, as in duty bound. It is satisfactory, and is accepted. There is no instance in the history of the primitive church of a minister claiming special privileges in discipline. The Church at Ephesus (Rev. ii. 2) is praised by the Apostle John, for having "tried them which say they are apostles, and are not."

The common argument for "a council" in the discipline of ministers, that "as the agency of the Presbytery was called in to invest him with the ministerial office, it is equally necessary in order to divest him of it," is untenable, simply because it is unscriptural, the Scriptures making but one law of discipline for all members of the church, with the single exception we have noticed. But it may also be added, that the Presbytery is not necessary to his becoming a minister. The church is competent to make her own ministers, as far as man can make them, and this she always does in the Baptist Church. She authorizes him to preach by her own license, which is granted or withheld as she deems best. The essential act in ordination is her election of him for the purpose, and he may become a minister or a pastor, without the agency of the Presbytery.

5. *Treatment of Excluded Members of the Church.*

As they may be excluded for a variety of offences, of greater or less criminality, so it is obvious they should be treated differently afterwards. For this the Scriptures provide. "But now I have written unto you not to keep company, if any man that is called a brother, be a fornicator, or covetous, or an idolator, or a railer, or a drunkard, or an extortioner: with such an one no not to eat." 1 Cor. v. 11. This is quite a different rule from the following: "And if any man obey not our word in this epistle, note that man, and have no company with him, that he may be ashamed. Yet count him not an enemy, but admonish him as a brother." 2 Thess. iii. 14, 15. The distinction in *character* is between those grossly immoral, and those to some extent disobedient to the "word," and the distinction in *treatment* is non-intercourse with the former as brethren, and attention to the latter as such, "admonishing them." In the former case, however, it is obvious that the prohibition "not to eat" with nim does not extend to the act as man with man, but as brother with brother. Well does the Apostle remark, (1 Cor. v. 10,) if we were to have literally no intercourse with the grossly immoral, "then must we needs go out of the world." The prohibition relates to them as professed Christians. Those excluded for gross immoralities are not to be admitted to society under circumstances implying those present to be Christians. It does not, however, follow that even such are to be forgotten. We may seek the reform of "heathen and publicans," aye, are under obligations to; and so we may and should that of all excluded persons. At the same time, there is more hope of those excluded for disobedience to the "word;" and they are more suitable companions for Christians, and should be treated with less severity.

At the same time, great charity is required toward all persons who repent of their trespasses. "If thy brother trespass against thee, rebuke him; and if he repent, forgive him." Luke xvii. 3. "Then Peter came to him, and said, Lord, how oft shall my brother sin against me, and I forgive him? till seven times? Jesus saith unto him, I say not unto thee until seven times, but until seventy times seven." Matt. xviii. 21, 22. It is obvious that by "seventy times seven" is meant an indefinite number of times. It is equally obvious that this rule does not apply to those who merely profess to repent; for it were trifling with serious things, and casting contempt upon all discipline, to exclude and restore persons with such frequency, and on so slight evidence of repentance. But where there is evidence of genuine repentance, including reform, restoration is necessary in all cases.

6. *The Reception of Excluded Members by other Churches.*

It sometimes occurs that excluded members, failing to obtain restoration to their own church, apply for admission to some other one of the same faith and order. In the absence of a special scriptural rule in such case, we must be governed by general rules, and these are ample for such a purpose. The Church is one, and yet composed of numerous independent, but harmonious parts. For the sake of harmony, and as essential to it, great courtesy must be used by different churches toward each other. It is obvious that the church excluding a member is the one upon whom rests the first responsibility of his restoration. It should be taken for granted, in the absence of evidence, that his exclusion is just, and to his own church he should be referred for a settlement of his difficulty. At the same time, churches may err, and individuals have rights, and any church may, on conviction that a sister church has erred, either intentionally or ignorantly, receive those they deem entitled to such privilege. It is obvious that such questions need the control of great wisdom and justice and courtesy. Churches receiving the excluded members of sister churches, without ample evidence of duty in the case, are guilty of introducing disorder into the body; at the same time they are under obligation to God and his wronged disciples, to rebuke any erring church, and undo, as far as it may, its error, by receiving those wrongly excluded, who fail to obtain redress in the right quarter.

PART IV.

BAPTIST MARTYRS AND PERESCUTIONS, FOR THE FOREGOING PRINCIPLES.

CHAPTER I.

1. The Uses of Persecutions. 2. Evidence of Discipleship. 3. They prove how idle is the wrath of man against God. 4. The Martyrs as an Example.

1. SOME minds recoil from the heart-rending and sickening details of suffering for conscience sake, which abound in the history of the church, and condemn their recital. But they are matters of fact, and of Scripture recognition, and have most important uses. They should be studied until the mind is imbued with their lessons.

2. *Sufferings for Christ are evidence of discipleship.* "Then shall they deliver you up to be afflicted, and shall kill you, and ye shall be hated of all nations, for my name's sake." Matt. xxiv. 9. "Blessed are ye when men shall revile you, and persecute you, and shall say all manner of evil of you falsely, for my name's sake. Rejoice and be exceeding glad, for great is your reward in heaven; for so persecuted they the prophets which were before you." Matt. v. 11, 12. Aware that his disciples would be subject to intense persecutions, the Saviour provided, as far as possible, for them, not only admonishing them of the fact, but that their endurance was essential to discipleship, and that he would be with them, and bless them, and give them strength equal to their day. It is well known to all readers of the Bible how amply passages of

this nature abound. It is equally obvious to all readers of church history, how fully the truths of the Bible have been verified in this respect. Just as it predicts, persecutions have abounded; the false have fallen away, unable to stand before their fires; and myriads of the genuine disciples of the Saviour have unflinchingly endured all manner of indignities, and sufferings, in comparison with which their ultimate death was as nothing. The evidence of the inspiration of the Scriptures would have been defective, without the historical confirmation of them furnished in persecutions.

It does not follow that he is a disciple of Christ who suffers; but that he is, who suffers innocently "for righteousness' sake." No doubt many have claimed merit from their sufferings, not understanding this important distinction; but this detracts not from their elevated position, by the Master's side, who have borne indignities and ultimate death, in unshrinking, undying love for the truth, as it is in Jesus. Noble, glorious martyrs! though dead, they yet speak.

Troublous times may come again to the Church of Christ. Well, let them come. They will be nothing new or strange. Though there would undoubtedly be a great falling away, among professing Christians, there would still be, as of old, those true to Christ in all circumstances. Indeed, such times are now in different parts of the world, and probably will be, as they ever have been, until the millennium. They are now the feeble efforts of the dying demon of persecution. As ever, they develop now the true martyr spirit. Fear not, disciple of Christ; mistrust not the principle of religion, which has been implanted within thee; it is as undying as the throne of Omnipotence. It is said of martyrs of a former day: "By this love (the love of Christ) they overcame all things, and performed glorious deeds, beyond human power. Feeble women showed more than manly strength. Maidens and young men, in the bloom of youth, were able, by God's help, to despise the alluring world, with all its fair and mighty promises. These young and tender plants overcame, by faith and patience, the mighty of this world." So it shall be again, if it please God to suffer it. Human nature is the same in all ages; and Christianity is the same in fact, and in its operations upon the heart, and "Jesus Christ is the same, yesterday, to-day, and forever."

3. *Persecution for conscience sake is Anti-Christian.* Another use of persecutions and martyrdoms is to distinguish the enemies of Christ "And in nothing terrified by your adversaries, which is to them an evident token of perdition, but to you of salvation and that of God." Phil. i. 28.

It is worthy of remark, that no fact has done more to fasten upon the Papal Church the odium of the description in Rev. xvii. 3–7, than her persecuting spirit, which, all history shows, is identical with her. Rev. Dr. Dowling remarks, in his history of Romanism: "Among the scriptural marks of the predicted Romish Apostasy, the Babylonish harlot of the Apocalypse, is the following—'And I saw the woman drunken with the blood of the martyrs of Jesus.'" The whole history of Popery is a commentary upon the truthfulness of this description. That history is written in lines of blood. Compared with the butcheries of holy men and women by the papal anti-Christ, the persecutions of the Pagan emperors of the first three centuries sink into comparative insignificance. For not a tithe of the blood of the martyrs was shed by Paganism, that has been poured forth by Popery; and the persecutors of Pagan Rome never dreamed of the thousand ingenious contrivances of torture, which the malignity of Popish inquisitors succeeded in inventing, when, in the language of Pollok, they

* * * * "Sat and planned
Deliberately, and with most musing pains,
How to extremest thrill of agony
The flesh, and blood, and souls, of holy men,
Her victim, might be wrought."

From the birth of popery, in 606, to the present time, it is estimated by careful and credible historians, that "more than fifty millions of the human family have been slaughtered for the crime of heresy, by popish persecutors, an average of more than forty thousand religious murders for every year in the existence of popery."

It is said these things should be forgotten, as barbarities of a bygone day. Forgotten, indeed! Impossible! It were less impossible if Romanism had repented of these enormities; and if it were not amply evident that persecution is an integral part of her; indeed, her pet method of promoting her cause of sin and crime; but still impossible, because her persecutions are not only matter of prophecy, but of scriptural evidence of her anti-Christian character. When these things can be blotted from the Bible, where they stand written by the pen of the Almighty, an ever-living, burning sentence against her, then they may be forgotten, not before.

That Protestants have been guilty of persecuting men for conscience sake is greatly to be deplored, but cannot be denied. These differences, however, are obvious between such, and those of Pagans and Papists. There are Protestant sects which have never resorted to persecutions and martyrdoms. *There is not an instance on record against the Baptist Church. She has ever protested against every thing of the kind, by precept and example.* And in numerous cases of Protestant persecutions, they have been the result of mistaken views, prevailing for a short time, rather than of fixed laws. Better views have speedily taken their place, and bitterly have different ones been lamented. Where Protestants have persecuted under other circumstances than these, they must be placed in the same category with Pagans and Papists, as the enemies of Christ and his people.

4. *Persecutions and martyrdoms prove how idle is the wrath of man against Christ and his people.* Well has Luther sung:

"Flung to the heedless winds,
  On the waters cast,
Their ashes shall be watched,
  And gathered at the last:
And from that scattered dust,
  Around us and abroad,
Shall spring a plenteous seed
  Of witnesses for God.

Jesus hath now received
  Their latest, dying breath;
Yet vain is Satan's boast
  Of victory in their death.
Still, still, though dead, they speak,
  And triumph-tongued proclaim
To many a waking land
  The one availing name."

So it has ever been, and so it shall continue. Let the people of God take courage and never "fear what man shall do unto them."

"The blood of the martyrs is the seed of the church."

And let their enemies profit by past experience, as they read the second Psalm:

"Why do the heathen rage,
And the people imagine a vain thing?
The kings of the earth set themselves,
And the rulers take council together
Against the Lord, and against his anointed, saying,
Let us break their bands asunder,
And cast away their cords from us.
He that sitteth in the heavens shall laugh:
The Lord shall have them in derision.
Then shall he speak unto them in his wrath
And vex them in his sore displeasure.
'Yet have I set my king
Upon my holy hill of Zion.'
I will declare the decree:
The Lord hath said unto me
'Thou art my Son;
This day have I begotten thee.
Ask of me and I shall give thee the heathen for thine inheritance,

And the uttermost parts of the earth for thy possession.
Thou shalt break them with a rod of iron;
Thou shalt dash them in pieces like a potter's vessel.'
Be wise now, therefore, O ye kings;
Be instructed, ye judges of the earth.
Serve the Lord with fear,
And rejoice with trembling.
Kiss the Son, lest he be angry,
And ye perish from the way,
When his wrath is kindled but a little.
Blessed are all they that put their trust in him."

5. *The martyrs are an example to their fellow-disciples.* We commend to our readers, in this connection, the 10th, 11th, and 12th chapters of Hebrews. In these chapters, the Apostle Paul, who knew so well what persecution was, (from his own experience as a persecutor "unto death," before his conversion, and as persecuted afterwards,) beautifully illustrates this use of martyrdoms.

"Let us hold fast the profession of our faith without wavering; (for he is faithful that promised;) and let us consider one another, to provoke unto love and good works." (x. 23, 24.) "Now faith is the substance of things hoped for, the evidence of things not seen; for by it the elders obtained a good report." (xi. 1, 2.) He then, in a most eloquent manner, shows the triumphs of faith in all ages, and among them, those of martyrs: "And what shall I more say? for the time would fail me to tell of Gideon and of Barak, and of Samson, and of Jephthah; of David also, and Samuel, and of the prophets, who through faith subdued kingdoms, wrought righteousness, obtained promises, stopped the mouths of lions, quenched the violence of fire, escaped the edge of the sword, out of weakness were made strong, waxed valiant in fight, turned to flight the armies of the aliens. Women received their dead raised to life again; and others were tortured, not accepting deliverance, that they might obtain a better resurrection; and others had trials of cruel mockings and scourgings, yea, moreover, in bonds and imprisonments; they were stoned, they were sawn asunder, were tempted, were slain with the sword; they wandered about in sheep skins and goat skins; being destitute, afflicted, tormented; (of whom the world was not worthy:) they wandered in deserts, and in mountains, and in dens and caves of the earth. And these all, having obtained a good report through faith, received not the promise: God having provided some better things for us, that they without us should not be made perfect. Wherefore, seeing we also are compassed about with so great a cloud of witnesses, let us lay aside every weight, and the sin which doth so easily beset us, and let us run with patience the race which is set before us." (xi. 32–40, i. 1.)

"Encompassed about by such a cloud of witnesses," we ought indeed to "lay aside every weight," even (?) "the sin that doth so easily beset us," (timidity?) "and run with patience the race set before us." O, how should we blush for our timidity, in the presence of the trifling sacrifices required of us! Well may we sing, as often we do, (God grant that we may be innocent in so singing!)—

"Am I a soldier of the cross—
  A follower of the Lamb?
And shall I fear to own his cause,
  Or blush to speak his name?
Must I be carried to the skies,
  On flowery beds of ease,
While others fought to win the prize,
  And sailed through bloody seas?"

Our brethren, for the blessed privileges we enjoy, literally sailed to heaven through seas of blood; and yet we, with this hymn upon our lips, halt and desert, for comparatively the most trifling obstacles. O, shame, shame on us, in this day, that we are not more faithful to Christ! One thousandth part of the sacrifice they made would fill to overflowing the treasury of the Lord, and elevate the disciples of Christ beyond any thing now exhibited of disposition and ability to toil and suffer for the truth.

This is not the martyr, but the victorious age of the Church. We could not, if we would, make such sacrifices as have our brethren of a different day. But as much as they, are we under obligations to possess the martyr spirit, which would, did the circumstances require it, cause us to rejoice in the extremest persecutions, and whose office, in different times, it is, to make us equally faithful to such sacrifices as may fall to our lot. Disciple of Christ, thou mayest deny thyself, if thou wilt, in illustrating the graces of Christianity, as thou dost live for God and his cause. By a well-ordered life and godly conversation—by industry, and benevolence to the charities of the church, and of philanthropy, you may be soldiers of the cross, and hardly otherwise can you. What else can you do? O, then, call not these hardships, nor dream of desertion on their account.

CHAPTER II.

1. The Abundance of the Sufferings of Baptists. 2. New Testament Martyrs.

1. We claim not for Baptists a monopoly of these glories, through grace, of the Church of Christ. Far, far from it. Instances are numerous of most noble sufferings, for the truth, in other denominations. We delight to honor the spirit of Christ, wherever it is found; but neither our limits, nor our plan in this work, permit us to linger about the edifying lessons abounding in most Christian denominations.

That Baptists, however, have had by far the largest share of suffering from the persecutions and martyrdoms of the church, is obvious. They have suffered from Jews, Pagans, Papists, Greeks, and Protestants, and have retaliated upon neither. Rev. J. Newton Brown, D. D., in his preliminary historical essay to the Baptist martyrs, says, speaking of the martyrdom of Stephen, and of John the Baptist, and of James: "Thus began, with names never to be forgotten, the long, bright roll of New Testament martyrs. And thus, from year to year, and from age to age, that illustrious roll received accessions from the violence of Jewish or heathen persecutions, for three centuries. But, with only one known exception, all this time, these Christian martyrs were Baptists."

Cardinal Hosius, President of the Council of Trent, (A. D. 1545,) a distinguished dignitary of the Church of Rome, says: "If you behold their cheerfulness in suffering persecution, the Anabaptists run before all the heretics. If you have regard to the number, it is likely that in multitude they would swarm above all others, if they were not grievously plagued, and cut off with the knife of persecution. If you have an eye to the outward appearance of godliness, both the Lutherans and the Zuinglians must needs grant that they far pass them. If you will be moved by the boasting of the word of God, these be no less bold than Calvin to preach, and their doctrine must stand aloft above all the glory of the world, and stand invincible above all power, because it is not their word, but the word of the living God." The testimony of these two writers covers the ground from the first Christian martyrdom to the reformation of the sixteenth century.

Any amount of facts, illustrating the truth of this testimony, may be found in the New Testament, in the various Church Histories, and Baptist Histories; in Fox's Book of Martyrs, in Dutch Martyrology, in Dowling's History of Romanism, and in Baptist Martyrs. It is true, that in some of these works the denominational character of the martyrs is sedulously concealed; still it often appears, and there is no mistaking their baptistical tendencies. In the New Testament, and the Baptist works, no attempt being made to conceal the real character of the sufferers, it cannot be mistaken; and it is remarkable, for how much of these sufferings the world is indebted directly to sprinkling, and *infant* sprinkling particularly. When it is remembered for how long a period of the world Christians were to so great an extent Baptists, namely, fifteen hundred years, (See chapters in this work on the origin and history of the church,) it will be perceived that, of necessity, the martyrs of the same period were Baptists to a similar extent.

Our limits admit of only a few instances of persecutions and martyrdom, selected from materials ample for volumes of a similar character. In tracing them, we follow the path, every where marked with blood, which we have sketched in Part First of this work.

2. *Persecutions and Martyrdoms of New Testament times.*

These are so well known, that we feel compelled, though they are so important, to confine ourselves to the briefest possible recital of them.

"The time and age of the New Testament" (see Preface to Dutch Martyrology) "afford abundant matter of confirmation. John, the forerunner of Jesus, had to bare his neck, in prison, to the sword. Our Captain, the leader of our faith, Jesus Christ, had to enter into his glory through many scoffs, much suffering and reproach, and, at last, by the shameful death of the cross. His apostles and disciples, as the history of those times bears witness, followed their Master. Peter and Paul were slain by the Emperor Nero. James, the brother of John, was put to death by Herod, with the sword. Matthew was nailed to the ground in India. Bartholomew was flayed alive. Andrew was crucified. Thomas was pierced with spears. Philip was nailed to a cross, and then stoned to death. Simon Zelotes was scourged and crucified. James, the son of Alpheus, was thrown down from the temple at Jerusalem, and afterwards beaten with staves. Judas Thaddeus was murdered in Persia by the ungodly heathen priests. Matthias also obtained the crown of martyrdom. The evangelical Mark was dragged about at Alexandria, by a cord round his neck, until he died. John, the Apostle, being banished to the Isle of Patmos, adorned the gospel by suffering. Pollycarp, the disciple of John, was burned alive at Smyrna. Ignatius, Bishop of Antioch, was torn in pieces by wild beasts. Even the Roman bishops (pastors) were in the first 300 years nearly all martyred, and, in common with Christians in general, were subjected to the persecutions of heathen emperors. Under the Emperor Diocletian, there was such a terrible persecution that it seemed as if the Christian name would be entirely rooted out. Thus the first churches, until the time of Constantine, were so accustomed to persecution, that with premeditated counsel they prepared themselves entirely to suffer."

CHAPTER III

1. Persecutions of the Montanist Baptists terrible in the extreme. 2. Of the Novatian Baptists by the Emperors.

1. *The Montanist Baptists.*

NEANDER seems in some doubt as to whether Montanus and his numerous adherents flourished "during the catastrophies of nature which led to the tumultuary attacks of the populace on the Christians; or during the bloody persecutions of the Emperor Marcus Aurelius." Whichever it was, they undoubtedly came in for a full share of suffering. Either of these persecutions were terrible in the extreme; and it is perfectly obvious, that a people so uncompromising in their defence of the truth, must have been great sufferers. The distinguished historian just quoted, says of them: "Accordingly, Montanism tended to fasten a fanatic longing after martyrdom. It set up the principle, that, in submitting to the divine will, men should do nothing to avoid those persecutions which it was God's will to suspend over Christians, for the trial of their faith. This spirit of Montanism characteristically expresses itself in the following oracle: 'Let it not be your wish to die on your beds—but desire to die as martyrs, that He may be glorified who suffered for you.' The same tendency of spirit pushed Montanism, in its anxiety to avoid an accommodating disposition, which might prove injurious to the faith, to the other extreme, of sternly renouncing all those usages of civil and social life, which could in any way be traced to a pagan origin; of despising all those prudential maxims, by which it was possible to avert the suspicion of the pagan authorities. It seems, among other things, to have been objected to the Montanists, that, by their frequent meetings for fasting and prayer, they defied the established laws against secret assemblies." Such a people were not likely to escape the very dregs of a tyrant's cup.

Thanks to Neander for the above account of our brethren; for, notwithstanding his attempts slily to cast odium upon them, and admitting the possibility of their having extreme views of martyrdom, who cannot see in them the true Christian hero; just such disciples as Christ requires for such times, and always secures? How marvelously were these like certain men we read of in the New Testament! On one occasion they were thrust into prison, for their imprudence in going contrary to the commands of tyrants. An angel opened the prison door, and (fanatical angel also?) bid them in the morning "go, stand and speak in the very temple all the words of this life." They did it, and were brought before the council; "and the high priest asked them, Did we not straitly command you not to teach in this name? and behold you have filled Jerusalem with your doctrine, and intend to bring this man's blood upon us. Then Peter and the other apostles answered and said, We ought to obey God rather than men." You know the sequel. They were "beaten;" "and they departed from the presence of the council, rejoicing that they were counted worthy to suffer shame for his name. And daily still, in the very temple, and in every house, they ceased not to teach and preach Jesus Christ." Just as well might Neander say of these men, that they were indebted for their ultimate sufferings "to a fanatical longing after martyrdom," which pushed them on in their defiance of tyrants. When historians can find no better place for such men, let them turn them over to Baptists. God grant that they may ever be welcome.

2. *Persecutions and Martyrdoms of the Novatian Baptists.* We quote a few facts of this people from Lardner: "In 331, he (Constantine) changed his policy towards these people, (Novatians,) and they were involved with other denominations in distress and sufferings. Their books were sought for, they were forbidden assembling together, and many lost their places of worship. Constantine's oppressive measures prompted many to leave the scene of sufferings, and retire into some more sequestered spots. Claudius Lyssel, the popish archbishop, traces the rise of the Waldensean heresy to a pastor named Leo, leaving Rome at this period for the valleys."

"In 375, the emperor Valens embraced the Arian creed. He closed the Novatian churches, and banished their ministers. During this severe trial, the benevolent feelings of the Novatians became so apparent as to extort admiration from their enemies."

"In the fourth lateral council, canons were made to banish them as heretics; and these canons were supported by an edict, in 413, issued by the emperors Theodosius and Honorius, declaring that all persons re-baptized, and the re-baptizers, should be punished with death. Accordingly, Albanus, a zealous minister, with others, were punished with death for re-baptizing. These combined modes of oppression led the faithful to abandon the cities, and seek retreats in the country, which they did, particularly in the valleys of Piedmont, the inhabitants of which began to be called Waldenses."

How precisely do these persecutions answer the description of those in New Testament times! "At that time there was a great persecution against the church which was at Jerusalem ; and they were all scattered abroad throughout the regions of Judea and Samaria." . . "Therefore they that were scattered abroad went every where preaching the word." In the Novatian persecutions, when they fled to the valleys, we no doubt have the germ (as Claudius Lyssel supposes) of what he terms "the Waldensean heresy." How, in their case, did "the blood of the martyrs prove the seed of the church!" Here undoubtedly is the solution of Mosheim's "difficulty" in regard to the Anabaptists, whose "origin is had in the remote depths of antiquity." Here we are enabled to account for his admission of the fact, that "before the rise of Luther and Calvin, there lay concealed in almost all the countries of Europe, particularly in Bohemia, Moravia, Switzerland and Germany, many persons who adhered tenaciously to the spiritual nature of the kingdom of Christ." Thus has it pleased God to pass along, from age to age, and from country to country, his church, never for a moment allowing it to become extinct.

CHAPTER IV.

1. Persecutions of the Donatist Baptists ; their Defence of Religious Liberty. 2. Of the Paulician Baptists, eminent in piety and suffering.

1. *The Donatists.*

According to Mosheim, "the Donatists were a most powerful and numerous body of dissenters, almost as numerous as the Catholics." Jones says : "There was hardly a city or town in Africa, in which there was not a Donatist church."

Constantine was now (A. D. 314) fully invested with imperial power. The Papists claim his interference in their difficulties with the Donatists. He complies apparently at first, in kindness, but ultimately in great severity. The Donatists inquire indignantly, as Roger Williams in substance did, at a much later day: "*What has the Emperor to do with the Church? What have Christians to do with Kings? What have Bishops to do at Court?*"

Surely, there need be no dispute as to where the doctrine of the separation of the State and Church appeared, after New Testament times. We presume that so important a doctrine never died out of the creed of the genuine disciples of Christ. From the moment the Saviour gave form to it, in the ever-memorable declaration: "My kingdom is not of this world; if my kingdom were of this world, then would my servants fight, that I should not be delivered to the Jews; but now is my kingdom not from hence;" from that moment it has been cherished, and has gone with Christians into the "valleys," as they have fled from persecution. If it appears not before, here at all events we have it, in "the first persecution which realized the support of a Christian emperor" (A. D. 314), thundered by the Novatian Baptists in the very ears of Constantine, when he presumed in his secular capacity to preside in person over the affairs of religion.

Constantine did not relish such a method of receiving his interference in the affairs of religion. He listened to the more flattering representations of Papal bishops; and deprived the Donatists of their houses of worship, and put some of them to death. Wavering between the parties, like a weak man, he repealed the laws against them only to enact more severe ones, and finally died in the full career of persecution for conscience sake.

Now, for many years, the Donatists received a vacillating treatment from their enemies, sometimes fully tolerated, and then the sad reverse, until about A. D. 413, when the Papists prevailed upon Honorius and Theodosius, emperors of the East and the West, to issue that bloody edict against those rebaptizing and rebaptized. Gibbon remarks on this edict, that "three hundred bishops, with many thousands of the inferior clergy, were torn from their churches, stripped of their ecclesiastical possessions, banished to the islands, proscribed by law, if they presumed to conceal themselves in the provinces of Africa. Their numerous congregations, both in the cities and the country, were deprived of the rights of citizens, and the exercise of religious worship. A regular scale of fines, from ten to two hundred pounds of silver, was curiously ascertained, according to the distinction of rank and fortune, to punish the crime of assisting at a schismatic conventicle; and if the fine had been levied five times without subduing the obstinacy of the offender, his future punishment was referred to the discretion of the imperial court."

2. *Persecutions and martyrdoms of the Paulician Baptists.*

"I hope it may be shortly evident" (says Milnor, in his confidence in the Paulicians), "that they originated from a heavenly influence, teaching and converting them; and that in them we have one of those extraordinary effusions of the Divine Spirit, on his word, by which the knowledge of Christ, and the practice of godliness, was kept alive in the world."

But these brethren did not escape the fate of the faithful in such a day. Indeed, in proportion as error became prevalent in the world, did the fires of persecution burn with the greater violence. We quote from Orchard's account of this people, in relation to their sufferings for the truth. His positions are sustained by such authorities as Milner, Gibbon, Lardner, Robinson, and Jones.

"Alarmed at the progress their novel opinions were making, and discovering the growing importance of their opinions, the church party engaged in the most bitter and virulent controversy with them. Ineffectual in their efforts, the Greek emperors began to persecute them with the most sanguinary severity. They were sentenced to be capitally punished, and their books, wherever found, to be committed to the flames. If any person was found to have secreted them, he was to be put to death, and his goods confiscated."

"A Greek officer, armed with legal and military authority, appeared at Coronia, to strike the shepherd, and to reclaim if possible the sheep. By a refinement of cruelty, he placed Sylvanus (their pastor) before a line of his disciples, who were commanded, as the price of their pardon, and as proof of their penitence, to stone to death their spiritual father. The affectionate flock turned aside from the impious office, the stones dropped from their filial hands, and, of the whole number, only one executioner could be found. This apostate, after putting Sylvanus to death, gained, by some means, admittance into communion, and again deceived and betrayed his unsuspecting brethren; and as many as were treacherously ascertained, and could be collected, were massed together into an immense pile, and, by order of the emperor, consumed to ashes. Simeon, the officer, struck with the readiness with which the Paulicians could die for their religion, examined their arguments and became himself a convert, renounced his honors and fortune, and three years afterwards went to Cabossa, and became the successor of Constantine Sylvanus, a zealous preacher among the Paulicians, and at last sealed his testimony with his blood. Many were banished into Thrace, from whence they passed into Bulgaria and Sclavonia, where they took root and settled in their own church order. From the blood and ashes of the first Paulician victims, a succession of teachers and congregations arose. The Greeks, to subdue them, made use both of arguments and of arms, with all the terror of penal laws, without effecting their object. The emperors, in conjunction with the clergy, exerted their zeal with a peculiar degree of bitterness and fury, against this people. Though every kind of oppressive measures and means were used, yet all efforts for their suppression proved fruitless; nor could all their power, and all their barbarity, exhaust the patience, or conquer the obstinacy of that inflexible people, who possessed, says Mosheim, a fortitude worthy of a better cause."

Towards the end of the eighth century, a better state of things prevailed for a time, when the Paulicians became very numerous; but, under Michael and Leo, persecutions were resumed. "They made strict inquisition throughout every province of the Grecian empire, and inflicted capital punishment upon such of them as refused to return to the bosom of the church."

"The severest persecution experienced by them, was encouraged by the Empress Theodora, A. D. 835. Her decrees were severe, but the cruelty with which they were executed by her officers, was horrible beyond expression. Her sanguinary inquisitors explored cities and mountains in lesser Asia. After confiscating the goods and property of *one hundred thousand* of this people, the owners, to that number, were put to death in the most barbarous manner, and made to expire slowly under a variety of the most excruciating tortures."

It must here be admitted that some of the Paulicians, driven to madness by what they suffered, did retaliate upon their enemies, contrary to the custom of ancient Christians and the teachings of the Saviour. Whilst we cannot approve this exception, we cannot be surprised at it. The only matter of astonishment is, that the exceptions were so rare under such provocations. Gibbon finds an apology for them; and better men have done it, and no doubt will continue to, at least in that "charity which hopeth all things." Though we may not now see how, there must be some extenuation of their conduct in this affair, who were generally so correct.

CHAPTER V.

1. Persecutions and Martyrdoms of the Paterine Baptists. 2. Gundulphas arises. 3. Arnold of Brescia; his intrepidity and martyrdom.

1. *The Paterine Baptists.*

THERE is some little uncertainty attending the origin of the term Paterines, and hence how it came to be applied to this excellent and numerous class of Baptists. The probability, however, is, that the term is about equivalent to sufferers or martyrs, and that it was well applied to this people. So claims Mezeray: " A name which came from the glory they took in suffering patiently for the truth." Orchard remarks in regard to it: " In a previous section we have given the outlines of this suffering people, under the denomination of Novationists, and endeavored to trace their history till the penal laws compelled them to retire into caves and dens to worship God. While oppressed by the Catholic party, they obtained the name of Paterines, which means sufferers, or what is nearly synonymous with our modern acceptation of the word martyrs, and which indicated an afflicted and poor people, trusting in the name of the Lord."

So pious and unoffending were this people, that it is unaccountable how any could persecute them. And yet not unaccountable, with the Bible in our hands, teaching man's natural enmity to holiness, and the essentially persecuting spirit of Anti-Christ. Common consent ascribes to them the following distinguished character: " They took no oaths and bore no arms. Were decent in their deportment, modest in their dress and discourse, and their morals were irreproachable. In their conversation, there was no levity, no scurrility, no detraction, no falsehood, no swearing. Their dress was neither fine nor mean. They were chaste and temperate, never frequenting taverns or places of amusement. They were not given to anger or violent passions. They were not eager to accumulate wealth, but were content with the plain necessaries of life. They avoided commerce, because they thought it would expose them to the temptations of collusion, falsehood and oaths; and they chose to live by labor or handicraft. They were always employed in spare hours, either in giving or receiving instruction." Surely such a people could not deserve persecution. We shall see whether they received it or not.

We find the first traces of the Paterines as early as A. D. 330; and the last of them, when they probably were merged in the Waldensian churches, in A. D. 1260, covering a period of more than nine hundred years. The theatre of their sufferings and victories was Germany, Italy, France, and Spain. All reliable authorities agree not only in this, but in the statement of Mosheim, that "they passed out of Italy, and spread like an inundation throughout all the European provinces." Rome itself, the boasted "Capital of Christendom," resounded to the eloquence of the Puritans.

This period and theatre in the history of the church, marked by the fortunes of the Paterine Baptists, are of intense interest. Well might a volume of no ordinary size be written of them. The men who appeared, the scenes which transpired, the results reached, all conspire to cause the intelligent Christian to linger around them. Our limits, however, admit of but a brief notice of a few instances of persecution. We follow Orchard's data, sustained by such authorities as Allix, Jorton, Milnor, M'Crie, Mosheim, and Robinson.

2. Gundulphas, a distinguished preacher among the Paterines, arose about A. D. 1020. Some of his followers were arrested in Flanders, charged with abhorring Catholic baptisms. They replied, "The law and the discipline we have received of our Master, will not appear contrary either to the gospel decrees, or apostolic institutions, if carefully looked into." They objected to the baptism of unconverted men, as adminis-

tering or receiving the ordinance, and of infants, "because," they claimed, "the reprobate life of ministers can afford no saving remedy to the persons baptized: because what sins are renounced at the font, are afterwards taken up again in the life and practice; and because a strange will, a strange faith, and strange confession, do not seem to belong to a little child, who neither wills nor runs, who knoweth nothing of faith, and is altogether ignorant of his own good and salvation, in whom there can be no desire of salvation or regeneration, and from whom no confession of faith can be expected."

"During the kingdom of the Goths and Lombards, (from A. D. 954 to 1059,) the Anabaptists, as the Catholics called them, had their share of churches and baptisteries, during which time they held no communion with any hierarchy, that is, churches having different orders of clergy. After the union of those kingdoms, laws were issued by the emperors to deprive dissenters of baptismal churches, and to secure them to the Catholic clergy. Consequently the brethren worshiped in private houses, under different names. Each of the houses, where they met, seemed to be occupied by one of the brethren. They were marked, so as to be known only among themselves, and they never met in large companies." Alas, alas! for this secresy. Those familiar at all with church history know what it means. Such measures were resorted to, to save themselves and children from violent persecution.

3. Arnold of Brescia now (A. D. 1137) appeared, in the providence of God, a man of singular piety, learning and intrepidity. He carried the war, bloodless on his part, into the enemy's very camp. The anathemas of the church were thundered against him; "he was condemned to perpetual silence. He fled to Switzerland; and then, persecuted by Bernard, fled again, all the time gathering strength for the conflict yet before him, until, far in advance of Luther, he goes to Rome itself, resolved to rear there the standard of the cross, or perish in the attempt. Success crowned his efforts. Arnold maintained

his station above ten years, while two Popes either trembled in the Vatican, or wandered as exiles in the adjacent cities." To the end "his friends were numerous, but the sword was no weapon in the articles of his faith." The persecutors finally triumphed, and "in 1155, this noble champion was seized, crucified, and burnt. His ashes were thrown into the river. The clergy triumphed in his death; with his ashes his sect was dispersed; his memory still lives in the minds of the Romans." Jones has well remarked: "Though no corporeal relic could be preserved to animate his followers, the efforts of Arnold, in civil and religious liberty, were cherished in the breasts of future reforming spirits, and inspired those mighty attempts in Wickliffe, Huss, and others."

Numerous have been the charges brought against this martyr; but, as Davenport remarks: "his real crime was his having taught that the church ought to be divested of its worldly possessions, and reduced to its primitive simplicity;" or, as Dr. Wall has it: "he was condemned along with Peter de Bruys for rejecting infant baptism." But we must linger no longer with this interesting, suffering, and victorious people.

CHAPTER VI.

1. The persecutions and martyrs of the Waldensian Baptists; the inquisition originated for them. 2. The boy and the priest. 3. Bartholomew Copin. 4. Cromwell and Milton interfere in behalf of Baptists.

1. *The Waldensian Baptists and the Inquisition.*

THE fires of persecution now began to burn with a lurid glare, which it is impossible to look upon, at this distant point, without shuddering. As never before or since, we seem to see "the Mystery of Babylon the great, the mother of harlots, and abominations of the earth, drunken with the blood of the saints, and with the blood of the martyrs of Jesus." See Rev. xvii. 5, 6. God grant that the period here predicted may have been passed, for it seems impossible to conceive of anything more terrible than this persecution. The Inquisition now (12th century) makes its appearance. The Papists, maddened by their ill success against the Almighty and his people, and apparently "given up to believe a lie that they might be damned," consummate their malignity in that infernal instrument of persecution, the Inquisition—originated, it is generally supposed, particularly for the punishment and extirpation of the Waldenses. The Inquisition established by the spiritual tyrants, it must be sustained by corresponding edicts from the secular tyrants; and now appear those incredible edicts of the European princes, particularly those of Frederick II. and Louis IX., which enshrouded the world in gloom.

It is impossible to do anything like justice to the terrific, heaven-defying results of this coalescence of the spiritual and secular power against the church. Nothing but a miracle of mercy could have saved the wretches of it from his wrath, which those of them who did not repent must now be suffering, whilst multitudes of their victims help to swell the company of those described in Revelations vi. 13, 14, "arrayed in white robes," "who came out of great tribulation, and have washed their robes and made them white in the blood of the Lamb."

Disciple of Jesus, brother of these martyrs, turn not away from their sufferings, until thou hast learned to look upon thy own sacrifices, made, or likely to be, as nothing, and less than nothing, in comparison. Passing with a mournful tribute of respect what they endured for Christ for so many long, long years, we come at once to some of their darkest days, in the valleys of Piedmont, whither they had fled, in the vain hope of rearing their families in the fear of God, unmolested by his enemies.

The valleys of Piedmont, where "Alps on Alps arise," must ever be classic ground to the Christian. Alas! could those mountains and valleys speak, were those fissures in the rocks mouths with tongues, how sad a tale would they tell of murdered, bleeding, burning fathers and mothers, and youths and infants! "A spectator, taking his stand on the top of the ridge of these mountains, will observe, that at the foot, on the Spanish side, lie Asturias, Old Castile, Aragon, and Catalonia; and on the French side, Guienne and Languedoc, Toulouse, Bearn, Alby, Roussillon, and Narbonne, all of which places were remarkable in the darkest times for harboring Christians, who were reputed heretics. Indeed, from the borders of Spain, throughout the greatest part of the south of France, among and below the Alps, along the Rhine, and even to Bohemia, thousands of the disciples of Christ were found, even in the very worst of times, preserving the faith in its purity, adhering to the simplicity of Christian worship, patiently bearing the cross of Christ: men distinguished for the fear of God, and obedience to his will, and persecuted only for righteousness' sake."

"About the year 1400, a violent outrage was committed upon the Waldenses inhabiting the valley Pragela, in Piedmont, by a Catholic party residing in the neighborhood. The attack, which seems to have been of the most furious kind, was made towards the end of December, when the mountains were covered with snow, and thereby rendered so difficult of access, that the peaceable inhabitants of those valleys were wholly unapprized that any such attempt was meditated; and the persecutors were in actual possession of their caves ere the owners seem to have been apprized of any hostile design against them. In this pitiable strait, they had recourse to the only alternative which remained for saving their lives—they fled, though at that inauspicious season of the year, to one of the highest mountains of the Alps, with their wives and children; the unhappy mothers carrying the cradle in one hand,

and in the other leading such of the children as were able to walk. Their inhuman invaders pursued them in their flight, until darkness obscured the objects of their fury. Many were slain before they could reach the mountains. Overtaken by the shades of night, these afflicted outcasts wandered up and down the mountains covered with snow, destitute of the means of shelter from the inclemency of the weather, or of supporting themselves under it, by any of the comforts which Providence had designed for that purpose. Benumbed with cold, some fell asleep, and became an easy prey to the severity of the climate; and when the night had passed away, there were found in their cradles, or lying on the snow, four score of their infants deprived of life; and many of their mothers were dead by their side, and others just on the point of expiring. During the night, their enemies had plundered their abodes of every thing that was of value. This seems to have been the first general attack made by the Catholic peasantry opon the Waldenses. They had been hitherto sheltered from the Pontiff's measures by the Dukes of Savoy, so that the rage of their enemies had been restrained to a few solitary cases of arrested heresy; but this kind of assault, planned no doubt by the clergy, was of a novel character; and so deeply impressed were the minds of these people with the circumstances of the sufferers, as to speak of it for centuries after with feelings of apparent horror."

"Innocent the 8th was promoted to the tiara in 1484. This pontiff, in the spirit of his predecessor of infamous notoriety, Innocent III., issued his bulls for the extirpation of the Waldenses, and appointed officers to carry the same into effect. 'We have heard,' said the Pope, 'and it is come to our knowledge, not without much displeasure, that certain sons of iniquity, followers of that abominable and pernicious sect of malignant men, called the "*poor of Lyons*," or Waldenses, who have so long ago endeavored, in Piedmont and in other places, to ensnare the sheep belonging to God,' &c."

The Pontiff's menaces were not vapor. An army was soon raised by Albert, the Pope's legate, and marched directly into the valley of Loyse. The inhabitants, apprized of their approach, fled to their caves at the tops of the mountains, carrying with them their children, and whatever valuables they possessed, as well as what was thought necessary for their support. The lieutenant, finding the inhabitants all fled, and that not an individual appeared with whom he could converse, had considerable trouble in discovering their retreats; when causing quantities of wood to be placed at the entrance to their caves, he ordered it to be set on fire. The consequence of this inhuman conduct was, four hundred children were suffocated in their cradles, or in the arms of their dead mothers, while multitudes, to avoid death by suffocation, or being committed to the flames, precipitated themselves headlong from their caverns upon the rocks below, where they were dashed to pieces; and if any escaped death by the fall, they were immediately slaughtered by the brutal soldiers. It appears that more than three thousand men and women perished on this occasion. Measures equally ferocious were adopted against the inoffensive inhabitants of other valleys, and with a like cruel success."

"Sentences were now publicly given against them in various churches. Innocent VIII. appeared as resolved at this period (A. D. 1484) to free the world from these dissenters as Innocent III. had been in the 13th century to rid Languedoc of the Albigenses. The Pontiff was filled with terrible apprehensions of danger, and exhorted the European princes to put a stop to all opposition. In order to have pecuniary means adequate to the expenses of these undertakings, indulgences to sin were sold by the servants of the church, and pardons for crimes past, or to be committed, could be purchased of these panders of hell. So effectual were the Papal measures that the inhabitants were wholly extirpated in the above-named valleys."

"In 1487, scenes of barbarous cruelty awaited those long privileged people, who inhabited other districts of Piedmont; and in the ensuing year, to complete the work of destruction, an army of 18,000 men marched into those sequestered parts. The early Waldenses forbade war and even prohibited self-defence; but their patience was now worn out (Dan. vii. 25), and they departed from their ancestors' creed. They armed themselves with wooden targets and cross-bows, availing themselves of the advantages of their situation and country, every where defended the defiles of the mountains and repulsed the invaders. The women and children, (an affecting sight,) were on their knees during the conflict, and in the simplest language, arising from overwhelming distress, and the prospect of losing all, their religion and their lives, entreated the Lord to spare and protect his people."

We select from the persecutions and martyrdoms of the Waldenses, two cases illustrating the times to which they relate. The former is given by McCrie, and the latter by Jones.

2. *The boy and the priest.*

"A monk was exhorting the people to purchase heaven by the merit of good works. A boy who was present exclaimed, 'That's blasphemy, for the Bible tells us that Christ purchased heaven by his sufferings and death, and bestows it on us freely by his mercy.' A dispute of considerable length ensued between the youth and the preacher. Provoked at the pertinent replies of his juvenile opponent, and at the favorable reception which the audience gave them, 'Get you gone, you young rascal!' exclaimed the monk. 'You are just come from the cradle, and will you take it upon you to judge of sacred things, which the most learned cannot explain?' 'Did you never read these words, "out of the mouths of babes and sucklings God perfects praise?"' rejoined the youth. Upon which the preacher quitted the pulpit in wrathful confusion, breathing out threatenings against the poor boy, who was instantly thrown into prison, where he still lies, says the writer, Dec. 31, 1544."

3. *Bartholomew Copin.*

This man suffered death in 1601, at Ast, a city of Piedmont, and the only crime that was laid to his charge, was an occasional remark one evening, at the table, against the doctrine of transubstantiation. He was a merchant, and the fatal expression was made in the company of men of his own vocation. But some spy carried the tale to the bishop; a long and tedious prosecution was commenced against him; he was thrown into prison, where it was supposed he was strangled, and his dead body was committed to the flames."

4. In May, 1665, the persecution of the Waldenses was arrested by the interference of Oliver Cromwell, then "protector" of England, who, according to Moreland, immediately on hearing of them, "arose like a lion out of his place, and by the most pathetic appeals to the Protestant princes upon the Continent, awoke the whole Christian world, exciting their hearts to pity and commiseration. Milton was now Cromwell's secretary, and one of the staunchest friends of religious liberty. His Christian and poetic heart gave birth to the following well-known and beautiful sonnet:

"Avenge, O Lord, thy slaughtered saints, whose bones
Lie scattered on the Alpine mountains cold;
E'en them who kept thy truth so pure of old,
When all our fathers worshiped stocks and stones,
Forget not: In thy book record their groans,
Who were thy sheep, and in their ancient fold
Slain by the bloody Piedmontese that roll'd
Mother and infant down the rocks. Their moans
The vales redoubled to the hills, and they
To heaven. Their martyr'd blood and ashes sow
O'er all the Italian fields, where still doth sway
The tripled tyrant; that from these may grow
A hundred fold, who, having learned thy way,
Early may fly the Babylonian woe."

It is said by writers of Milton's time, that the eighth line relates to the following affecting incident: "A mother was hurled down a mighty rock with a little infant in her arms; and three days after, was found dead with the little child alive, but fast clasped between the arms of its dead mother, which were cold and stiff, insomuch that those who found them had much ado to get the young child out."

In evidence that this persecution was not only wrong, in the sense that all persecution is, but was now inflicted upon a most pious and excellent people, it should be remarked, that though they had peculiarities, which no one will now defend, they sustained a most excellent character, even though their enemies judge them. Archbishop Claudius Seisselius says of them, in 1480, "Their heresy excepted, they generally lived a purer life than other Christians." Their "heresy" was such an opposition to the Papal Church as all Protestants now agree in. A monk, who was sent under the pretence of reforming them, returned confounded, and confessed that: "in his whole life, he had never known so much of the Scriptures as he had learned during those few days he had conversed with the heretics." Any amount of such testimony can be produced.

CHAPTER VII.

1. Persecutions and martyrs of the Anabaptists by Luther and the Reformers; difference between Muncer and Munster. 2. Adrian Pan and wife. 3. John Deswarte, his wife, children, and neighbors.

As early as A. D. 1522, our brethren were called Anabaptists, (rebaptizers,) because they would not acknowledge the validity of the baptisms of the Papal Church, and baptized again those converted to Christ, who had previously received the ordinance from her hand.

We are pained to be compelled, in faithfulness to history, to record the fact that the Papists now had Protestant aid in persecution. The Reformers, with Luther at their head, were now upon the stage. Robinson, in his "Ecclesiastical Researches" (a work of learning and faithfulness, of which any one must be convinced who will give it an examination), quoting numerous authors, not Baptists, gives a full and painful account of what our brethren suffered from the Reformers. Many other writers agree essentially with him.

It is unfair, however, to make Luther and his associates responsible for all the Anabaptists suffered at this period. Luther's position was one of great difficulty. He had been the apparent cause of the reform now progressing, which involved not only himself and his church, but his political protectors in difficulty with the higher government. The Anabaptists, who, at first, could hardly be distinguished from the Lutherans, carried things further than they, and were more obnoxious to the State; and Luther and his defenders were of necessity involved with them. Some things, severe to them, Luther had no part in procuring; and others, he could not have prevented if he would. Others he was strongly tempted to approve and promote, by his desire to save the reform from unnecessary unpopularity with the powers that were. Of course, he should have adopted the thorough principles of reform, which characterized the Anabaptists; and if he had, no one can tell how glorious the result might have been. But, on the other hand, it is at least possible, that the age was unprepared for any thing else; and that more severity and correctness might have resulted, for the time being, in the suppression of the whole movement. It is easier to blame Luther than it would have been to have acted a better part in such circumstances. But, of course, all this is no justification of his participation in what they wrongly suffered.

Rev. Dr. Sears, whose account of this matter, in his Life

of Luther, is one of eminent charity for the Reformers (we suspect of much more than the facts will warrant), remarks: "Luther has been accused of inhumanity toward the Anabaptists; and when we compare him with the mild Brentz, who opposed putting them to death for their sentiments, and with religious men of modern times, we must, in part at least, admit the charge." After apologizing, for even this admission, he continues: "Without dwelling on these painful details, we will adduce one brief letter, as giving a fair specimen of Luther's feelings, and thus dismiss the subject. The letter is addressed to Menius and Myconius, in 1530. 'I am pleased,' he says, 'that you intend to publish a book against the Anabaptists, as soon as possible. Since they are not only blasphemous, but also seditious men, *let the sword exercise its right over them; for this is the will of God, that he shall have judgment who resisteth the power.* Let us not, therefore, think better of these men than God himself, and all the saints have done.'" This is indeed a brief letter, but a most bitter, persecuting one; and if it is "a fair specimen of Luther's feelings," it is a strong confirmation of all Robinson and his authorities claim upon the subject.

After minor acts of intolerance, in which Luther and his associates *did* participate, we come to others for which they may be, more or less, or not at all, accountable. "The first edict against the Anabaptists was published at Zurich, 1522, in which there was a penalty of a silver mark set upon all such as should suffer themselves to be rebaptized, or should withhold baptism from their children. And it was further declared, that those who should openly oppose this order, should be yet more severely treated. This being insufficient to check immersion, the senate decreed, like Honorious (A. D. 413), that all persons who professed anabaptism, or harbored the professors of the doctrine, should be punished with death by drowning. In defiance of this law, the Baptists persevered in their regular discipline; and some of their ministers of learned celebrity, realized the severity of the sentence. Many Baptists were drowned and burnt."

"An edict issued by Frederick, at a later period, shows how unpalitable these views (of the Anabaptists) were. His majesty expressed his astonishment at the number of Anabaptists, and his horror at the principal error which they embraced, which was that, according to the express declaration of the Holy Scriptures (1 Cor. vii. 23), they were to submit to no human authority. He adds that his conscience compels him to proscribe them, and accordingly he banished them from his dominions on pain of death."

It is now evident, that many persons of the Baptist persuasion and views existed on the continent long before the affair of Munster blackened their escutcheon; and the characters of these people have awakened admiration in men of distinguished parts, who have left testimonies of their piety, which may be brought into comparison with any denomination of the present age. Among their admirers may be found the names of Commenius, Scultetus, Beza, Cloppenburg, Cassander, Erasmus, Heyden, Hoornbeck, Cocceius, and Cardinal Hossius. The latter says: "If the truth of religion were to be judged by the readiness and cheerfulness which a man of any sect shows in suffering, then the opinions and persuasions of no sect can be truer or surer than those of the Anabaptists, since there have been none for these twelve hundred years past, that have been more grievously punished."

Erasmus says of the Anabaptists of Switzerland, in 1529: "Although they are very numerous, they have no church in their possession. These persons are worthy of greater commendation than others, on account of the harmlessness of their lives, but they are oppressed by all other sects."

"In almost all the countries of Europe, an unspeakable number of Baptists preferred death in its worst forms," says Mosheim, "to the retraction of their sentiments. Neither the view of the flames that were kindled to consume them, nor the ignominy of the gibbet, nor the terrors of the sword, could shake their invincible constancy, or make them abandon tenets that appeared dearer to them than life and all its enjoyments."

"It is indeed true, that many Baptists suffered death, not on account of their being considered rebellious subjects, but merely because they were judged to be incurable heretics; for in this century the error of limiting the administration of baptism to adult persons only, and the practice of re-baptizing such as had received that sacrament in a state of infancy, were looked upon as most flagitious and intolerable heresies. Those who had no other marks of peculiarity than their administering baptism to the adult, and their excluding the unrighteous from the external communion of the church, ought to have met with milder treatment. Many of those who followed the wiser class of Baptists—nay, some who adhered to the most extravagant factions, were men of upright intentions and sincere piety, who were seduced into fanaticism by their ignorance and simplicity, on the one hand, and by a laudable desire of reforming the corrupt state of religion, on the other. While the terrors of death, in the most awful forms, were presented to the view of this people, and numbers of them were executed every day, without any distinction being made between the innocent and the guilty, those who escaped the severity of the sword, were found in the most discouraging situations that can be imagined. On the one hand, they saw with sorrow all their hopes blasted by the ravages of Munster; and on the other, they were filled with the most anxious apprehensions of the perils that threatened them on all sides."

It is important, in tracing the persecutions of the Anabaptists, to distinguish between Mun*cer* and Mun*ster*, terms frequently occurring in this connection. *Muncer* was a distinguished man, at one time admired by Luther, but ultimately condemned and persecuted by him for his Anabaptist conduct. It seems incredible that Martin Luther, persecuted himself, and giving utterance to sentiments so noble on the subject, could treat Muncer with so much injustice. But, alas for poor human nature ! it makes all the difference in the world, whether one is the assailed or the assailer. When the "Peasant War" broke out, Muncer became deeply interested in it, and is supposed to have drawn up its memorial, a noble document, which, says Voltaire, "a Lycurgus might have signed." He was undoubtedly a Baptist, and though, like many of his brethren, he participated in the peasants' war, which was as just, on their part, as the war of the American Revolution, there is no evidence of his approving of all to which it led. It is stated, on the authority of Mosheim, in regard to the peasants' war, and the death of Muncer, "these oppressed men were consequently met by their lords with a sword, instead of redress ; being defeated, they were slaughtered and reproached, the invariable results and concomitants of defeat. Muncer, their friend and chief, was put to death."

Munster was a city, in which, some ten years after the death of Muncer, a violent and fanatical disturbance took place. This affair did not originate with the Anabaptists. That more or less of them participated in it, is probable, but not more so than that they generally condemned it. The Anabaptists being well known as reformers, holding to some of the opinions of the Munster affair, were too readily accused by their enemies of a participation in it which they never had. It resulted, however, in some of the severe measures against them which we have contemplated.

In confirmation of this opinion in regard to the Munster affair, Benedict says : "We see them almost daily on trial in the criminal courts ; and never were a people so uniform, and, I may say, so dauntless in their religious professions, as were the German Anabaptists, for the century and a half now under review. The charges against them seem to have been stereotyped by the inquisitors, and their answers were uniform as to matters of fact, and always mild and explicit as to the men of

Munster or Amsterdam, for the scenes at both places are often referred to. They uniformly answered, 'These were not our brethren; we have no fellowship with such men. The men of Munster are among yourselves, or of your party. They did not admit, or even intimate, that they went off from them, or were ever in their connection. But they bitterly complained of having to suffer for the faults of others, that they knew nothing about, because some of them agreed with them in rejecting infant baptism. They treated the whole story much as Baptists would at the present day, if any thing which had happened among the Mormons should be laid to their charge."

We select a few instances of martyrdom of the German Anabaptists:

2. *Adrian Pan and Wife.*

They suffered martyrdom in Antwerp, in 1559. When they lay in prison, he wrote to his friends thus: "They accused us much concerning those of Munster and Amsterdam; but I told them that I had nothing to do with them, but that we suffered for the truth's sake; and that I am not thirty years old, and how could I have possibly taken part with them? Some blasphemed, and others sympathized with us." This is a remarkable instance of Anabaptist suffering for the errors of others. Adrian Pan was not born at the time of the Munster and Amsterdam riots, but dies notwithstanding, being a Bap tist. He was *beheaded;* and his wife, shortly after giving birth to a child, was *drowned.*

3. *Martyrdom of John Deswarte, his wife and six children, with some of their neighbors.*

At about the same time with the martyrdom of Pan and his wife, the above-named cases occurred: "Brant, in his history of the Reformation, in the sixteenth century, at Halwin, in Flanders, states that John Deswarte, whom he calls an Anabaptist, and his family, who had been betrayed by the professedly Christian pastor of that town, were carried away by the Dean of Rousen to Lisle.

"Deswarte was taken with his wife and four sons. The two youngest of his children, not being at home when the inquisitor broke into the house, were warned by the neighbors to escape; but one of them said to the other, 'Let us not seek to save ourselves, but rather die with our father and mother.' In the mean time they carried the father out, who, seeing his sons, said to them, 'Will ye also go to the new Jerusalem?' One of them, who was scarcely sixteen, cried out, 'Yes, we will, father;' and they at once surrendered themselves. These, with two other persons of the same faith, who happened to be in the house, as also two married couples, and a man who had endeavored to comfort them, were at several times all burnt at Lisle."

So numerous and thrilling are such instances in this period, that volumes might be extracted. We hasten on.

CHAPTER VIII.

1. Persecutions and Martyrs in Britain. 2. Jeffreys and Baxter. 3. John Bunyan. 4. Kiffin and the Hewling Family.

1. *Baptists in Britain.*

AN intelligent article, originating in the English Baptist Jubilee Memorial, furnishes valuable facts upon this topic:

"But early in the 12th century, some of the Waldenses coming into England to propagate the gospel, were apprehended and examined before a council assembled at Oxford, by command of Henry II., and on confessing themselves followers of the Apostles, and rejecting infant baptism, they were branded on the forehead with a red hot iron, and treated with merciless rigor."

"Two circumstances connected with that period are prominent in the history of Baptists; the publicity into which they emerged, and the hostility which was evinced against them.

In 1536, the national clergy met in convocation, declared the sentiments of the Baptists to be 'detestable heresies, utterly to be condemned.' In 1538 a commission was given to Cranmer, Archbishop of Canterbury, and others, to proceed against Baptists, and burn their books; and on the 16th of November, in the same year, a royal proclamation was issued against them, and instructions sent to the justices throughout England, directing them to see that the laws against the Baptists were executed. Several were burnt to death in Smithfield."

"The reign of Mary is well known to have been cruel even to ferocity. One circumstance in Baptist history accords with the spirit of that execrable reign. A man named David George was disinterred at St. Lawrence church, three years after his death, and his body burnt, because it was discovered that he had been a Baptist."

It was during her reign that John Rogers suffered martyr dom, for we are in a period now, (1555,) rich with the blood of eminent saints of all Protestant sects.

"This relentless cruelty against the Baptists continued even under Queen Elizabeth. A royal proclamation was issued, in which it was ordained that all Baptists, and other heretics, should leave the land; but they seemed to gather fortitude. In 1575, the 17th year of Elizabeth's reign, a congregation of them was found without Aldgate, London, of whom some were banished, twenty-seven were imprisoned, and two were burnt to death in Smithfield."

For a time now, 1650, including the period of the commonwealth, and Cromwell's reign, and Milton, the poet's secretaryship, our brethren were tolerated. But soon the demon persecution began again to revive, and especially in the hands of James II., and his tool, Lord Chief Justice Jeffreys, that insolent persecutor. Well known names, Baptists and others, appear in this period; such as Bunyan, Kiffin and Hewling, among the Baptists; and Baxter, How and Owen, among Pedobaptists. In illustration of the insolence and injustice of persecution in power, observe Richard Baxter's treatment before Jeffreys, as given by Macaulay.

2. "Baxter begged that he might have some time to prepare for his defence. It was on the day that Oates was pilloried at Palace Yard, that the illustrious chief of the Puritans, oppressed by age and infirmities, came to Westminster Hall to make this request. Jeffreys burst into a storm of rage. 'Not a minute,' he cried, 'to save his life. I can deal with saints as well as with sinners. There stands Oates on one side of the pillory; and if Baxter stood on the other, the two greatest rogues in the kingdom would stand together.'

"When the trial came on at Guildhall, a crowd of those who loved and honored Baxter filled the court. At his side stood Doctor William Bates, one of the most eminent Non-conformist divines. Two Whig barristers of great note, Pollexfen and Wallop, appeared for the defendant. Pollexfen had scarce begun his address to the jury, when the chief justice broke forth: 'Pollexfen, I know you well. I will set a mark on you. You are the patron of the faction. This is an old rogue, a schismatical knave, a hypocritical villain. He hates the Liturgy. He would have nothing but long-winded cant without book;' and then his lordship turned up his eyes, clasped his hands, and began to sing through his nose, in imitation of what he supposed to be Baxter's style of praying, 'Lord, we are thy people, thy peculiar people, thy dear people.' Pollexfen gently reminded the court that his late majesty had thought Baxter deserving of a bishopric. 'And what ailed the old blockhead then,' cried Jeffreys, 'that he did not take it?' His fury now rose almost to madness. He called Baxter a dog, and swore that it would be no more than justice to whip such a villain through the whole city.

"Wallop interposed, but fared no better than his leader. 'You are in all these dirty causes, Mr. Wallop,' said the judge. 'Gentlemen of the long robe ought to be ashamed to assist such factious knaves.' The advocate made another attempt to obtain a hearing, but to no purpose. 'If you do not know your duty,' said Jeffreys, 'I will teach it you.'

"Wallop sat down, and Baxter himself attempted to put in a word; but the chief justice drowned all expostulation in a torrent of ribaldry and invective, mingled with scraps of Hudibras. 'My lord,' said the old man, 'I have been much blamed by Dissenters for speaking respectfully of bishops.' 'Baxter for bishops!' cried the judge; 'that's a merry conceit indeed. I know what you mean by bishops—rascals like yourself, Kidderminster bishops, factious, snivelling Presbyterians!' Again Baxter essayed to speak, and again Jeffreys bellowed, 'Richard, Richard, dost thou think we will let thee poison the court? Richard, thou art an old knave. Thou hast written books enough to load a cart, and every book as full of sedition as an egg is full of meat. By the grace of God, I'll look after thee. I see a great many of your brotherhood waiting to know what will befall their mighty Don. And there,' he continued, fixing his savage eye on Bates, 'there is a doctor of the party at your elbow. But, by the grace of God Almighty, I will crush you all!'

"Baxter held his peace. But one of the junior counsel for the defence made a last effort, and undertook to show that the words of which complaint was made would not bear the construction put on them by the information. With this view he began to read the context. In a moment he was roared down. 'You sha'n't turn the court into a conventicle!' The noise of weeping was heard from some of those who surrounded Baxter. 'Snivelling calves!' said the judge.

"Witnesses of character were in attendance, and among them were several clergymen of the Established Church. But the chief justice would hear nothing. 'Does your lordship think,' said Baxter, 'that any jury will convict a man on such a trial as this?' 'I warrant you, Mr. Baxter,' said Jeffreys. 'Don't trouble yourself about that.' Jeffreys was right. The sheriffs were the tools of the government. The juries, selected by the sheriffs from among the fiercest zealots of the Tory party, conferred for a moment, and returned a verdict of guilty. 'My lord,' said Baxter, as he left the court, 'there was once a chief justice who would have treated me very differently.' He alluded to his learned and virtuous friend, Sir Matthew Hale. 'There is not an honest man in England,' said Jeffreys, 'but looks on thee as a knave.'

"The sentence was, for those times, a lenient one. What passed in conference among the judges cannot be certainly known. It was believed among the Nonconformists, and is highly probable, that the chief justice was overruled by his three brethren. He proposed, it is said, that Baxter should be whipped through London at the cart's tail. The majority thought that an eminent divine who, a quarter of a century before, had been offered a mitre, and who was now in his seventieth year, would be sufficiently punished for a few sharp words with fine and imprisonment.

"The manner in which Baxter was treated by a judge who was a member of the cabinet, and a favorite of the sovereign, indicated, in a manner not to be mistaken, the feeling with which the government at this time regarded the Protestant Nonconformists. But already that feeling had been indicated by still stronger and more terrible signs."

In 1665, the "Five Mile Act" was passed. According to this act, "it was a crime for a Nonconformist minister to reside within five miles of any city or borough, or even to approach within that distance of any parish or place where they had stated service in the Established Church, unless in passing on the public road. The violation of this law exposed them to a fine of forty pounds"—two hundred dollars. The "Conventicle Act" rendered "the meeting of more than five persons for the worship of God illegal, in any other place than that allowed by the liturgy, and sanctioned by the compulsory church. For the first offence, persons suffered three months' imprisonment, or paid a fine of five pounds; for the second offence, the fine was doubled; for the third, it was a fine of one hundred pounds, or seven years' transportation—and in the event of their returning without permission, they were doomed to death, without benefit of clergy."

"The Baptists," says Sir James McIntosh, "suffered more than any others under Charles II., because they had publicly professed the principles of religious liberty." "It has been computed," says Orchard, "that from the Restoration to the Revolution, seventy thousand persons suffered on account of religion; eight thousand persons were destroyed; and twelve million pounds sterling, sixty million dollars, were paid in fines."

3. *Persecution of John Bunyan.*

Bunyan was arrested in Nov., 1660. What was his crime? In the language of the warrant upon which he was arrested: "He went about to several conventicles in the country, to the great disparagement of the government of the Church of England." His own account of his preaching is: "I had great desire, in fulfilling my ministry, to get into the darkest places in the country. I never cared to meddle with things controverted. It pleased me to contend, with great earnestness, for the word of faith, and the remission of sins by the death and sufferings of Jesus; but as to other things, I would let them alone, because I saw they engendered strife." No man could be more inoffensive in doing the bidding of the Son of God. But the Conventicle act had passed; and the Justice had resolved, as he said, "to break the neck of such meetings" as people dared to hold out of the Established Church.

As to the period of his imprisonment, he says: "I was had home to prison, and there have lain now complete twelve years, waiting to see what God would suffer these men to do to me." Dr. Southey, the poet, coldly supposes: "their condition was not worsened by their imprisonment, since it would render them objects of compassion to their neighbors; and that Bunyan was on the whole very comfortable. He had the society of some who suffered for the same cause. He had his Bible, and his book of martyrs, and had leisure to brood over his thoughts." No doubt he was more comfortable than some prelates in their palaces, but no thanks for this to the laws, or their executors, or abettors.

"The oppressor holds
His body bound; but knows not what a range
His spirit takes, unconscious of a chain;
And that to bind him is a vain attempt,
Whom God delights in, and in whom he dwells."

The only sunshine in his prison was such as God and truth and a clear conscience gave him. Out of prison he might have had these, and been spared all he suffered. The consequences of his firmness to lay in prison until doomsday, rather than relinquish his right and duty to preach, were severe.

"I found myself," he says, "a man encompassed with infirmities: the parting with my wife and poor children hath often been to me in this place as the pulling of the flesh from my bones; and that not only because I am somewhat too fond of these great mercies, but also because I should have often brought to my mind the many hardships, miseries, and wants, that my poor family was likely to meet with, should I be taken from them; especially my poor blind child, who lay nearer my heart than all beside. O! the thoughts of the hardship my poor blind one might undergo, would break my heart to pieces. Poor child, thought I, what sorrow art thou to have for thy portion in this world! Thou must be beaten, must beg, suffer hunger, cold, nakedness, and a thousand calamities, though I cannot now endure the wind should blow on thee. But yet, recalling myself, thought I, I must venture you all with God, though it goeth to the quick to leave you."

We leave to Macaulay what remains to be said of Bunyan:

"It may be doubted whether any English Dissenter had

suffered more severely under the penal laws than John Bunyan. Of the twenty-seven years which had elapsed since the Restoration, he had passed twelve in confinement. He still persisted in preaching; but, that he might preach, he was under the necessity of disguising himself like a carter. He was often introduced into meetings through back doors, with a smock frock on his back and a whip in his hand. If he had thought only of his own ease and safety, he would have hailed the Indulgence with delight. He was now, at length, free to pray and exhort in open day. His congregation rapidly increased; thousands hung upon his words; and at Bedford, where he originally resided, money was plentifully contributed to build a meeting-house for him. His influence among the common people was such that the government would willingly have bestowed on him some municipal office; but his vigorous understanding and his stout English heart were proof against all delusion and all temptation. He felt assured that the proffered toleration was merely a bait, intended to lure the Puritan party to destruction; nor would he, by accepting a place for which he was not legally qualified, recognize the validity of the dispensing power. One of the last acts of his virtuous life was to decline an interview to which he was invited by an agent of the government."

4. *Persecution of William Kiffin and the Hewling Family.* We insert here Macaulay's account of this instance of the sufferings of a most deserving family:

"Great as was the authority of Bunyan with the Baptists, that of William Kiffin was still greater. Kiffin was the first man among them in wealth and station. He was in the habit of exercising his spiritual gifts at their meetings; but he did not live by preaching. He traded largely; his credit on the Exchange of London stood high; and he had accumulated an ample fortune. Perhaps no man could, at that conjuncture, have rendered more valuable services to the court. But between him and the court was interposed the remembrance of one terrible event. He was the grandfather of the two Hewlings, those gallant youths, who, of all the victims of the Bloody Assizes, had been the most generally lamented. For the sad fate of one of them, James was in a peculiar manner responsible. Jeffreys had respited the younger brother. The poor lad's sister had been ushered by Churchill into the royal presence, and had begged for mercy; but the king's heart had been obdurate. The misery of the whole family had been great; but Kiffin was most to be pitied. He was seventy years old when he was left destitute, the survivor of those who should have survived him. The heartless and venal sycophants of Whitehall, judging by themselves, thought that the old man would be easily propitiated by an alderman's gown, and by some compensation in money for the property which his grandsons had forfeited. Penn was employed in the work of seduction, but to no purpose. The king determined to try what effect his own civilities would produce. Kiffin was ordered to attend at the palace. He found a brilliant circle of noblemen and gentlemen assembled. James immediately came to him, spoke to him very graciously, and concluded by saying, 'I have put you down, Mr. Kiffin, for an alderman of London.' The old mau looked fixedly at the king, burst into tears, and made answer, 'Sir, I am worn out; I am unfit to serve your majesty or the city. And, sir, the death of my poor boys broke my heart. That wound is as fresh as ever. I shall carry it to my grave.' The king stood silent for a minute in some confusion, and then said, 'Mr. Kiffin, I will find a balsam for that sore.' Assuredly James did not mean to say any thing cruel or insolent; on the contrary, he seems to have been in an unusually gentle mood. Yet no speech that is recorded of him gives so unfavorable a notion of his character as these few words. They are the words of a hard-hearted and low-minded man, unable to conceive any laceration of the affections for which a place or a pension would not be a full compensation."

CHAPTER IX.

Persecutions of Baptists in America. 1. By the Pilgrim Fathers in New England. 2. Roger Williams; his sufferings for conscience sake; his true place in the history of religious liberty. 3. The Sufferings of Obediah Holmes and others in Boston; the Contrast in Boston. 4. The Sufferings of Baptists in Virginia; the Defence of three Baptist Ministers by Patrick Henry.

1. THE Pilgrim Fathers were now in New England; and the scene of the sufferings of our brethren, for conscience sake, is transferred there. O, how long had the angel of religious liberty to struggle for a free and full existence! Though the Pilgrim Fathers fled from persecution, when they came to this country, they neither understood the principles of liberty, nor possessed its spirit. The germ of all the troubles of New England, in regard to religious liberty, was planted in her institutions, on ship-board, before the Pilgrims had yet landed upon our shores. The "Court of Assistants" are on their way to New England, in the ship Arabella, and before they arrive, on the 23d August, 1630, they pass the fatal law. The question was, "How shall the ministers of the new country be supported?" "It was ordered that houses be built for them, with convenient speed, at the public charge, and their salaries were established."

Here we have the Church and State combined—that certain method of forcing men to sustain churches; and to sustain them in opposition to their serious convictions. From this principle, originating, in this case at least, in desire to promote and provide for religion, our fathers had suffered, and are yet to suffer. Experience has since amply proved, that in addition to the better policy of a free toleration, it answers a good purpose, practically, for the pecuniary support of religion.

In the early history of New England, November, 1644, an

additional law, the necessary concomitant of the first, was passed in Boston, Mass., namely, a law for the suppression of anti-Church and State sects.

The language of this law is positive confirmation of the fact, that Baptists were now multiplying; and that it was made for their special benefit. It runs: "Forasmuch as experience hath plentifully and often proved, that since the first rising of the Anabaptists." It then goes on, in the language of the old persecutors, to denounce the Anabaptists, in consideration of their multiplication, and rigid adherence to their old opposition to infant baptism.

The penalty of this law runs thus: "It is ordered and agreed, that if any person or persons within this jurisdiction, shall either openly oppose or condemn the baptizing of infants, or go about secretly to seduce others from the approbation or use thereof; or shall purposely depart from the congregation at the ministration of the ordinance, * * every such person or persons shall be sentenced to banishment."

Backus says he "had diligently searched all the books, records and papers, which he could find on all sides, and could not find an instance then, (1777,) of any real Baptist in Massachusetts being convicted of, or suffering for any crime, except the denying of infant baptism, and the use of secular force in religious affairs."

As strange as it may now seem, for many long, long years, they, in common with the Quakers, did suffer incredible hardships from such laws as these, in different parts of this country, particularly in New England. "It would take a volume," says Morgan Edwards, "to contain an account of all their sufferings for ten or twelve years." Yes, we may add, and extending the time to the entire period, volumes on volumes would not do it.

We proceed to detail a few instances of these sufferings:

2. *Roger Williams; his sufferings for conscience sake;*

the Champions of Soul Liberty in Modern Times; the working of our Principles.

He was born in Wales, in 1599; was educated at Oxford University, England, under the patronage of Sir Edward Coke, and is supposed to have been a relative of Oliver Cromwell. He studied law; but finally received orders in the Episcopal Church. He was an intelligent, serious youth, as is evident from his own statement, and from his gaining the esteem of his patron. His education was a liberal one, as we infer from his Alma Mater and from his writings.

Roger Williams did not leave England until he was about thirty-two years old. Living in the eventful time of the Puritans, and possessing an intelligent, devout, independent mind, he had ample opportunities to espouse their cause, and suffer with them. He was intimate with Oliver Cromwell, for he speaks of "a close conference with Oliver." His puritanical principles, also, in advance of the Pilgrim Fathers, appearing immediately on his arrival in this country, is evidence that his character was fixed at that time.

He arrived at Nantucket, near Boston, in 1630, in the prime of life, with an excellent reputation. Gov. Winthrop, speaking of the arrival of the ship, says: "She brought Mr. Williams, a godly minister, and his wife." He immediately begins to develop the principles which resulted in his becoming a Baptist, and the champion of soul liberty, and a sufferer for conscience sake. Though it was eight years later before he was baptized, and formed the first Baptist church in America, at Providence, it is plain to see that his ideas were, from the commencement, very different from those of the Pilgrim Fathers.

He refused to join the church at Boston, for reasons which shortly appear, when his trouble commences.

Receiving a call from a church in Salem, thirteen miles from Boston, he proceeds thither to commence his labors, the news of which soon reaches the church in Boston, which he had refused to join, when the cruel war commences. According to Gov. Winthrop: "On the 25th of April, at a court held in Boston, (upon information of the governor, that they of Salem had called Mr. Williams to the office of teacher,) a letter was written from the court to Mr. Endicott to this effect: 'that whereas, Mr. Williams had refused to join the church at Boston, because they would not make a public declaration of their repentance for having communion with the churches of England while they lived there; and, besides, had declared his opinion that the magistrate might not punish a breach of the Sabbath, or any other offence, because it was a breach of the first table; therefore they marveled that they would choose him without advising with the council; and, withal, desiring him that he would forbear to proceed until they had conferred about it.' No one would presume to defend such interference on the part of the government with the church now; or to dispute Mr. Williams' right to decline joining any church, on any grounds. But those were different times. Though the church at Salem stood upon their rights and retained him, he was not suffered to remain in peace; for, says Dr. Bentley: 'Persecution, instead of calm expostulation, immediately commenced; and Williams, before the close of summer, was obliged to retire to Plymouth.'"

He remained at Plymouth about two years. But here, also, he was guilty of being in advance of the times, and suffered accordingly. His friends at Salem insisted on his return there, which was at length secured, when, with a few others who had adopted his views, he removed there. He was now accused of anabaptistical tendencies. Mr. Brewster, the ruling elder at Plymouth, "prevailed on the church there to dismiss him and his adherents. He alarmed the church by expressing his fears that he would run the same course of rigid separation and anabaptistry, which Mr. John Smith, the Se-Baptist, had done at Amsterdam."

Quite soon, Mr. Williams' writings make him further trouble

with the authorities, for which he is called to an account, but on his disavowing any intention of wrong, and conducting himself in the most humble and conciliatory manner possible, they affected to forgive him. But now a new pretext occurred for them to assail him. The teacher of the church at Salem died, and Mr. Williams was invited to take his place. "The magistrates sent a request to the church that they would not ordain him;" but in vain; he was regularly inducted into the pastorate of the church; and now commence the proceedings which resulted in his banishment, and in the settlement of Rhode Island and of Providence, and Mr. Williams' baptism, and the formation of the first Baptist church in America. How mysterious are the ways of Providence! Mr. Williams undoubtedly exclaimed with Jacob of old, in somewhat analogous circumstances: "All these things are against me." But no; *they* meant it for evil, but God meant it for good. Henceforth, a free toleration begins to dawn again upon the world.

After sundry oppressive measures against the church at Salem and Mr. Williams, without success in crushing them, he is summoned before the court for the last time. Gov. Winthrop says: "At this general court, Mr. Williams, the teacher of Salem, was again convented, and all the ministers of the bay being desired to be present, he was charged with the said two letters—that to the churches, complaining of the magistrates for injustice, extreme oppression, &c.; and the other to his own church, to persuade them to renounce communion with all the churches of the bay, as full of anti-Christian pollution, &c. He justified both of these lettters, and maintained all his opinions; and being offered further conference and disputation, and a month's respite, he chose to dispute presently. So Mr. Hooker was chosen to dispute with him, but could not reduce him from his errors. So the next morning the court sentenced him to depart out of our jurisdiction within six weeks, all the ministers save one approving the sentence; and his own church had him under question also for the same cause; and he, at his return home, refused communion with his own church, who openly disclaimed his errors and wrote an humble submission to the magistrates."

Poor Williams! Like Paul, he was "cast down, but not destroyed." Aye, what is better, like his Master, he was "forsaken by all," but firmly drained the "cup" to its very dregs. And what was his crime? Thanks to the progress of the age, it is not now necessary to defend him. His posterity have effectually done it, by adopting his views. We may, however, remark, that admitting he sometimes exceeded the truth, and was to be blamed (and what human reformer is not in the same condemnation?) the brunt of his offending was his sound views of religious liberty. More than sixteen hundred years before, the Son of God had given the principle involved; and more than thirteen hundred years before, had his Donatist brethren, before Constantine, assumed a similar position when they asked: "What has the emperor to do with the church? What have Christians to do with kings? What have bishops to do at court?"

Mr. Williams had permission to remain in Salem until spring, but because he would not refrain from using his blood-bought liberty, but did "go about to draw others to his opinions; and did use to entertain company in his house, and to preach to them even of such points as he had been censured for, it was agreed to send him into England by a ship then ready to depart." But God's servants are not so easily disposed of. When the warrant commanding him "to come presently to Boston to be shipped," &c., failed to produce him, a "pinnace was sent, with commission to apprehend him, and carry him on board the ship; but when they came at his house, they found he had been gone three days before, but whither they could not learn."

The bird had flown, but "whither," *we* can tell. Judge Durfee, in a poem entitled "What Cheer," has given an account of his flight, probably nearer the truth than any cold prose description of it:

Morn came at last, and by the dawning gray
  Our founder rose, his secret flight to take;
His wife and infant still in slumber lay.
* * * * * *
Mary! (she woke) prepare my traveling gear,
  My pocket compass and my raiment strong;
My flint and steel to yield the needful fire;
  Food for a week, if that be not too long;
My hatchet too—its service I require,
  To clip my fuel desert wilds among;
With these I go to found in forests drear
A state where none shall persecution fear.
What! goest thou, Roger, in this thrilling storm?
Wait! wait at least until its rage is o'er.
Its wrath will bar e'en persecution's arm
From thee and me until it cease to roar.
* * * * *
So forth he ventured.
* * * * *
In boundless forest now our founder trod,
And south-west for his doubtful course he took.
* * * * *
He encamps for the night, when the wolves appear.
  Growling they come, and in dark groups they stand,
Show their white fangs, and roll their bright'ning eye;
  Till urged by hunger seemed the shaggy band,
Even the flames' bright terrors to defy—
  Then 'mid the group he hurled the blazing brand;
Swift they disperse, and raise the scattered cry;
But rallying soon, back to the siege they came,
And scarce their rage paused at the mountain flame."
* * * * * *

But little is known of the particulars of his flight, as *he*, who alone could give them, is too silent on the subject. So much, however, appears to be true from his own account and other circumstances. It was mid-winter. He fled to the forests, inhabited only by wild beasts and Indians. For fourteen weeks, "in winter snow, which I feel yet," as he remarks, he lived thus "not knowing what bread or bed did mean." In the mean time, at the peril of his life, he was promoting fraternity among the Indians, and effecting his own settlement at Seekonk or Rehoboth, some fifty miles from Salem.

Settled here, his family and a few friends having joined him; rude houses having been erected, and seed placed in the ground, he began to feel free as the winds which blew around him. But not yet. He was within fettered limits still, and Gov. Winslow "lovingly advised" him to cross the Pawtucket (now Seekonk) River. For the sake of peace, he accepted this advice, and in a canoe, with five other persons, proceeded to a spot near the mouth of Moshassuck River, and commenced the settlement of the City of Providence and State of Rhode Island. From this point, the sun of freedom already arising, ascends higher and still higher to the meridian, flashing its rays in every direction.

It is impossible to describe what Roger Williams must have suffered. Poor in the things of this world; a beloved wife and children dependent upon him for support in a strange land; the stigma attaching to one of whom all persons of consequence spake evil; threatened with violence at which his noble spirit recoiled; flying from civilized life, to contend with forest, cold, snow, wild beasts, and Indians; on these and numerous other accounts, he suffered more than martyrdom.

We are compelled to press into a few lines here, what has occupied volumes in its discussion, namely, Roger Williams' true place in the history of religious liberty. We concur in the following just remark on the subject: "Roger Williams' is neither the father of the Baptists, nor of religious liberty; he belongs to the chain—to the true apostolic succession—a foremost man of his age, but himself the child of like-minded apostles and martyrs of earlier times." The evidence of this position is detailed in this part of this volume. It is amply evident that religious liberty has been from the days of John the Baptist until now a cardinal Baptist principle. Individuals

26*

among the Donatists (A. D. 314) were as loud in their remonstrance against persecution for conscience sake, and as patient in suffering, as was Roger Williams. All through the chain of Baptists, the same faithfulness appears to this principle, until intolerance received its death-blow in the Constitution of the United States. The demon persecution will find no quarters, from Baptists at least, in any country or age.

3. *Persecution of Obadiah Holmes and others in Boston; the contrast in Boston.*

I cannot do better than give these in the language of Rev. Dr. Dowling:

"Let us roll back the dial of the world to the month of September, in the year 1651, and place ourselves in imagination in one of the streets of old Boston town. See! there is a crowd passsing along toward the place of public punishment and disgrace. In their midst is a man, bound and handled by the rude officers of the law as a criminal; but showing in his meek, upturned countenance, no tokens of guilt; and uttering with his lips the language of Christian exhortation and prayer. Who is he? what is his name? and what is the crime with which he is charged?

"He is a minister of the Lord Jesus Christ, a Baptist minister. His name is Obadiah Holmes, and his crime is that he has dared to preach the same gospel, and administer the same ordinances, as those which have been maintained on the same spot, by the venerated and beloved Stillman, and Baldwin, and Sharp, in succession, now for more than three-quarters of a century. But see! his clothes are rudely torn from his person by the coarse and brutal executioner, and this minister of Christ is tied securely to the whipping-post. Hark! he speaks. 'Good people all, I am now about to be baptized in afflictions, that so I may have fellowship with my Lord; and am not ashamed of his sufferings, for by his stripes I am healed.' His voice is silenced for a moment by the cruel thongs of 'the three-corded whip,' dashing the crimson gore from the quivering flesh of the man of God; and again he cries aloud: 'though my flesh should fail, and my spirit should fail, yet God would not fail me!' 'And so,' to use the language of the meek sufferer, in relating this cruel scene to his brethren in England, 'and so it pleased the Lord to come in, and to fill my heart and tongue as a vessel full, and with an audible voice I broke forth praying the Lord not to lay this sin to their charge, and telling the people that now I found God did not fail me, and therefore I should trust him for ever. For, in truth, as the strokes fell upon me, I had such a spiritual manifestation of God's presence, as I never had before; and the outward pain was so removed from me, that I could well bear it: yea, and in a manner, felt it not; although it was grievous, as the spectators said, the man striking with all his strength, spitting in his hand three times, with a three-corded whip, giving me therewith thirty strokes.'

"A few days later, and that meek sufferer, bruised and wounded so that for weeks he could rest only on his hands and knees, might have been seen stealthily threading his way through the forest wilderness between Boston and Providence, to escape the constable, who, with a second warrant, was hunting again for his prey; and as he drew near to the Rhode Island asylum of freedom, the voice of thanksgiving and songs of praise might have been heard 'for miles in the woods,' where pioneers of soul-liberty had gone to meet their suffering brother, to thank God for his deliverance, and to pour oil into his wounds.

"It may serve as an index to the prevailing opinions, even in New England, two centuries ago, to mention that when this act of cruel persecution was severely rebuked in a letter from Sir Richard Saltonstall, in England, the Rev. John Cotton, author of the reply to Williams, entitled 'the Bloody tenet washed and made white in the blood of the Lamb,' boldly justified and defended the whipping of Holmes, and the right of the magistrate to persecute, by the flimsy sophism that 'if the worship be lawful in itself, the magistrate compelling a man to it, compelleth him to sin, but the sin is in the man's will that needs to be compelled:' and at that time, not a minister in New England could be found, with the exception of the Baptists of Rhode Island, to dissent from the views of Mr. Cotton, or to speak a word in favor of freedom to worship God.

"On the 28th of May, 1665, fourteen years after the scene of persecution we have described, Thomas Gould, a member of a Pædobaptist church in Charleston, Richard Goodall, a member of the Baptist Church in London, of which Mr. Kiffin was then pastor, and seven other humble disciples, after wading through a sea of persecution, formed themselves into the First Baptist church of Boston. Fifteen years later, on the 8th of March, 1680, the doors of their humble sanctuary were nailed up by the marshal, and a notice posted thereon, warning 'all persons' against holding any meetings, or opening the doors, 'as they will answer the contrary at their peril.' And the little despised band were compelled to meet to worship God under a temporary covering in the yard of their meeting-house.

"But soon a brighter day begins to dawn. Every experiment has only proved the utter folly of attempting to control the conscience by coercive means. The sun of soul-liberty, shining so brightly over the neighboring colony of Rhode Island, sends its rays beyond the limits of the noble little state; and at length, light burst into the minds of the ministers of Boston, and they began to look with a more favorable eye upon the little company of Baptists in their midst, who have so long and so nobly struggled for 'freedom to worship God.' The march of freedom is onward, still onward. Not all at once, but by sure, though gradual steps, and not one step backward, till at length the New England mind becomes emancipated, freedom of conscience is declared the right of all, and the doctrine of Roger Williams is at last triumphant.

At the present time, throughout all New England, and in all the United States, equality of civil and religious privileges is conceded to every sect, with a single obsolete exception in the statute book of New Hampshire, which the intelligence of the people of the Granite State, we are sure, will soon erase.

"One more scene in this panorama of the champions and the triumphs of soul-liberty, and we have done. It is the 8th day of January, in the year 1852. Just two hundred years and four months have passed away since the whipping of the Baptist minister Holmes. A vast assembly have convened in one of the most venerable and stately church edifices of the New England metropolis. Among that assembly are the flower of New England's true nobility, not the empty title, but of intellect and heart. The honored chief magistrate of the commonwealth is there, and a long train of "grave and reverend" senators, and legislators, and judges, and divines, the ornaments of the workshop, the farm, or the counting-house, the bar, the bench, or the pulpit. They have met to listen to lessons of instruction from the minister of God, on the occasion of their annual election sermon, and to implore wisdom from on high to qualify them for the duties to which they have been chosen.

"And who is that servant of Christ, who by their own appointment, rises before them, and announces as his theme, 'RELIGIOUS LIBERTY, such as is enjoyed in these United States, derived directly from the king of heaven; not regarded as a matter of toleration, but a heaven-descended and inalienable right?' Who is he? He is simply an humble minister of Christ, a Baptist minister, occupying only the platform of equality with his brother ministers of other sects; a position which was just as much the right of his brethren in the faith and in the ministry, Williams and Holmes, two hundred years ago, as it is the right of himself; a minister, who has long preached the very same truths, for declaring which, his brother Baptist ministers, two centuries before, had been so shamefully scourged at the whipping-post, almost on the very spot where that preacher stands. Who is he? He is the pastor of that self-same first Baptist church of Boston, whose persecuted members were shut out of their humble sanctuary, when its doors were nailed up by the marshal, one hundred and seventy-two years before; a successor, moreover, to the principles of Roger Williams, cherishing as dearly as that noble champion, the blessing of soul-liberty; but instead of being driven, like him, from the abodes of civilized men, to seek in the wilderness a home for liberty of conscience, standing up in the assembly of honorable men, to defend the same glorious principle for which Williams became a sufferer, a fugitive, and an exile; while now, and in that assembly, every countenance beams with a smile of approval, and every heart does homage to the truth.

"While we contemplate the wonderful contrast, between the Boston scenes of 1651 and 1680, which we have described, on the one hand, and the far different scenes of 1852, on the other; well may we exclaim, in the words of the Latin adage,

'Tempora mutantur, et nos mutamur in ills.'

Or, in the paraphrase of the words given by an English poet,

'Men change with fortune, manners change with climes,
Tenets with books, and principles with times.'

"Yet amidst all these changes which time has produced in the tenets or principles of others, it may well be the glory of our denomination, that Baptists have continued steadily true to their mission as witnesses for soul-liberty. On this subject, their principles have varied neither with 'climes' nor 'times;' but alike in adversity and in prosperity, in evil report and good report, in the beginning of the seventeenth century as in the middle of the nineteenth, in the old world as well as in the new, they have persevered, as the firm, unflinching, undeviating advocates for perfect liberty of conscience to all the family of man. Thank God! we have lived to see this glorious principle triumphant in America. May our children live to see it triumphant throughout the world!"

4. *The sufferings of Baptists in Virginia; the defence of three ministers by Patrick Henry.*

Numerous instances of persecution for conscience sake, occurred in different parts of the United States from the time of Williams' sufferings, onward to the Declaration of Independence, July 4th, 1776. In Virginia, as late as 1768–75, Baptists suffered from Episcopal persecutions. Preaching contrary to law, was construed into a breach of the peace, and devoted ministers were incarcerated in common with the vilest men. June 4, 1768, three men were arraigned as disturbers of the peace; and the prosecuting attorney brought this charge against them: "May it please your worship, these men are great disturbers of the peace; they cannot meet a man on the road, but they must ram a text of Scripture down his throat."

The following instance of persecution seems to have been one of the last struggles of the demon, just before the Declaration of Independence. The facts were derived from two men in the court-room at the time of the trial, by a gentleman who communicated them to John M. Peck, who published them in the Baptist Memorial in 1845.

Go back to the period just prior to the Declaration of Independence. Imagine yourself in the old court-house at Fredericksburg, Spotsylvania Co., Virginia. The king's judges are upon the bench, in great dignity, and the king's attorney is present to aid in dealing justice to all offenders. Numerous are the spectators on the present occasion, for three ministers are to be tried, for no other offence than, "*preaching the Gospel of the Son of God,* contrary to the statute in that case provided, and consequently disturbers of the peace." The thunders which soon reverberated in the Revolution, had begun their mutterings, and many were the brave hearts in that audience, indignant at what was transpiring, and at the impending fate of those inoffensive men, which apparently nothing could avert. But whilst these portentous preparations are going on within the court-house, a plain man dismounts his horse at the door. This was Patrick Henry, beginning to be known as a talented, patriotic lawyer. He had heard of this approaching trial, and true to his noble principles, unsolicited, he had rode fifty or sixty miles from his residence in Hanover County, to volunteer his services in defence of these prisoners. No one can tell the feelings which agitated his noble heart at that time. What might seem to a common observer of little consequence, the punishment of three unimportant men, to him was freighted with moment, as embracing the principles of the Revolution. As Henry entered the court room, unknown to most present, and attracting no attention, the clerk was reading the indictment, in a slow, formal manner, in harmony with the august court assembled. "He pronounced the crime with emphasis, *for preaching the Gospel of the Son of God.*" The reading of the indictment finished, the prosecuting attorney submitted a few words, all he supposed necessary to convict the prisoners; and all which would have been necessary under ordinary circumstances. The judges were about to pronounce the ordinary verdict of condemnation, when Henry, who had entered the bar among the lawyers, arose, stretched out his hand, and received the paper. The first sentence of the indictment, which was being read as he entered, which had fallen upon his ear was: "*for preaching the Gospel of the Son of God.*" This was his key note. He commenced:

"May it please your worships. I think I heard read, as I entered this house, the paper I now hold in my hand. If I have rightly understood, the king's attorney of this county has framed an indictment for the purpose of arraigning and punishing by imprisonment, three inoffensive persons, before the bar of this court, for a crime of great magnitude, as disturbers of the peace. May it please the court, what did I hear read? Did I hear it distinctly, or was it a mistake of my own? Did I hear an expression, as if a crime, that these men, whom your worships are about to try for a misdemeanor, are charged with, what? and continuing in a low, solemn, heavy tone, '*for preaching the Gospel of the Son of God!*' Pausing amidst the most profound silence and breathless astonishment of his hearers, he slowly waved the paper three times around his head, then lifting up his hands and eyes to heaven, with extraordinary and impressive energy, he exclaimed, '*great God!*' The exclamation—the action—the burst of feeling from the audience, were all overpowering. Mr. Henry resumed:

"May it please your worships: In a day like this, when truth is about to burst her fetters—when mankind are about to be raised to claim their natural and inalienable rights—when the yoke of oppression which has reached the wilderness of America, and the unnatural alliance of ecclesiastical and civil power, is about to be dissevered—at such a period, when liberty—liberty of conscience—is about to awake from her slumberings, and inquire into the reason of such charges as I find exhibited here to-day in this indictment!" * *
"Another fearful pause, while the speaker alternately cast his sharp piercing eyes on the court and the prisoners, and resumed—'If I am not deceived, according to the contents of the paper which I hold in my hand, these men are accused of *preaching the Gospel of the Son of God. Great God!*' Another long pause, during which he again waved the indictment around his head, while a deeper impression was made on the auditory. Resuming his speech—May it please your worships: There are periods in the history of man when corruption and depravity have so long debased the human character, that man sinks under the weight of the oppressor's hand, and becomes his servile, his abject slave; he licks the hand that smites him; he bows in passive obedience to the mandates of the despot, and in this state of servility he re-

ceives his fetters of perpetual bondage. But, may it please your worship, such a day has passed away? From the period when our fathers left the land of their nativity for settlement in these American wilds, for liberty—for civil and religious liberty—for liberty of conscience, to worship their Creator according to their conceptions of Heaven's revealed will; from the moment they placed their feet on the American continent, and in the deeply imbedded forests sought an asylum from persecution and tyranny—from that moment despotism was crushed; her fetters of darkness were broken, and Heaven decreed that man should be free—free to worship God according to the Bible. Were it not for this, in vain have been the efforts and sacrifices of the colonists; in vain were all their sufferings and bloodshed to subjugate this new world, if we, their offspring, must still be oppressed and persecuted. But, may it please your worships, let me inquire once more, for what are these men about to be tried? This paper says, '*for preaching the Gospel of the Son of God.' Great God.* For preaching the Saviour to Adam's fallen race.'

"After another pause, in tones of thunder he inquired—'*What law have they violated?*' Then for the third time, in a slow dignified manner, he lifted his eyes to Heaven, and waved the indictment around his head. The court and the audience were now wrought up to the most intense pitch of excitement. The face of the prosecuting attorney was pale and ghastly, and he appeared unconscious that his whole frame was agitated with alarm; and the judge, in a tremulous voice, put an end to the scene, now becoming extremely painful, by the authoritative command—'*Sheriff, discharge those men.*'"

PART V.

FACTS AND STATISTICS OF BAPTIST MISSIONARY INSTITUTIONS, SCHOOLS OF LEARNING, PERIODICALS AND CHURCHES; AND CONCLUDING CHAPTERS ON THE INDEBTEDNESS OF THE WORLD TO BAPTISTS, AND THEIR DUTY TO THE WORLD.

CHAPTER I.

1. Baptists ever the friends of Missions. 2. The first money raised in the United States for Foreign Missions. 3. Missionary Institutions in the United States and Great Britain. 4. Statistics of Benevolence, Pastor's Salaries and Church Edifices. 5. Institutions of Learning. 6. Periodicals. 7. Baptist Associations, Churches, Ministers and Baptisms. 8. Reflections upon the increase of Churches. 9. Ministers, Churches aud Members.

1. Baptists have ever been the active friends of missions. This is seen in their history and persecutions in the different ages of Christianity. Ample evidence of this is found in the parts of this volume *on History and Persecutions.*

Early in the history of modern missions, they are found in the front rank. To the Moravians belongs the honor of being pioneers in *modern* missions. As early as 1732, at that time few and in extreme poverty, they established a mission in Greenland. In 1784, the Baptists of England originated the since world-wide "Monthly Concert of Prayer for the spread of the Gospel." This was ten years before the "London Missionary Society" was formed; and twenty-six years before the formation of the "American Board of Commissioners for Foreign Missions.

2. Dr. Belcher, in his valuable "Life of Carey," gives an interesting account of the first (as far as has been ascertained, probably *the* first) money raised in the United States for foreign missions. Captain Benjamin Wickes received from the Baptist Missionary Society, in England, one thousand guineas for their missionaries in Serampore. Arriving in Philadelphia, he deposited the money with Robert Ralston, Esq., for safe keeping, until he sailed for India. He published in the newspapers the fact, under the caption of "Propagation of the Gospel;" "to all who love the prosperity of Zion, and are disposed to aid in the propagation of the gospel among the heathen," requesting additions to the sum. Five thousand dollars were immediately raised in Philadelphia, and other sums were received from Boston. This was in the winter of 1806, four years before the formation of the American Board, the oldest missionary organization in this country. It is not known who the persons were contributing this money, but it is probable they belonged to different denominations. It is an interesting fact, that in the providence of God the first money for foreign missions from this country was contributed without regard to sect.

3. *Baptist Missionary Institutions in the order of their origin.*

The first in this order, now sustained in this country, is the American Baptist Missionary Union. If our memory is correct, (we have not the means at hand to state all the facts,) the Salem Bible Translation and Foreign Mission Society, a Baptist society for many years in existence, now extinct, was formed prior to the Missionary Union. The immediate cause of the formation of the Missionary Union, was the fact that Mr. and Mrs. Judson, and Mr. Rice, became Baptists. Mr. Judson was one of the four young men from the Theological Seminary, at Andover, Massachusetts, who were the instruments of the organization of the "American Board of Commissioners for Foreign Missions," in 1810, by the presentation of a memorial to the "General Association of Massachusetts." He is the author of the memorial. He, with Mr. Rice, were sent out, though in different ships, among the first missionaries of that board. On their passage they became Baptists, the result of an examination of the subject. Mr. Rice returned to this country, and laid their case before the Baptists, when, in 1814, the "American Baptist Triennial Convention" was originated, which finally took the present name, American Baptist Missionary Union. Its career has been one of great prosperity and usefulness. Its present condition is as follows:

The annual meeting of the Board and the Union was held in the city of Chicago, Ill., May 15–18, 1855. The receipts for the year, $114,907 58; expenditures, $145,528 31; deficit in two years, $61,333 25. Of the Missionary Magazine, 5558 copies, and of the Macedonian, 33,258 copies, were circulated monthly.

Number of missions under the care of the Board, 22; stations, 84; out-stations, 574, including 406 in Germany. Missionaries, 57; female assistants, 63; native pastors and preachers, 237; total, 357. Added during the year, 3 missionaries and 3 female assistants; retired, 3 missionaries and 2 female assistants; died, 5 missionaries and 2 female assistants. Under appointment, 2; applicants, 6. Mission churches abroad, 218: baptized the past year, 2910; whole number of members, 17,548. Schools, 107; pupils, 2500.

OFFICERS.—Hon. Geo. N. Briggs, LL. D., of Mass., President; Hon. Ira Harris, LL. D., of N. Y., Chairman of the Board; Rev. Solomon Peck, D. D., Foreign Secretary; Rev. Jonah G. Warren, Home Secretary; Nehemiah Boynton, Esq., Treasurer.

Missionary rooms, 33 Somerset Street, Boston.

American Baptist Publication Society.—This society originated in 1824. Its cause has been onward from the commencement, until, from a somewhat limited position, it has attained its present important one. Its object is thus stated in the second article of its revised Constitution—"The object of this Society shall be to promote evangelical religion, by means of the printing press, Colportage, and the Sunday School."

The Society held its thirty-first anniversary at Chicago, Ill., May 11–14, 1855. Receipts, $52,705 74; expenditures, $52,660 22. Net value of property, $63,666 98.

New publications in the year, 44; besides 20,000 copies of the Baptist Almanac, and 10,000 of the Baptist Record. Total number of pages *issued* during the year, 26,598,000, of which 9,050,000 are of new publications. Total number *printed*, 32,149,000.

The number of publications now on the Society's Catalogue is 476; of which 218 are bound volumes, and 255 Tracts, in English, French, Swedish and German.

The whole number of Colporteurs employed during the year, 111, including 34 students; now in commission, 69, of whom 35 are sustained by funds specifically designated. As the result of their labors, 6,722 volumes have been sold; 2107 volumes, and 485,980 pages of Tracts gratuitously distributed; 3201 sermons preached; 1816 prayer meetings held: 368 hopeful converts baptized; 73,314 families visited; 15 new churches and 43 new Sunday schools organized.

OFFICERS.—Mason Brayman, Esq., of Chicago, Ill., President; Rev. Wm. Shadrach, D. D., Corresponding Secretary; Rev. J. Newton Brown, D. D., Editor; W. W. Keen, Esq., Treasurer; Rev. B. R. Loxley, Depository Agent. Depository, 118 Arch Street, Philadelphia.

American Baptist Historical Society, (connected with the A. B. Publication Society.)—The second anniversary was held in Brooklyn, New York, May 7, 1855. The annual address was delivered by Rev. W. R. Williams, D. D., of New York, on "Roger Williams."

OFFICERS.—President, Rev. Wm. R. Williams, D. D.;

Corresponding Secretary, Rev. J. Newton Brown, D. D.; Recording Secretary, H. G. Jones, Esq., Philadelphia.

American Baptist Home Mission Society.—This Society was founded in 1832. Its object is thus stated in the second article of its Constitution: "The object of this Society shall be to promote the preaching of the Gospel in North America." Its present prosperous condition is thus given:

The twenty-third annual meeting was held at Brooklyn, N. Y., May 9, 1855. Receipts, $64,346 33; expenditures, $64,205 85.

Missionaries and agents employed, 179; preaching in twelve languages, and in 16 States and Territories. Stations and out-stations, supplied, 481; baptisms, 1026; churches organized, 55; ministers ordained, 36; church edifices completed, 12; in progress, 22.

Sermons preached, 17,926; lectures and addresses, 1561; pastoral visits, 36,857; prayer and other meetings, 9547; temperance pledges, 346; Sabbath schools, 227; teachers, 1492; scholars, 10,614; volumes, 25,392; preparing for the ministry, 26; contributions from churches aided, $5183 49.

Officers.—Hon. Albert Day, Hartford, Conn., President; Corresponding Secretary, Rev. Benjamin M. Hill, D.D.; Treasurer, Charles J. Martin. Office, 115 Nassau Street, New York.

American and Foreign Bible Society, [1838.]—Annual meeting at Brooklyn, N. Y., May 8, 1855. Receipts, $40,034 28, exclusive of $19,000 for the Bible House; expenditures, $39,989 79.

Of the $55,000 subscription for the new house, $43,065 95 have been collected. Rooms have been rented in the building, yielding an annual income to the amount of $11,925, and others remain, valued at $850 a year.

Central Europe has received liberal appropriations. Bibles are also on their way to New Mexico, and Mexico, California, Hayti, and New Grenada; besides the usual grants to missions in South-eastern Asia. Total grants, $23,500; in America, $3,090; in Europe, $14,859; and in Asia, $5,544. In 18 years the Society has received $700,000; and sent forth more than a million and a quarter copies of God s word, in thirty or forty different languages.

A resolution was adopted to employ Colporteurs to circulate the Scriptures more extensively in our own country.

OFFICERS.—Rev. Bartholomew T. Welch, D. D., President; Rev. Rufus Babcock, D. D., Corresponding Secretary; Rev. J. B. Stone, Financial Secretary; Nathan E. Platt, Treasurer. Rooms, 117 Nassau Street, New York.

5. *American Baptist Free Mission Society.* [1843.]—The annual meeting was held in New York, May 10–11, 1855. Receipts for the year, $7,533 08; expenditures, $4,356 97. Balance, $3,176 11. Mission in Hayti, 3 stations; 1 missionary, 3 female assistants, 2 native preachers and 3 native assistants, and 3 churches.

OFFICERS.—Rev. H. Hutchins, President; Rev. S. Howe, Corresponding Secretary; Geo. Curtis, of Utica, Treasurer.

Southern Baptist Convention. [1845.]—The biennial meeting was held at Montgomery, Ala., May 11, 1855. President, Rev. R. B. T. Howell, D. D.; B. C. Pressly, of Charleston, Treasurer.

FOREIGN MISSION BOARD.—President of the Board, Rev. J. B. Jeter, D. D.; Corresponding Secretaries, Rev. J. B. Taylor, and Rev. A. M. Poindexter; Treasurer, Archibald Thomas, Esq. Office, Richmond, Va. Receipts, $36,274 48; expenditures, $31,549 11.

DOMESTIC MISSION BOARD.—Receipts, $21,153 74; increase over $2,000; expenditures, $22,132 06. Agents, 9; missionaries employed, 99; more accomplished than in any two former years, notwithstanding pestilence and famine. President, Rev. J. H. De Votie; Corresponding Secretary, Rev. J. Walker; Treasurer, W. Hornbuckle. Office, Marion, Ala.

BIBLE BOARD.—Receipts, $10,176; increase, $2000; expenditures, $8862. President, Rev. W. H. Bayless; Corresponding Secretary, Rev. A. C. Dayton; Treasurer, C. A. Fuller. Office, Nashville, Tenn.

PUBLICATION BOARD.—Receipts from donations, $2167. Corresponding Secretary, Rev. J. P. Tustin; Treasurer, A. C. Smith, Esq. Office, Charleston, S. C.

AMERICAN INDIAN MISSION ASSOCIATION.—This body it was agreed at the meetings of the Convention, should be merged in the Southern Board of Domestic Missions.

The next meeting is appointed to be at Louisville, Ky., the second Friday in May, 1857. Rev. Wm. Cary Crane to preach the Annual Sermon; Rev. A. M. Poindexter, of Va., alternate.

American Bible Union. [1850.]—The fifth annual meeting was held Oct. 5, 1854, at New York. Receipts, $36,050 63; pledges, $140,000, payable in annual instalments. Expenditures, $35,378 80; distributed thus, Spanish Scriptures, $931 45; French, $281 05; Italian, $665 55; German, $880 68; Rev. J. G. Oncken, $5000 for German Bibles and $395 designated for Mission Chapels; Home and Foreign Missions by request, $139 50; English Scriptures, $19,278 43; Rent of rooms, $500; Salaries and general expenses, $7,303 44. The Board publish a quarterly, entitled the Bible Union Reporter. The revised versions of 2d Peter, the three epistles of John and the epistles of Jude have been published in an elegant quarto form, with notes. The Gospels of Matthew and John are in press.

OFFICERS.—Rev. Spencer H. Cone, D. D., President; Wm. B. Wyckoff, Corresponding Secretary; Wm. Colgate, Treasurer. Rooms, 354 Broome Street, New York.

Besides these national missionary institutions, numerous sectional ones exist of more or less consequence, for similar purposes. There are also 25 "State Conventions" and 519 "Associations," all of them more or less missionary in their object and influence. Some of the money which they raise for missionary purposes is included in the receipts of the national societies, but a large sum, which we have not the means of giving, is raised besides. There are also several Ministerial Education Societies; and societies for the aid of superannuated ministers, and the widows and orphans of deceased ministers.

PRINCIPAL BAPTIST SOCIETIES IN GREAT BRITAIN.

NAMES.	WHEN FOUNDED.	INCOME.
Baptist Missionary Society,	1792	£123,705
Baptist Home Missionary Society,	1797	19,690
Baptist Irish Society,	1814	10,750
General Baptist Missionary Society,	1816	9,180
Bible Translation Society,	1840	10,785
Baptist Building Fund,	1824	7,345
Particular Baptist Fund, for aiding Ministers and Churches,	1817	12,605
Baptist Union,	1813	710
Baptist Tract Society,	1841	665
Society for aged or infirm Baptist Ministers,	1816	2,145
Young Men's Association in aid of Baptist Missionary Societies,	1848	650

4. *Statistics of Benovolence, Pastors' Salaries and Church Edifices.*—The sum total of annual Baptist expenditure for the objects given, taking the year 1854–5, is as follows:—Baptist Missionary Societies of Great Britain, reckoning $4 84 to the pound, $959,868 80. United States Baptist Missionary Societies, $444,729 11. From Baptists in the two countries, $1,404,597 91.

The amount paid by Baptists in the United States, annually, to their Pastors, (supposing there are 7,479 of them, averaging $400 per annum, and these are as near the facts as we are able to reach,) is $2,991,600. The annual interest on the value of Baptist Church edifices in the United States, at six per cent., is $583,785 90. Add to these two items, the annual expenditure of National Missionary Institutions in the United States, and you have for the three objects, $4,020,106 01. This sum is large in the aggregate, but divided among the 1,000,000 of Baptist Church members, and the immense Baptist population, it is inconsiderable. While the masses of them are not rich, they are not poor, and many of them are worth sums varying from $5,000 to $2,000,000.

The statistics of Baptist church edifices in the United

States, as given in 1850, is 7,111 houses of worship, furnishing seats for 2,590,325 hearers, valued at $9,729,765. It is worthy of remark, that as large as the sum is supposed to be, raised for missionary purposes, and as loud as the cry has been, we do too much for others and too little for ourselves, the mere annual interest upon the value of church edifices in the United States, is greater by $139,056 79, than the sum raised for all national missionary societies.

5. *Baptist Institutions of Learning.*—We have said that Baptists have ever been the fast friends of missions: the same remark is true of general and ministerial education. Nothing is more unjust than the charge, still reiterated, that the regular Baptists have ever been indifferent to education for the ministry. In illustration of the injustice of our opponents, the American translators of the church history of Professor Hase, Messrs. Blumenthal and Wing, among other singular mistakes of Baptists in this country say: "*Of late years some portions* of this denomination have done much to redeem their order from the reproach of indifference to education." Baptists have ever been more or less active in this work, and have had learned men in their ranks, from the time of Luke the evangelist, and Paul the apostle.

They *do not*, indeed, deem education *essential* to the ministry; but *desirable*, as is amply proved by their entire history. See in this work the parts on their history and persecution. What are the facts in this country? Brown University, the first Baptist College, was established as early as A. D., 1764, and has had a large share in education, general and ministerial, and stands as high at the present time as any college in the land. It is well known that Mr. Hollis, of London, who became a Baptist A. D., 1679, and died in A. D., 1731, early in the history of Harvard University was one of its benefactors. "He founded in it two professorships, one of divinity and the other of mathematics. He presented it with a valuable apparatus for philosophical experiments, and with many valuable books. He made provision there for ten students in divinity." A recent controversy has shown that Baptists have still a claim on that university on account of Mr. Hollis.

In 1855, it is said of Baptist schools of learning in the United States: "more than $1,500,000 have been subscribed within the last six years for their endowment, the greater part of which has been collected and invested."

BAPTIST COLLEGES IN THE UNITED STATES.

Name.	*Location.*	*Presidents.*	*Founded.*
Brown University,	Providence, R. I.	Francis Wayland, D. D., L. L. D.,	1764
Madison University,	Hamilton, N. Y.	Stephen W. Taylor, L. L. D.,	1819
Waterville College,	Waterville, Me.	R. E. Pattison, D. D.,	1820
Columbian College,	Washington, D. C.	J. G. Binney, D. D.,	1821
Georgetown College,	Georgetown, Ky.	D. R. Campbell, L. L. D.,	1829
Richmond College,	Richmond, Va.	Robert Ryland, D. D.,	1832
Denison University,	Granville, Ohio.	Rev. Jeremiah Hall, D. D.,	1832
Mercer University,	Penfield, Ga.	N. Crawford, D. D.,	1833
Shurtleff College,	Upper Alton, Ill.	N. N. Wood, D. D.,	1835
Wake Forest Colleg	Wake Forest, N. C.	W. M. Wyngate, A. M.,	1838
Rector College,	Pruntytown, Va.		1839
Union University,	Murfreesboro', Tenn.	J. H. Eaton, L. L. D.,	1840
Howard College,	Marion, Ala.	Henry Talbird. D. D.,	1841
Franklin College,	Franklin, Ia.	Silas Baily, D. D.,	1844
Baylor University,	Independence, Texas,	Rufus C. Burleson, A. M.,	1845
Central College,	McGrawville, N. Y.	I. J. Calkins,	1848
University at Lewisburg,	Lewisburg, Pa.	Howard Malcom, D. D.,	1849
William Jewell College,	Liberty, Mo.	R. W. Thomas, A. M.,	1849
University of Rochester,	Rochester, N. Y	M. B. Anderson, L. L. D.,	1850
Oregon College,	Oregon City.	George C. Chandler, A. M.,	1850
Furman University,	Greenville, S. C.	James C. Furman, A. M.,	1851
Mississippi College,	Clinton, Miss.	I. N. Urner, A. M.,	1851
Enon College,	Sumner Co., Tenn.	O. J. Fisk, A. M.,	1851
Central University,	Pella, Iowa.	G. W. Gunnison, A. M.,	1853
Mt. Lebanon University,	Mt. Lebanon, La.	J. Q. Prescott, A. M.,	1853
Wayland University,	Beaver Dam, Wis.		1854

BAPTIST THEOLOGICAL INSTITUTIONS IN THE UNITED STATES.

		Senior Professors.	
Theol. Dep. Madison Univ.,	Hamilton, N. Y.	George W. Easton, D. D.	1820
New Hampton Theol. Sem.,	Fairfax, Vt.	Eli B. Smith, D. D.	1825
Newton Theol. Inst.,	Newton Center, Mass.	Henry J. Ripley, D. D.	1826
Mercer Theol. Sem.,	Penfield, Ga.	John L. Dagg, D. D.	1833
Furman Theol. Sem.,	Greenville, S. C.	J. C. Furman, A. M.	1835
Western Bap. Theol. Inst.,	Georgetown, Ky.	Samuel W. Lynd, D. D.	1840
Theol. Dep. Howard Col.,	Marion, Ala.	Henry Talbird, D. D.	1843
Kalamazoo Theol. Sem.,	Kalamazoo, Mich.	J. A. B. Stone, A. M.	1846
Rochester Theol. Sem.,	Rochester N. Y.	Thomas J. Conant, D. D	1850
Fairmount Theol. Inst.,	Cincinnati, Ohio.	E. Turney, A. M.	1851

BAPTIST THEOLOGICAL COLLEGES IN GREAT BRITAIN.

Name.	*Presidents.*	*Founded.*	*Income.*	*Students.*
Bristol,	Rev. T. S. Crisp,	1770	£10035	20
Bradford,	Rev. James Ackworth, L. L. D.,	1804	5180	24
Stepney,	Rev. Jos. Angus, D. D.,	1810	7235	22
Pontypool,	Rev. Thomas Thomas,	1807	3250	14
Haverford West,	Rev. D. Davis,	1839	1855	18
Leicester, (General Bap.)	Rev. Joseph Wallis,		2200	11

The gentlemen to whom I have before referred, in relation to injustice to Baptists on this subject, say, "they have now under their control fourteen colleges, and eight theological seminaries." But here we have a list of twenty-six colleges and ten theological seminaries. Whilst Baptists still insist that education is not essential to a minister, and can never atone for want of piety and a divine call, they everywhere deem education desirable, and there is an imperative demand for it in favorable circumstances.

The number of Baptist academies, male and female, is too numerous to admit of even a conjecture. Particularly do they abound in this country.

6. BAPTIST PERIODICALS IN THE UNITED STATES.

Names.	*Editors.*	*Issued.*	*Where Published.*	
South Western Baptist,	S. Henderson, J. M. Watt,	*Weekly.*	Tuscogee,	Ala.
Pacific Recorder,	B. Brierly,	"	San Francisco,	Cal.
Christian Secretary,	Normand Burr,	"	Hartford,	Conn.
Christian Index,	J. F. Dagg,	"	Penfield,	Ga.
The Christian Times,	J. A. Smith, Leroy Church,	"	Chicago,	Ill.
Western Recorder,	S. W. Lynd, S. H. Ford,	"	Louisville,	Ky.
N. Orleans Bapt. Chronicle,	W. C. Duncan,	"	New Orleans,	La.
Zion's Advocate,	J. B. Foster,	"	Portland,	Me.
The True Union,	F. Wilson,	"	Baltimore,	Md.
Christian Watchman and Reflector,	J. W. Olmstead,	"	Boston,	Mass.
The Christian Era,	J. M. Burtt,	"	Lowell,	Mass.
Michigan Christian Herald,	George W. Harris,	"	Detroit,	Mich.
Western Watchman,	Wm. Crowell, S. B. Johnson,	"	St. Louis,	Mo.
The Gospel Banner,	J. D. Fulton,	"	"	Mo.
New York Examiner,	S. S. Cutting, E. Bright, A. M. Beebee,	"	New York,	N. Y.
New York Chronicle,	P. Church, J. S. Backus,	"	"	N. Y.
American Baptist,	W. Walker,	"	Utica,	N. Y.
Biblical Recorder,	J. J. James,	"	Raleigh,	N. C.
Carolina Baptist,	James Blythe, J. M. Bryan,	"	Hender'nville,	N. C.
Carolina Intelligencer,	Alex'r J. Cansler,	"	Shelby,	N. C.

Names.	*Editors.*	*Issued*	*Where Published.*	
Journal and Messenger,	J. L. Batchelder,	"	Cincinnati,	Ohio.
Christian Chronicle,	W. B. Jacobs,	"	Philadelphia,	Pa.
Southern Baptist,	J. P. Tustin,	"	Charleston,	S. C.
The Tennessee Baptist,	J. R. Graves,	"	Nashville,	Tenn.
The Baptist Watchman,	M. Hillman,	"	Knoxville,	Tenn.
The Texas Baptist,				
Religious Herald,	Wm. Sands,	"	Richmond,	Va.
Mountain Messenger,	S. Siegfried,	"	Morgantown,	Va.
The Christian Repository,		*Monthly.*	Louisville,	Ky.
Bapt. Missionary Magazine,	Solomon Peck,	"	Boston,	Mass.
The Macedonian,	W. H. Shailer,	"	"	Mass.
Young Reaper,	Alfred Colburn,	"	"	Mass.
The Free Mission Visitor,	A. Kenyon,	"	Kirtland,	Ohio.
Home Mission Record,	James R. Stone,	"	New York,	N. Y.
Mother's Journal,	Mrs. M. G. Clarke,	"	Philadelphia,	Pa.
Western Star, (*Welch*)	R. Edwards,	"	Pottsville,	Pa.
Der Sendbote des Evangeliums, (*German*)	K. A. Fleischmán,	"	Philadelphia.	Pa.
Parlor Visitor,	Wm. P. Jones,	"	Nashville,	Tenn.
American Baptist Memorial,	J. L. Burrows,	"	Richmond,	Va.
Baptist Preacher.	H. Keeling,	"	"	Va.
Home and Foreign Journal,	James B. Taylor,	"	"	Va.
Western Evangelist,	Peter Long,	"	Rockwell,	Ill.
Christian Review,	R. Turnbull, J. N. Murdock,	*Quat'y,*	New York,	N. Y.
The Baptist Record,	J. Newton Brown, Wm. Shadrach,	"	Philadelphia,	Pa.

BAPTIST PERIODICALS IN THE BRITISH PROVINCES.

Names.	*Editors.*	*Issued.*	*Where Published.*	
Christian Observer,	James Pyper,	*Weekly.*	Toronto,	Can. W.
Christian Messenger,	T. L. Davidson,	"	Bradford,	Can. W.
Le Semeur Canadien,	N. Cyr,	"	Montreal,	Can. E.
Christian Messenger,	J. W. Nutting,	"	Halifax,	N. S.
Christian Visiter,	Rev. J. E. Bill,	"	St. John's,	N. B.
Grand Ligne Mission Reg'r,	C. Normandeau,	*Quarterly,*	St. John's,	Can. E.

We rejoice to be able to say of the above list of periodicals, with many of which, and their editors and publishers we are personally familiar, that they are all of an elevated, moral, and intellectual character. Some of them are unsurpassed in any denomination or country. The Christian Review, the denomination's quarterly, and the leading monthly magazines and weekly papers, have by their purity and ability obtained the highest encomiums from the press generally, both secular and religious.

7. GRAND TOTAL OF REGULAR BAPTISTS IN NORTH AMERICA.

STATES.	Associat's.	Churches.	Or. Minist.	Licentiates.	Bap. in '54.	Total.
Alabama,	24	614	358	28	4,182	46,162
Arkansas,	15	164	85	5	888	5,859
California,	1	20	11		5	494
Connecticut,	7	111	114	15	575	16,907
Florida,	3	93	45		441	4,031
Georgia,	37	903	508	84	5,934	72,516
Illinois,	28	438	347	4	2,661	24,058
Indiana,	26	498	253	23	2,870	24,682
Indian Territory,	3	35	33		182	3,179
Iowa,	5	90	47	4	519	3,533
Kentucky,	44	933	409	26	6,058	73,373
Louisiana,	8	146	66	5	622	5,681
Maine,	16	299	194	16	506	19,355
Maryland,	1	33	27	2	382	2,904
Massachusetts,	14	258	262	23	956	31,854
Michigan,	10	177	122	5	335	9,691
Minnesota,	1	8	8		4	202
Mississippi,	21	529	315	4	3,843	35,644
Missouri,	31	539	340	28	3,413	31,358
New Hampshire,	7	96	75	2	253	8,229
New Jersey,	4	107	124	14	851	14,074
New York,	43	828	741	96	4,358	87,754
North Carolina,	27	635	354	51	3,445	47,755
Ohio,	28	430	320	10	2,114	24,958
Oregon,	1	17	10	1	108	442
Pennsylvania,	16	343	265	44	2,568	34,105
Rhode Island,	2	52	55	9	311	7,357
South Carolina,	16	446	321	19	3,442	49,119
Tennessee,	26	567	377	30	3,756	40,344
Texas,	13	215	134		762	8,068
Vermont,	8	108	78	5	435	7,851
Virginia,	26	642	358	29	5,996	92,428
Wisconsin,	6	135	81		408	5,422
German and Dutch Churches in United States,	1	26	22	11	200	1,225
Swedish Churches in U. S.,	1	6	6		100	150
Welch Churches in U. S.,	3	34	20		240	1,000
Total in the United States,	523	10,488	6,887	592	63,727	842,660
British Provinces,	13	335	200		2,250	25,000
West India Islands,	4	110	125	38	1,200	35,450
Total in North America,	540	10,933	7,212	631	66,655	903,110

An entirely full list would give the regular Baptists in the United States, no doubt, *one million.* It is known that the statistics are incomplete. We subjoin the statistics of the irregular Baptists in the United States.

	Associat's.	Churches.	Or. Minist.	Bap. in '54.	Total.
Anti-Mission Baptists in U. S.,	155	1,720	825	1,500	58,000
Free-Will Baptists,		1,173	1,107		49,809
General Baptists,		17	15		2,189
Seventh-Day Baptists,		71	77		6,351
Church of God,		274	131		13,500
Disciples,					175,000
Tunkers,		150	200		8,000
Mennonites,		300	250		36,000
Total Irregular Baptists,					348,849

Regular Baptists in the United States,	1,000,000
Regular Baptists in British Provinces and West India Islands,	60,450
Irregular Baptists in the United States,	348,849
Grand total in North America,	1,408,939
Grand total Baptist *population* in United States,	5,200,000

8. We subjoin the following valuable editorial note of the Baptist Almanac for 1856, in regard to Baptist Churches in the United States: "Had all the associations sent in their minutes in due season, there would have been several thousands added to the general summary on the next page. The return of Licentiates is specially defective.

"It appears from calculations made on the minutes, that there is an average LOSS of 36,000 members every year by death, exclusion, and excess of dismissal over reception by letters. The proportion is nearly thus:—annual loss by *death,* 11,000; by *exclusion,* 12,000; by *excess of dismissal,* 13,000. To meet this loss in an average GAIN by *restoration* of about 2,500, besides the number *baptized.* From this it follows that if the number of converts *baptized* in any year should fall below 33,000, there would be a positive decrease of our churches. What a startling thought is this! What a call to dependence, to labor, and to prayer! And when we find, as in the past year, that the net gain, after all these deductions, is over 30,000, what shall we render to God for such a steady stream of grace to our churches, continuing and increasing year by year?

"What a solemn and sublime thought that our churches yield an annual revenue of 11,000 redeemed souls to Heaven!"

9. *Ministers, Churches and Members.*—In 1792, there were in the United States, 1,264 Baptist ministers, ordained and licensed. In 1812, there were 1,922. In 1832, there were 3,647. In 1852, there were 7,393.

In 1707, there were but 17 Baptist churches in the United States. In 1740, there were 37. In 1762, there were 56. In 1792, there were 1,000. In 1812, there were 2,433. In 1832, there were 5,322. In 1852, there were 9,552. In 1853, there were 10,131.

In 1792, there were 70,017 Baptist communicants in the United States. In 1812, there were 189,345. In 1832, there were 384,859. In 1852, there were 770,839. In 1853, there were 808,754.

CHAPTER II.

The Indebtedness of the World to Baptists. 1. On preserving pure the laws of God. 2. Baptists the only Christian people who have existed in all ages of the Christian era. 3. Defenders of Civil and Religious Liberty. 4. They have not altered the Ordinances. 5. They are the only consistent opponents of Popery. 6. They have contended for the truth against the World.

1. *It is of the first consequence to the world to keep pure the laws of the Messiah.*—It would seem that any one can appreciate this proposition. He alone is competent to make

infallible laws. Man knows nothing of the necessities of the church except what he derives from the Bible. The Messiah has delegated nothing to him but the execution of his laws. The moment man assumes to be a legislator, a maker of laws, instead of an executor, to do simply the bidding of deity, he assumes a place to which he was never appointed, to which he is incompetent, and which opens the door to innumerable mistakes and disasters.

The Scriptures as much forbid his assumption of executive power as does reason. The Messiah's laws are called "the glorious Gospel," and "the fullness of the blessing of the Gospel of Christ" and "the everlasting Gospel." The most terrible anathemas are pronounced upon those who shall "preach any other Gospel," and for "adding to or taking from" the word of God, the plagues of the Bible are to be inflicted upon men, and their "part is to be taken from the book of life, and the holy city, and the things written in the Bible."

Still men have been found who have assumed to change both the principles and ordinances of God. They perhaps have designed to make improvements upon them, to furnish principles more suited to depraved man, in compelling his conscience to choose correctly; and ordinances more convenient, to which he would be less disinclined, and which are better suited to all climates. The result has shown the consequences. What have seemed slight and even worthy innovations, have deluged the world in blood, in religious persecutions; and opened the doors of the church to the unconverted, by means of sprinkling and infant baptism. Strange that men cannot see the danger and impropriety of any innovations on the Messiah's laws, and that there is no difference, in *principle* between such innovations, and any, or all others. The only safe ground is to do his bidding—nothing more, nothing less. It is impossible to exaggerate the importance of this principle.

We have no desire to boast of the Baptist church, or to make false issues. Well do we know that boasting is forbidden to Christians, and that the world needs truth and not pretension. At the same time the declaration of the truth is not boasting, and it is due to it to make it known.

2. "Baptists are the only Christian people," to use the language of Drs. Ypeig and Durmont, learned men of another church, "who have stood since the days of the apostles, and preserved pure the doctrines of the Gospel in all ages." To repeat here the evidence of this position is of course unnecessary. The reader can refer to it in Part I. of this book. This position admitted, how great is the indebtedness of the world to Baptists? The claims of Romanism in this direction are idle in the extreme. The Greek church has its origin in the division of the Roman, and is but a little more primitive than its source. "The Church of England broke off from the Romish church, in the time of Henry the Eighth, when Luther began the reformation in Germany," and is no older than the Lutheran church. The whole family of Presbyterian churches originated in the same period. Congregationalism can claim no earlier origin, even admitting its rise in the Independents of England. Methodism has its origin in Morgan and John Wesley, in A. D., 1729.

3. *The Baptists have not altered the ordinances of the Saviour.* From the first it has been one of their characteristics to adhere rigidly to the Saviour's subjects of baptism, believers; to his mode of baptism, immersion; and to his supper, the simple reception of the bread and wine "in remembrance of him," after baptism. Of what other denomination can this be said? Indeed, all of them have not only united in adopting ordinances differing from the primitive, but in contemning Baptists for their singularity, in casting contemptuously at them the terms "dippers," "close communionists" and "bigots." But through all this they have persevered—sometimes suffering the loss of all things, as persecution has arisen to violence from contempt—in loyalty to Christ; and in defence of a principle laying at the foundation of all truth, namely, *no innova-*

tions upon the laws of Jehovah; or all innovations dangerous leading to others; or no perfect safety but in a rigid conformity to the Gospel. There is nothing nobler, in either an intellectual or moral point of view, than an unflinching adherence to principles. In this direction is one of the great dangers of the world. Short-sighted man, because the result is apparently separated from the principle; or because apparently undesirable results intervene between the principle and its legitimate end; denies the principle, accepting appearances for realities, and a present apparent good with certain loss, for the real good in the future. The true ground is to stand firmly by the truth at all hazards; and in all things trusting to the omnipotence of the truth of Jehovah for the result.

4. *Baptists have ever defended perfect freedom of conscience, sometimes to the loss of all things, and have never persecuted; and hence are, indirectly, pre-eminently the defenders of civil as well as religious liberty.* The evidence of this position is scattered over the preceding chapters, being an ever-present idea in Baptist principles and practice.

It is well known how free the New Testiment is from all physical coercion in religion. The Saviour suffered from violence, but never resorted to it. Witness particularly his arrest, trial and crucifixion. The Apostles imitated his example. Baptists have ever followed this rule implicitly.

The Donatist Baptists rejected the interference of Constantine, A. D., 314, indignantly exclaiming: "*What has the Emperor to do with the Church? What have Christians to do with Kings? What have bishops to do at court?*" The same thing is observable in Baptist history and sufferings up to the time of the American revolution, when the violence of persecution received so decided a check. Baptists, like John Bunyan, in England, and Roger Williams, in America, are well-known champions and sufferers for religious liberty. They share almost alone, with the Quakers, the honor of never having resorted to persecution. Suffering from Pagans, Papists,

Greeks, and Protestants, they have never retaliated upon either. They have freely abandoned property, companions, children, country, life itself, rather than acknowledge the right, for a moment of the demon coercion in religion.

Under these circumstances it were singular, if they had not had a remarkable influence in promoting *civil*, as well as religious liberty. The two are inseparable. They have never, in the history of the world, existed in any perfection in separation. The freest countries in the world, at the present time, are Great Britain and the United States; and in these, as nowhere else, is freedom of conscience understood and enjoyed. Of the two nations I need not say which is the freer, and has the more perfect realization of religious liberty. In the contest for freedom, religious liberty has the precedence in the history of the world. To go no farther back than the history of our own country, it was for freedom to worship God after the dictates of their own conscience, which first of all interested our fathers. The next step was civil liberty. If Baptists have had a large share in procuring the former, they have of necessity in procuring the latter.

The following is an interesting item in the history of our country, and of Baptists, given upon the authority of Rev. Dr. Fisher, of Lexington, Ky., who received it directly from Rev. Andrew Tribble, who died at the age of ninety-three years. Mr. Tribble was pastor of a Baptist church in Virginia, near the residence of Thomas Jefferson, the author of the American Declaration of Independence, some eight years before the birth of that immortal document. Jefferson attended the meetings of this church for several months in succession, and was on terms of intimacy with its pastor. He was asked how he liked Baptist church government? It is well known how democratic it is, and has been from the earliest times. To this day it surpasses all other churches in this respect. Mr. Jefferson replied, that its propriety had struck him with great force, and had greatly interested him; adding, that he considered it the only pure form of democracy then existing in the world, and had concluded that it would be the best plan of government for the American colonies. Who can tell the influence this little church had thus upon the destinies of our country and the world.

It is suppesed that Munster, a Baptist minister, drew up the memorial of the peasants in their war in Germany, in A. D., 1524. This memorial was presented to the lords and circulated all over Germany. It consists of twelve articles of civil and religious liberty, which any freeman might now be proud to sign. Though many things transpired in that war not to be defended, (and in what war have they not,) it was, on the whole, as just as that of the American revolution. This memorial is not, in principle, greatly unlike our Declaration of Independence, and Voltaire says, "a Lycurgus would have signed it."

5. *Baptists alone can contend consistently and successfully with the great enemy of the Gospel of the Son of God, and of civil and religious liberty; namely, Popery, in that they have no relic of Popery, and never had.* On this account they have suffered every thing, but defeat and extermination, from Romanism, with which it has been obliged to contend from the earliest times. They have no point of contact or coalescence with Romanism, and have never, for an instant, been on terms of fraternity with it. As the word of God points out this enemy to the truth pre-eminently; and as above all others obnoxious to God and right, and reserved for ultimate destruction; so Baptists have always regarded it, and it has been, between the two, war from the commencement, without intermission. The sword has been with us that of the Spirit, with it that of the flesh, as becomes its anti-Christian character.

Rome, in her contest with other churches, has acknowledged Baptist superiority as her opponent, and has taunted others with the fact. Do other denominations accuse her of being unscriptural; she throws back the charge by a repetition of it against themselves, in their sprinkling and infant baptism. Do they accuse her of her anti-Christian persecutions; she replies, who persecuted the Baptists in Germany, and the Baptists and Quakers in America? Does the essential tyranny of her church government pass in review, she replies, yours also is unscriptural, and but an imperfect imitation of ours; a little less obnoxious on your own grounds, but still in principle like our own. Particularly is this true of Episcopacy and Methodism, and to some extent of Presbyterianism, and even of Congregationalism, in that it has its councils of ministers superior to the church.

6. *Baptists have contended for the truth as it is in Christ against the world, and at immense sacrifice.* Until Luther and his coadjutors arose, numerous Baptists existed in different parts of the world poor and despised, but nevertheless firm to their principles, to contend alone against the whole world. Their sufferings for most of this time are, beyond description, severe. "Down to the time of Constantine," (A. D., 312, when Constantine declared himself a Christian, and for a time put an end to persecution,) "with the solitary exception of Cyprian, as we have shown, all the martyrs—and their number has been computed at three millions—were Baptists." Follow the history of Christians from this point through to Luther, and who were the sufferers? Not exclusively Baptists, but to an extent so great, as to justify giving them the highest possible elevation of the kind. Who were the "hordes" and "swarms" "thronging" different parts of Europe, and suffering every manner of indignity and cruelty for the truth in different ages of the world, until Luther's appearance, if they were not Baptists? From Luther onward to the present time, they have had the largest share in suffering for "righteousness sake."

The following extracts of an article in a recent "Christian Examiner," are so intelligent and directly to the point, that I quote them here. They are good illustrations of the fact that Baptists have contended for the truth against the world, for they have done it no more in England and America than in other countries.

"Earliest and alone in England, the Baptists raised aloft the banner of religious liberty. Others were content with toleration;—they demanded liberty. Their earliest distinctive literature shows them pleading for religious liberty, as the antagonists not only of churchmen, but of Presbyterians and Independents, who could not yet see that the magistrate had nothing to do with questions of conscience. John Knox thundered away at an Anabaptist "caviler," and declared if he could only catch him where a magistrate would do his duty, he would make him over, even if he were his own brother, to the pains and penalties of the law. John Robinson, the meek and holy pastor of the Pilgrims, himself an exile, and the leader of exiles, saw the truth but dimly, and pleaded for the authority of the magistrate, against the arguments of his Baptist brethren, Smyth and Helwisse. When the latter determined to go back to England, (A. D., 1610,) with his flock, "to challenge King and State to their faces, and not give way to them, no, not a foot"—Robinson poured upon the sublime heroism his reproaches, and clung with strange tenacity to the doctrine of the magistrate's power in matters of religion. The Baptists fulfilled their noble vow. They proclaimed their doctrines through the press, hurling them in the very face of the weak and pedantic despot who then sat upon the English throne, and accepting persecution and suffering for their constancy. The indebtedness of the world to this little band of spiritual heroes is not yet acknowledged.

"The contests of Helwisse and Robinson were renewed on this continent between Roger Williams and John Cotton. The banishment of Williams was the inauguration of American persecution. Earliest and alone in America, as in England, the Baptists contended for the highest type of religious liberty. Neither the doubtful toleration of Maryland, which was literally 'death on Unitarians,' nor the ampler toleration of Pennsylvania, where a Baptist magistrate interfered against Quaker intolerance, came up to the full measure of their principles on this subject. Honorable as was the tolerance of the Dutch, as compared with Episcopal intolerance in Virginia, and Congregational intolerance in Massachusetts, it fell short of the freedom for which Baptists contended. Accepting no alliance with the State, they were allured by no bribes, silenced by no frowns. Not till about the time of the revolution could they gain a fair hearing, and even then they were heard because they could be trampled upon no longer. They had been increasing with great rapidity since about 1745, in both Massachusetts and Virginia. They were familiar with fines and prisons. The best citizens of Sturbridge, Massachusetts, had been despoiled of their goods, and a Baptist minister who visited them, had been sent to the county jail at Worcester as a vagrant. At the very time when the patriots of the Bay State were combining to resist the stamp act, the Baptists were holding conventions to strengthen the common faith, and to unite in memorials to the king for protection against the insufferable tyranny of the standing order and the general court. Among the papers of the Second Baptist church in Boston, are precious memorials of those times, one of them a loose original memorandum of one of these meetings, with subscriptions made to send a messenger to England, to lay their grievances before the king, in council—on it the honored names of some of the Sturbridge sufferers. In Virginia, Patrick Henry, Thomas Jefferson, and James Madison, were their defenders, and the strenuous advocates of their views of the rights of conscience. 'James Madison,' said the venerable William Colgate, 'took up the cause of the Baptists, and made it the occasion of a plea for religious liberty, and God made him President of the United States.' The revolution made the struggle a home struggle. From the king the

Baptists turned to the Congress. They were numerous, and the fast friends of the revolution. They could not be treated with indifference or contempt. When the saintly Backus knocked at the door of Congress, John Adams growled his displeasure, but the meek minister was more than a match for him, and gained a hearing. The tide was now turning. The revolution was successful, and however persecution lingered in some of the States, the new General Government was inaugurated with religious freedom at its base. Virginia effaced at once the last traces of religious intolerance: Massachusetts and Connecticut still feared for the safety of religious institutions, under a system of voluntary support, but relaxed their laws, and in half a century came fully over to the Baptist side. The compact which gave rise to the Northwestern States, secured liberty of conscience over those vast regions, now populous, rich and powerful—and those who in their childhood witnessed the imprisonment of Baptists for their faith, lived to see, in their maturer years, a great nation united in the undisturbed enjoyment of their principles."

Does the world owe nothing to Baptists for all this? What, but for them, speaking humanly, would have become of the truth? What if they had yielded to the force of circumstances, and for riches, and honors, and ease, and life, had given up the contest? What if they had adopted the world-wise policy of multitudes then and now, for themselves and families, and made no resistance to the encroachments of error; or having contended for a time had shrewdly decided that they had made their share of sacrifice for the world, and would henceforth look to their own interest? What if they had abandoned the world to "Pagans" first; then to "Papists;" then to "Reformers," just emerging from total night; and then to the "Pilgrim fathers," whose eyes still were but partly opened to the sunshine of perfect liberty? What had been the consequence? How would the progress of the world have been retarded? Where now had been the boasted nineteenth century, with the bright tints of millennial day, marking its horizon, precursors of the glorious rising sun?

CHAPTER III.

The duty of Baptists to the world. 1. They should prove worthy of the honor conferred upon them. 2. They should not yield to the demands of the world. 3. They should contend earnestly with Romanism; its statistics. 4. The great number of Baptists should be consecrated; their statistics contrasted with other denominations.

1. God has highly honored them, let them not prove unworthy of the trust. The first great use which they should make of their history, is in this direction. God grant that they may appreciate the honor he has bestowed upon them; and may be elevated by it, to that usefulness which it demands. They may not scrutinize Jehovah's motives in this distinction. They may not make it a source of self-congratulation, as though they had merited such distinction, or derive from it personally any worldly elevation. They should be humbled by the divine condescension, and be grateful for his mercy. Especially should they pray that they may have grace to act worthily the part assigned them. May they never be left to bring reproach upon a cause, with which they have been in the providence of God so identified. Depositories of the truth, sons of the martyrs are they, and as such, should be the last to hesitate to enter the defiles of danger and toil; and the last to retreat intimidated by obstacles, or to bring the least reproach upon the Cross of Christ. Their song should ever be:

"In the cross of Christ I glory,
 Towering o'er the wrecks of time;
All the light of sacred story,
 Gathers round its head sublime."

Any one bearing the name of Baptist should feel, and must, as he reads their history, that there is for him no retreat from Christian ranks; and that the more severely the battle rages, the firmer he must stand at his post, "and having done all, still stand." Especially let him confess that "God is his helper," that "the race is not to the swift, or the battle to the strong." "The sword of the Lord and Gideon" should be his battle cry, as he rushes on, mingling in the thickest and hottest of the spiritual fight. Though he be but a child in years let him be bold, and humble, and live for God. Children have bled and died for the cause, sustained by all-sufficient grace. Though his steps are tottering to the grave, let him be young in the courage of God's people and never fear. The hoary-headed have found heaven the sooner in persecution's fire. Men with giant hearts have been children in faith and humility; and tender women have been endued with the courage and daring of heroes. Let none henceforth fear or doubt.

2. Baptists should not yield to the demands of the world with less sacrifices than their fathers made; they can hardly make greater ones. We, in some sense, have entered upon their labors, and live in the day of triumph, not of persecution. In this, it is our privilege to rejoice. Imagine not, however, that there remains nothing for us "to do and to dare." The devil has by no means yielded the point, and the world has still allurements and temptations. The advantage gained for us by our fathers is great, but it is the result of great sacrifices, and who can tell, if the sacrifices cease, how soon the victories may disappear. Indeed, much remains to be achieved, before the victory is complete; and if now we cease our efforts, we do great injustice to the sufferings of our fathers, and great injury to the cause. If the millenial day *has* dawned upon us, its sun has by no means reached the meridian. It still lingers in the horizon. Shall it tarry there through our indifference, and our want of the spirit of our fathers. God forbid it!

We may not, indeed, *die* for the cause. This seems not our office. But we may *live* for it, and this evidently is our responsibility. We may not suffer any very considerable reproach for Christ; for while the mutterings of its violence are still sometimes heard, they are far under ground, and we heed them not. Our triumphs, by God's mercy, have been too complete to leave much of all this to intimidate or even annoy us. Our sacrifices are in another direction, but equally important, and probably more difficult.

The violent obstacles overcome, there is danger that we lay down to rest, and sleep too long. The victories are to be pressed on to complete triumph before there is safety in repose. It is ours to live for the cause. This is more difficult than to die for it. There is in martyrdom an enthusiasm, which rarely attaches to ordinary holy living and enduring for God. Our brethren are now honored with distinctions and titles and wealth; and occupy places among men of the world, who care not for the honor and commands of God. "Evil communications corrupt good manners," and it were strange if they were uncontaminated. Here lies their danger; let them look to it before it is too late.

Disciples of the meek and lowly Jesus, children of the martyrs, what have you to do with worldly distinction and riches, except so far as you can and do consecrate them to God? "Ye cannot serve God and Mammon." You are not, indeed, to be slothful in business, but you are to be "fervent in spirit, serving the Lord." To draw the line here correctly, and keep on the right side of it, is important. Christians may, indeed, be enterprising and successful, and occupy high places in honor and riches, but *never* in denial of Christ. The more they acquire of influence and power, so much the more they have to consecrate to God, and the greater is their temptation to forget and forsake him. "It were better for them that a millstone were hanged about their neck, and that they were devoured in the depths of the sea," than that they should arise to the power of influence and wealth, to forget God, and especially to turn against him and his cause. Here, I repeat, lies their danger; and their office is, in the spirit of the martyrs, to live for God; to consecrate their peace, and comparative repose and victory, to him.

There is untold power in a holy life, though unattended by circumstances adapted to attract attention to it, or of peculiar influence. There is still greater power in a holy life under circumstances of temptation, in the possession of distinction, and of wealth. He who can carry the holy war into the very highest camps of the enemy, and conquer through grace, has an awful responsibility, and a usefulness in proportion, if there he is a true follower of the Lord Jesus. To live for God, is all we can do for him in a period like this. It is therefore enough, and of the same consequence, as to die for him in different times. Disciples of Christ, children of the martyrs, here is your vocation. "Dare and do" for God here, what others have done in a different sphere, and victory shall be yours—not otherwise.

It is not surely asking much of us to *live* for God, when others, no more accountable, have *died* for him; and when among the family of Christ there is to be "an equality," one is not to be "burdened" and another "eased." If our brethren have yielded all of this world for Christ, it can be no great hardship for us to do it, under circumstances so much more favorable, and attended with so little suffering. If they "took joyfully the spoiling of their goods" to the last dollar, it surely is no great thing for us to give a limited portion of ours. If they were not permitted to compete with other men for distinction and wealth; but, of necessity, must abandon all, on profession of their faith in Christ, it can be no hardship for us to consecrate a generous proportion of our attainments; and if in their extreme "poverty" the "riches of their liberality" abounded to the glory of God, shall we murmur, when of our abundance so little is required?

There are noble examples among us of consecration to God; disciples of small attainments consecrating them to him with a sincerity and earnestness worthy of all commendation. And there are those of distinguished attainments, imitating so worthy an example. Intellect and learning, to such, are gifts of God, to be his forever and entirely. And there are men of wealth, who look upon their talents in this direction, as the minister of the gospel looks upon his, to be consecrated to God; and they are replenishing the treasury of the Lord, as ministers labor for the conversion of souls. Some such, like the beloved Cobb, have passed away; and some like him, who would be surprised and pained to see their names recorded here, are still among us, daring to be singular, and consecrating their wealth to God.

There is, however, no stretch of charity which can compute such cases as numerous, in comparison with the whole number of our brethren. Why should not all be like the few? Disciples of Christ—children of the martyrs—reflect upon this question. *Why should not all be like the few?* This we owe to the world, to ourselves, to God. This we can render, and still come short of the sacrifices of "the cloud of witnesses" who surround us.

3. Baptists owe it to the world to contend earnestly with Romanism, inasmuch as they are armed above all others. They have no relic of popery, and never had. "The Bible, the Bible" is pre-eminently "the religion" of Baptists, in that from the earliest times the church and tradition have been to them, in comparison, without authority. No church and state; no tyrannical church government; no persecution for conscience sake; no sprinkling for baptism; no infant baptism or communion, do, or ever have, attached to them. On this account there is, to Romanism, no breach in the walls of their citadel; no rent in their armor.

They, as no others, have a warfare with Romanism, on the ground of injuries received, inasmuch as their anti-papal principles have made them peculiarly obnoxious to the Papacy. Their existence also, in all ages of the Christian era, for the most part contending alone with Romanism, in her power and glory, have exposed them to her contact, when she was able and amply willing to deal them blows of death. Historical research affords ample evidence of this position. The revenge of Christianity is to return good for evil. For the persecutions they have received at her hand, in tenfold proportion, they may, and should return her the gospel in its purity. To her poor priest-ridden people, they should be missionaries of the cross of Christ, until they, one and all, are as free from her tyrannical chains as ourselves. To her pope, and cardinals, and Jesuits, and priests, aye, to her very inquisitors, all these officers of Satan's army, from whom they have suffered so much, so innocently, to them all, they should go in the name of the Prince of peace, and mercy, and love, and beseech them in his stead to be reconciled to God. In this spirit, they are bound to prosecute a bloodless war of extermination, against this ancient enemy of our fathers, or they are unworthy of them. Their obligations here, as well as their facilities, exceed those of all others. We welcome the dupes of Romanism to our country. God is in the immense immigration. We are prepared for them. Here we have nothing to fear from persecution: nor have they. God has been preparing the final battle, where a bloodless contest may be waged between truth and error, that the world may see which is mightier. Some have trembled for the result, but the victory is beginning to appear. Robert Mullen, a Catholic missionary to this country, addresses to the priests of Ireland, under the caption of "A word in season," the earnest recommendation to keep the people at home, as otherwise they are, to a great extent, lost to the church. He shows that from the immigration and natural increase there ought to be in the United States 3,970,000 Catholics, while the actual number is only 1,980,000, showing a loss of 1,990,000, a little more than fifty per cent. Other statistics show that while in Ireland from 80 to 100,000 Catholics have been rescued from Romanism, during the last ten years, about one-third of all who have immigrated to this country from Ireland, and sixty per cent. of the children, are lost to Rome.

The actual condition of Romanism at the present time, in this country, is any thing but discouraging. The wildest opinions and conjectures have been indulged in, in regard to them; but the facts are as readily ascertained as of any of the Protestant sects. "The Metropolitan Catholic Almanac, and Laity's Directory for 1855" gives us the facts. They have in the United States 41 dioceses. They give the number of communicants in but 31 of these, and they are 1,844,500. Supposing the 10 dioceses whose numbers they do not give, to have a proportionate number of communicants, which on examination appears to be about the fact, and they have 405,000, which added to the preceding, gives us a sum total 2,249,500. The same authority gives us the number of colleges at 21, and female schools at 117. While these facts show us much work to be done, and while the entire history of the wily enemy admonishes us not to exult while he still lives, they also show us to which side victory inclines. When we add to the present facts in the case, that all the power of the Papacy has been brought to bear upon her mission here, with the avowed intention and determination of making ours a Catholic country, we may well thank God and take courage.

Let me not for a moment be supposed to make the mistake that Baptists have been the sole instruments of this dawning victory, in the present generation, as they were, up to the time of the Reformation, the chief enemy of the Papacy. They have had a part in it, but I fear have not had so large a part as was their duty. Let them henceforth furnish their full quota of men and munitions, until the war closes in complete victory to primitive Christianity. Reinerius Saccho, for many years a Waldensian Baptist, who became in A. D.

1220–50, a Roman Catholic inquisitor, takes the ground of Neander, that the Waldensians originated in the ancient Donatists. He says: "Their universal extension and high antiquity, makes them the most dangerous enemies of the Catholic Church." May this continue to be true of Baptists.

4. The immense number of Baptists should be consecrated to God for the subjugation of the world to Christianity. The whole number of regular Baptist church members in the United States, is now, 1856, just about one million, all of them adults, inasmuch as none are received into the Baptist Church, but those old enough to believe and choose for themselves. What may not one million of persons accomplish for the truth, if they are all truly consecrated to God! The regular Baptists of the United States are in numbers just about equal to six of the prominent denominations, not including the Methodists, who, perhaps, are a little more numerous than the Baptists. The American Almanac gives us the following statistics of seven denominations in the United States for 1853: Old School Presbyterians, 210,306; New School Presbyterians, 140,060; Cumberland Presbyterians, 50,000; Orthodox Congregationalists, 197,196; Episcopalians, 110,000; Dutch Reformed, 22,515; Regular Baptists, 719,290. The latter denomination has but a fraction less than the six former. Supposing the increase since 1853 to have been equal, of course the same proportion remains. Baptists have a much smaller proportion of pecuniary ability than the six denominations with whom they are here compared. This, however, is not so important a consideration as their numbers; for personal influence is greater than any other. Under these circumstances the obligation of Baptists to the world is very great. God has not given them so glorious a past and present, to excuse them from future usefulness of magnitude; and a part in the contest now waging for the supremacy of the Cross, of an ordinary character.

Let it, however, be observed that numbers must retard the

march of an army, if a large portion of it wants energy and courage. They hang upon the willing and obedient like lead. Nor is this all. They have an evil influence which enters into the entire discipline of the army. Numbers not of a desirable stamp, then, so far from being a favorable circumstance, is the reverse. One million of Baptists in the United States is one thing, and one million of consecrated Baptists is another.

There are two facts in their recent history which they should examine with great seriousness. I refer to their recent increase in numbers; and their expenditures for missionary purposes. The increase of Baptist church members, according to Baptist Almanac for 1854, in one year, was about 30,000. This is considered cause of congratulation. And so it is, when contemplated as a fact separate from the circumstances. But when it is remembered how rapidly our brethren multiplied in the most heart-rending times of persecution, and that we have now no such obstacles to contend with; and that the present is a period of great enterprise in every secular department, results being reached in a day once requiring months, and that Christians should not be outdone by men of the world; and that the population has had an increase natural and by immigration, unequaled, and much greater than that of the church; when these things are remembered, we ask, is an increase of 30,000 in a year a fair work for one million of soldiers of the cross? With the zeal of the martyrs, or even of worldly men; and with the facilities now enjoyed in the means of grace, which God has vouchsafed to us, what might not, and ought not, one million of Christians to accomplish in an entire year, in winning souls to Christ? If each one should win one soul in a year, instead of an increase of 30,000, we should have that of 1,000,000.

Look now at the expenditure of one year for missionary purposes, and see if we find there any more cause for congratulation. We have seen in a preceding chapter, that the sum total of money raised for, strictly speaking, missionary purposes, by one million of Baptists, in an entire year, is less than one half million of dollars. A half a million of money, in a year, seems a large sum in the aggregate, and so it is; but what is it divided among a million of church members? It is the paltry sum of fifty cents each—less money than multitudes of them spend in a day, for mere luxuries. Admit that great numbers of the one million are poor. Who so poor in the church in the United States that he could not give fifty cents in a year for the spread of the gospel if he desired to? And what is this sum for the great majority of them? If some are poor, many are rich; and some of them are worth, personally, the entire amount given; and some very much more.

If any one is surprised that so great an army should consummate so little in a given year, and inquires for the cause, let him visit the different regiments and companies of it, at their homes, in their associations and churches, and see if in the every-day practical working of it, he has any more cause of congratulation; or can he be in any doubt as to the result? Upon the Sabbath, of a fine day, indeed, all is promise, and his heart leaps for joy at the well-dressed, and in all respects noble-looking crowds, which throng the fine churches. But, alas! this is not the true criterion; and he can form thus but a slight estimate of the working disposition of the people. Let him go to the general prayer meeting, or the monthly concert of prayer for the spread of the gospel, and he will soon suspect the difficulty. Alas, alas! the few most consistent are hardly up to the mark of duty; and the masses, where are they? About all they do, is to go to church of a pleasant Sabbath, and this is doing but little for the cause—much more for themselves than for others. The difficulty lies just here: the masses are doing nothing; and the few, for the most part, but little. Whilst a million of persons can accomplish wonders in personal influence and charities if each one does his duty, they will accomplish but little if most of them do nothing, and the balance but a part of their duty.

We regret the necessity for remarks so discouraging, but the truth should be told, that delinquents may understand their position. The point to be gained is to secure the activity of the masses. This done, and little remains to be desired. So numerous an army may accomplish thus, any thing reasonable. Look at the success which has attended our efforts, notwithstanding the immense drawback to which we allude. What would it have been, with the same divine influences, if the masses had been like the noble few, who have "stood in the front rank, and borne the heat and burden of the day?"

Brethren, these are not the times for indifference and timidity. Every thing is upon the move, and seems imbued with an enterprise like that required of Christians in the passage, "Whatsoever thy hand findeth to do, do it with thy might." Evil influences are driven on with locomotive speed and power. Secular influences, business, and money-making, have a remarkable activity. Moral influences must have a similar impulse to keep pace, and not leave the world to destruction from its very activity and enterprise. Brethren, we are not the people to sleep at our post, or fold our arms in indolence, in times like these, with a history like ours; and with the commands of God ringing in our ears: "Be ye, therefore, steadfast, immovable, always abounding in the work of the Lord." "The field is the world." The world is to be won to Christ. There is work for all, and we should be the last to "be weighed in the balances, and found wanting;" or to suffer under the stigma, and "bitter curse of Meroz, because we come not up to the help of the Lord against the mighty."

INDEX.

D.

E.

F.

G.

H.

THE END.

www.ingramcontent.com/pod-product-compliance
Lightning Source LLC
LaVergne TN
LVHW010155110826
845151LV00002B/523
9781425537500